W9-DGU-886

Date: 10/5/17

GRA 741.5 DOC V.6
Abadzis, Nick,
Doctor Who : Sins of the
father /the tenth Doctor.

BBC

DOCTOR WHO

THE TENTH DOCTOR

VOL 6: SINS OF THE FATHER

"One of the best stories to be told via the comic book medium."

SNAP POW

"This book truly feels like a lost episode of the RTD era of *Doctor Who*."

MY GEEKY GEEKY WAYS

"Go buy this!"

COMICS VERSE

"The best of Titan Comics' slate of *Doctor Who* comics."

GIANT FREAKING ROBOT

"Abadzis does a wonderful job of drawing us in and weaving the world around us..."

GEEK GIRL PROJECT

"Perfectly captures the spirit of *Doctor Who*!"

KABOOOOOM!

"Writer Nick Abadzis, along with the smooth and engaging art by Giorgia Sposito, shows that traveling with the Doctor isn't just all alien planets and daring escapes. 8/10."

NEWSARAMA

"Wonderfully written and flows perfectly!"

POP CULTURE BANDIT

"*Doctor Who* fans are well-served."

SOUNDS ON SIGHT

"The *Doctor Who* comic fans have always deserved."

BLOODY DISGUSTING

"The Tenth Doctor will spirit you away with some cool horns, some hot jazz, and some superlative storytelling from four players at the top of their game."

WARPED FACTOR

TITAN COMICS

SENIOR COMICS EDITOR
Andrew James

ASSISTANT EDITORS
Jessica Burton, Amoona Saohin

COLLECTION DESIGNER
Andrew Leung

TITAN COMICS EDITORIAL
Tom Williams

PRODUCTION ASSISTANT
Peter James

PRODUCTION SUPERVISORS
Maria Pearson, Jackie Flook

PRODUCTION MANAGER
Obi Onuora

ART DIRECTOR
Oz Browne

SENIOR SALES MANAGER
Steve Tothill

PRESS OFFICER
Will O'Mullane

COMICS BRAND MANAGER
Lucy Ripper

For rights information
contact Jenny Boyce
jenny.boyce@titanemail.com

DIRECT SALES & MARKETING MANAGER
Ricky Claydon

COMMERCIAL MANAGER
Michelle Fairlamb

HEAD OF RIGHTS
Jenny Boyce

PUBLISHING MANAGER
Darryl Tothill

PUBLISHING DIRECTOR
Chris Teather

OPERATIONS DIRECTOR
Leigh Baulch

EXECUTIVE DIRECTOR
Vivian Cheung

PUBLISHER
Nick Landau

Special thanks to Steven Moffat, Brian Minchin, Mandy Thwaites, Matt Nicholls, James Dudley, Edward Russell, Derek Ritchie, Scott Handcock, Kirsty Mullan, Kate Bush, Julia Nocciolino and Ed Casey for their invaluable assistance.

BBC WORLDWIDE

DIRECTOR OF EDITORIAL GOVERNANCE
Nicholas Brett

DIRECTOR OF CONSUME PRODUCTS AND PUBLISH
Andrew Moultrie

HEAD OF UK PUBLISHING
Chris Kerwin

PUBLISHER
Mandy Thwaites

PUBLISHING CO-ORDINATOR
Eva Abramik

DOCTOR WHO: THE TENTH DOCTOR VOL 6: SINS OF THE FATHER
HB ISBN: 9781785853586
SB ISBN: 9781785856808
Published by Titan Comics, a division of Titan Publishing Group, Ltd. 144 Southwark Street, London, SE1 0UP.

A CIP catalogue record for this title is available from the British Library.
First edition: December 2016.

10 9 8 7 6 5 4 3 2 1

Printed in China.

Titan Comics does not read or accept unsolicited DOCTOR WHO submissions of ideas, stories or artwork.

www.titan-comics.co

BBC

DOCTOR WHO

THE TENTH DOCTOR

VOL 6: SINS OF THE FATHER

WRITER: NICK ABADZIS

ARTISTS: GIORGIA SPOSITO & ELEONORA CARLINI
WITH LEANDRO CASCO, SIMON FRASER & WALTER GEOVANNI

COLORISTS: ARIANNA FLOREAN,
WITH AZZURRA FLOREAN, MATTIA DE LULIS, ADELE MATERA, ROD FERNANDES & GARY CALDWELL

LETTERS: RICHARD STARKINGS AND COMICRAFT'S JIMMY BETANCOURT

Titan
COMICS

BBC

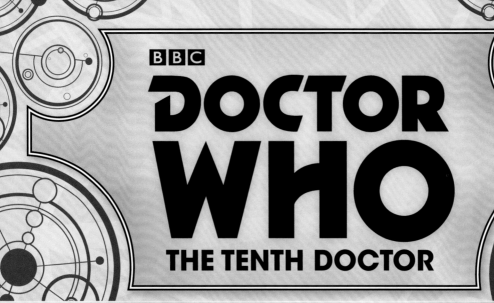

BBC

DOCTOR WHO

THE TENTH DOCTOR

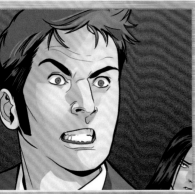

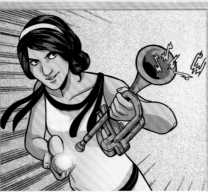

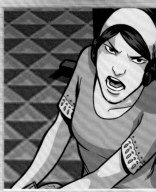

THE DOCTOR

Last of the Time Lords of Gallifrey, the Tenth Doctor still hides his post-Time War guilt beneath a happy-go-lucky guise. Never cruel or cowardly, he champions the oppressed across time and space – but his last adventure has left him shaken.

GABBY GONZALEZ

Gabriella Gonzalez is a young would-be artist from Sunset Park, Brooklyn, New York, who is traveling the universe at the Tenth Doctor's side. Her youthful spirit and artistic eye are coupled to an adventurous and quick-witted mind!

CINDY WU

Gabby's fiercely loyal best frien now traveling with her in the TARDIS. She has earned her place ten times over, but even Cindy can still be surpised by what their adventures can throw at her!

PREVIOUSLY...

The Doctor, Gabby, and Cindy are taking a well-earned break in New Orleans after beating the odds multiple times. First, there was their 'battle' with the Wishing Well Witch... in which they may have discovered a milennia-old Time Lord conspiracy!
Then the trip came under attack mid-flight! With the faithful ship creating multiple dimensional bubbles to save itself, Cindy found herself trapped! Luckily, the Doctor and Gabby managed to save her before she was lost to another dimension... but they suspect that their old friend Anubis might be up to his old tricks!

When you've finished reading this collection, please email your thoughts to doctorwhocomic@titanemail.com

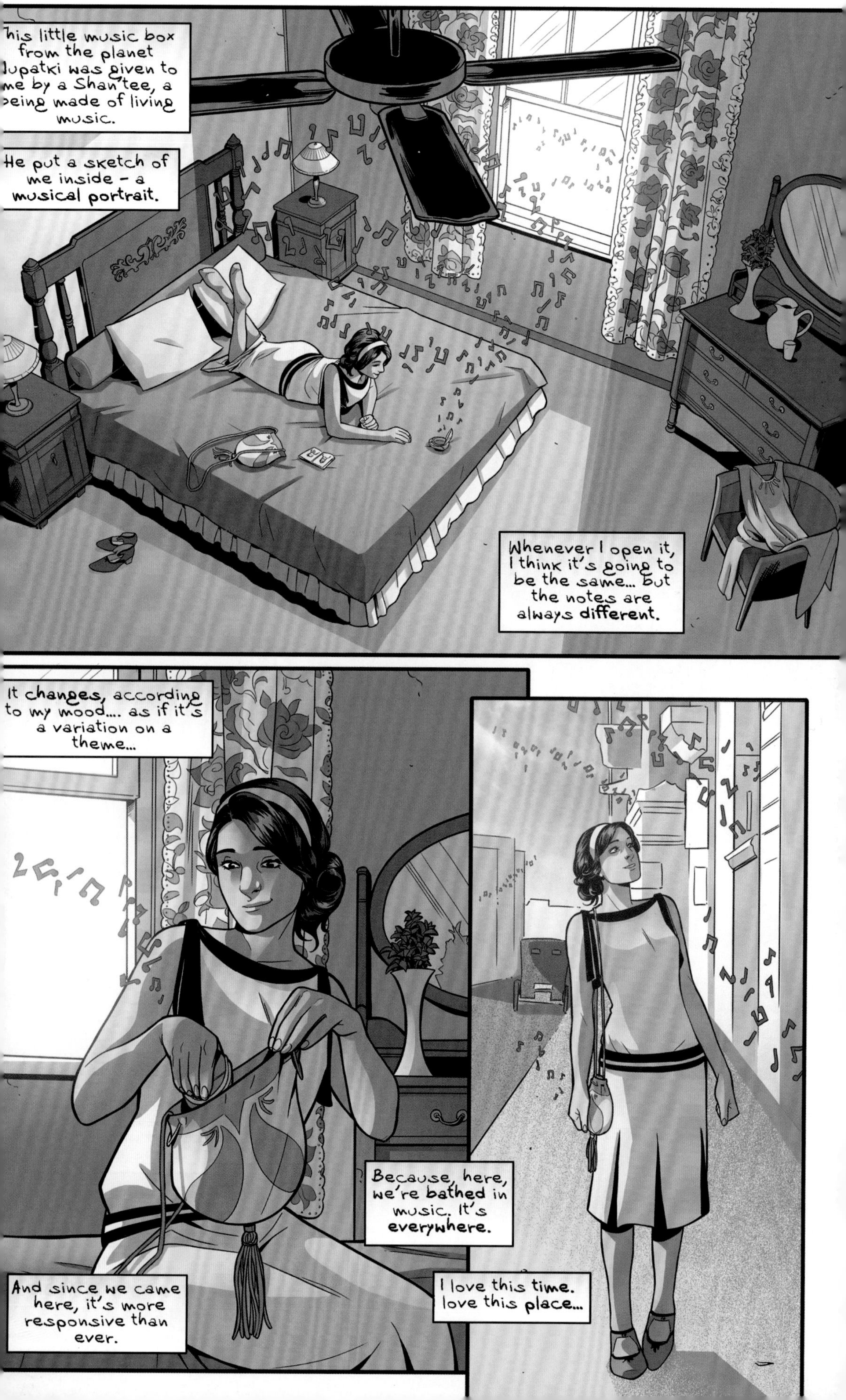
This little music box from the planet Jupatki was given to me by a Shan'tee, a being made of living music.
He put a sketch of me inside – a musical portrait.
Whenever I open it, I think it's going to be the same... but the notes are always different.
It changes, according to my mood.... as if it's a variation on a theme...
Because, here, we're bathed in music. It's everywhere.
And since we came here, it's more responsive than ever.
I love this time. love this place...

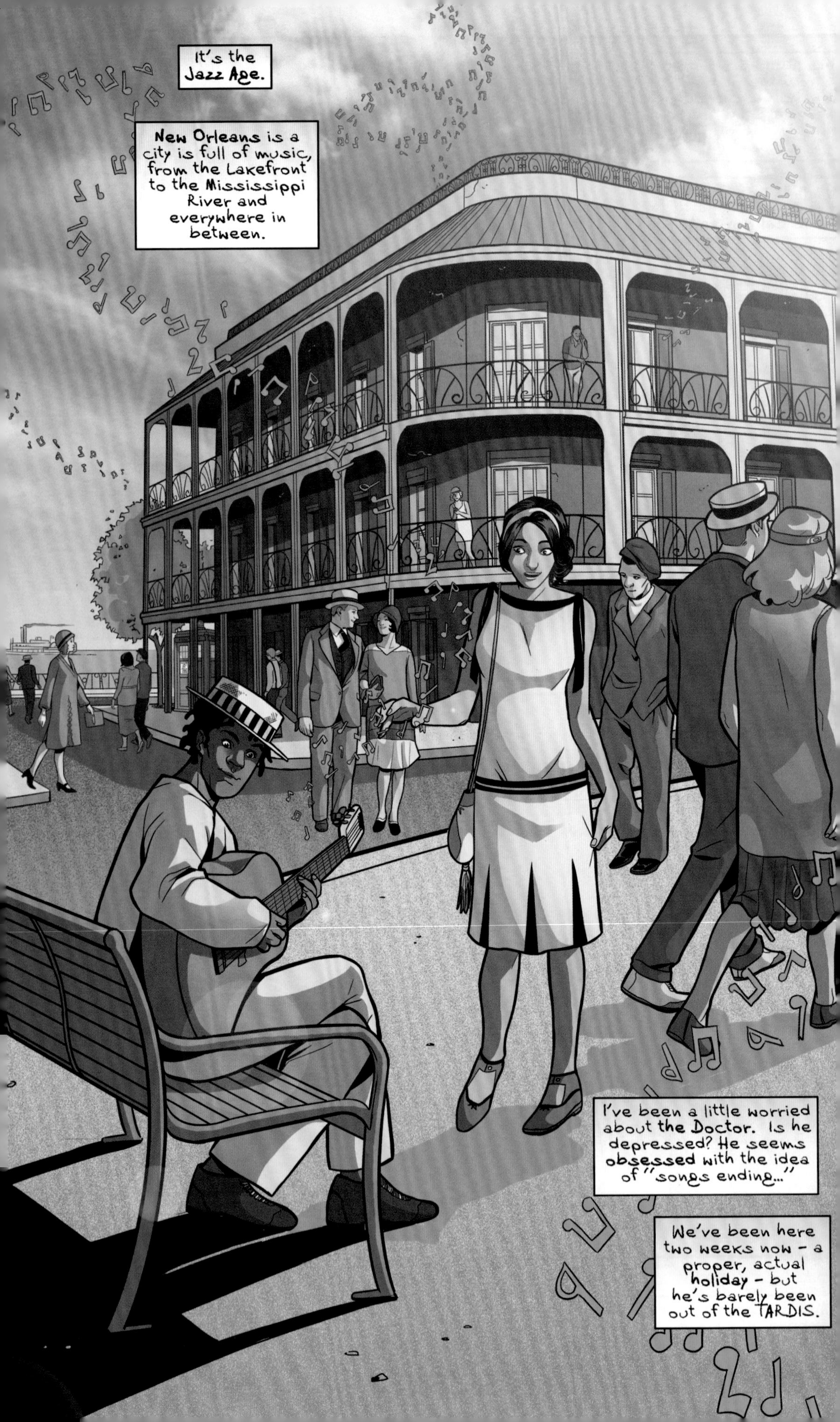
It's the Jazz Age.
New Orleans is a city is full of music, from the Lakefront to the Mississippi River and everywhere in between.
I've been a little worried about the Doctor. Is he depressed? He seems obsessed with the idea of "songs ending..."
We've been here two weeks now - a proper, actual holiday - but he's barely been out of the TARDIS.

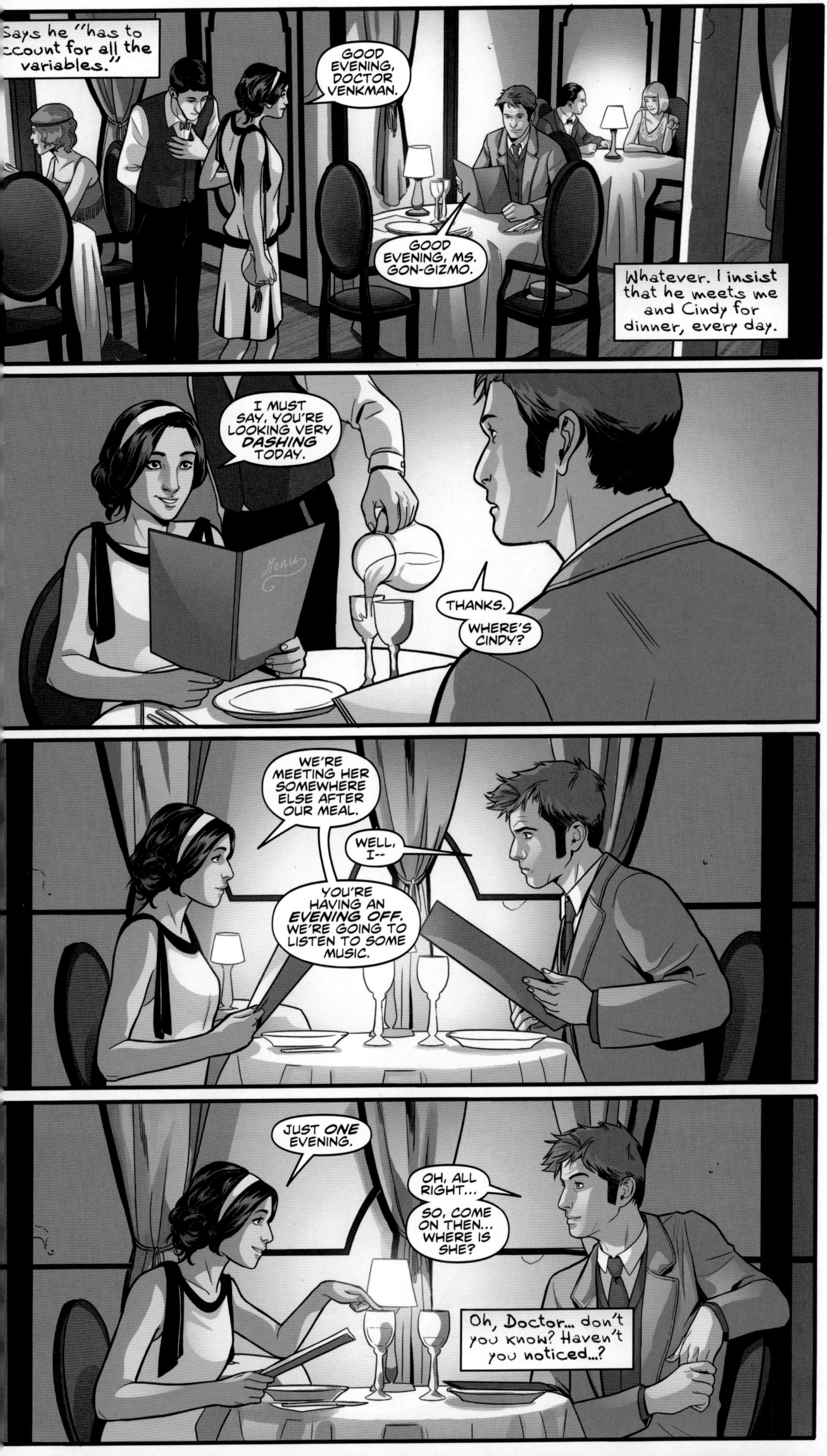
Says he "has to account for all the variables."
GOOD EVENING, DOCTOR VENKMAN.
GOOD EVENING, MS. GON-GIZMO.
Whatever. I insist that he meets me and Cindy for dinner, every day.
I MUST SAY, YOU'RE LOOKING VERY *DASHING* TODAY.
THANKS.
WHERE'S CINDY?
WE'RE MEETING HER SOMEWHERE ELSE AFTER OUR MEAL.
WELL, I--
YOU'RE HAVING AN *EVENING OFF.* WE'RE GOING TO LISTEN TO SOME MUSIC.
JUST *ONE* EVENING.
OH, ALL RIGHT...
SO, COME ON THEN... WHERE IS SHE?
Oh, Doctor... don't you know? Haven't you **noticed**...?

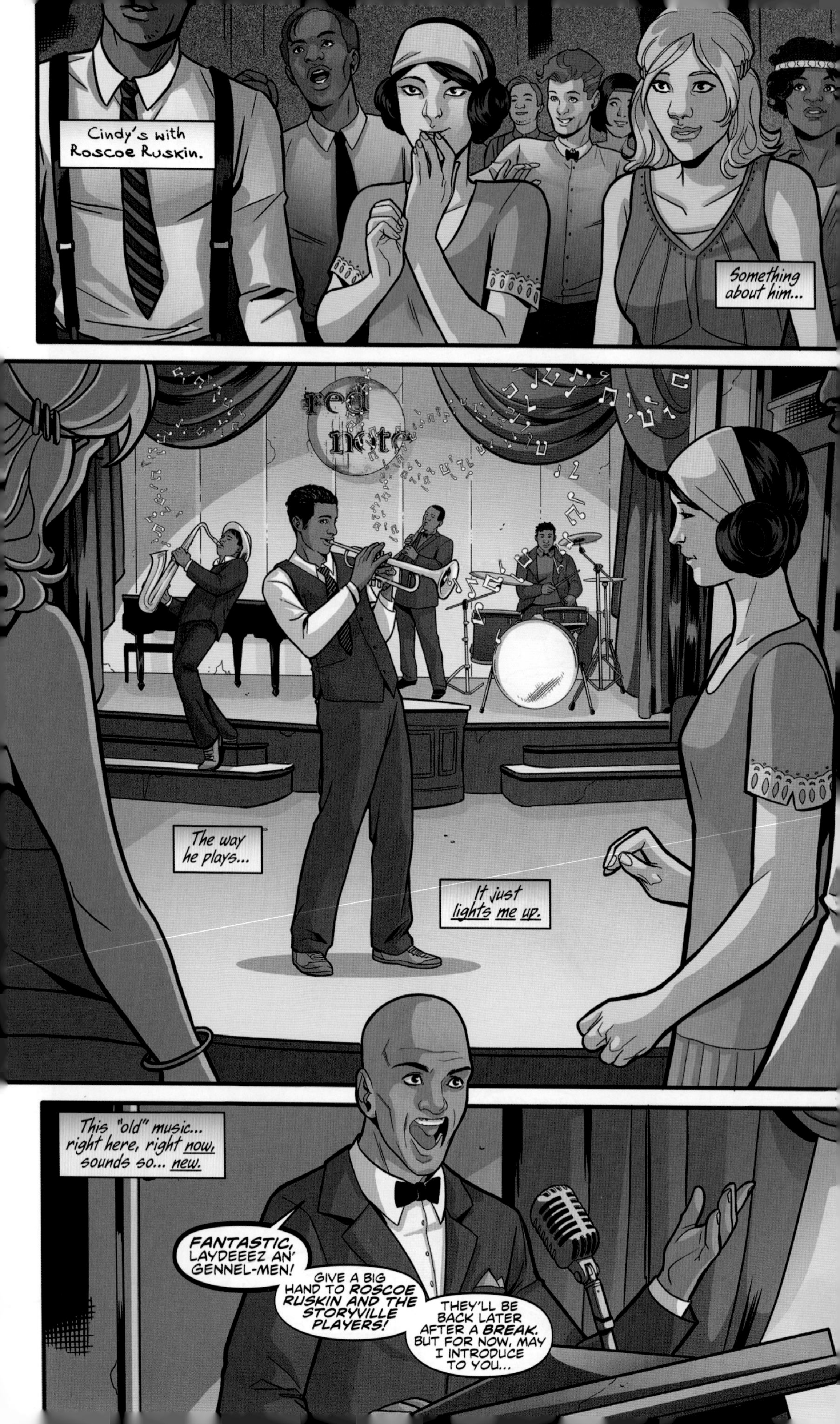
Cindy's with Roscoe Ruskin.
Something about him...
red note
The way he plays...
It just lights me up.
This "old" music... right here, right now, sounds so... new.
FANTASTIC, LAYDEEEZ AN' GENNEL-MEN!
GIVE A BIG HAND TO ROSCOE RUSKIN AND THE STORYVILLE PLAYERS!
THEY'LL BE BACK LATER AFTER A BREAK. BUT FOR NOW, MAY I INTRODUCE TO YOU...

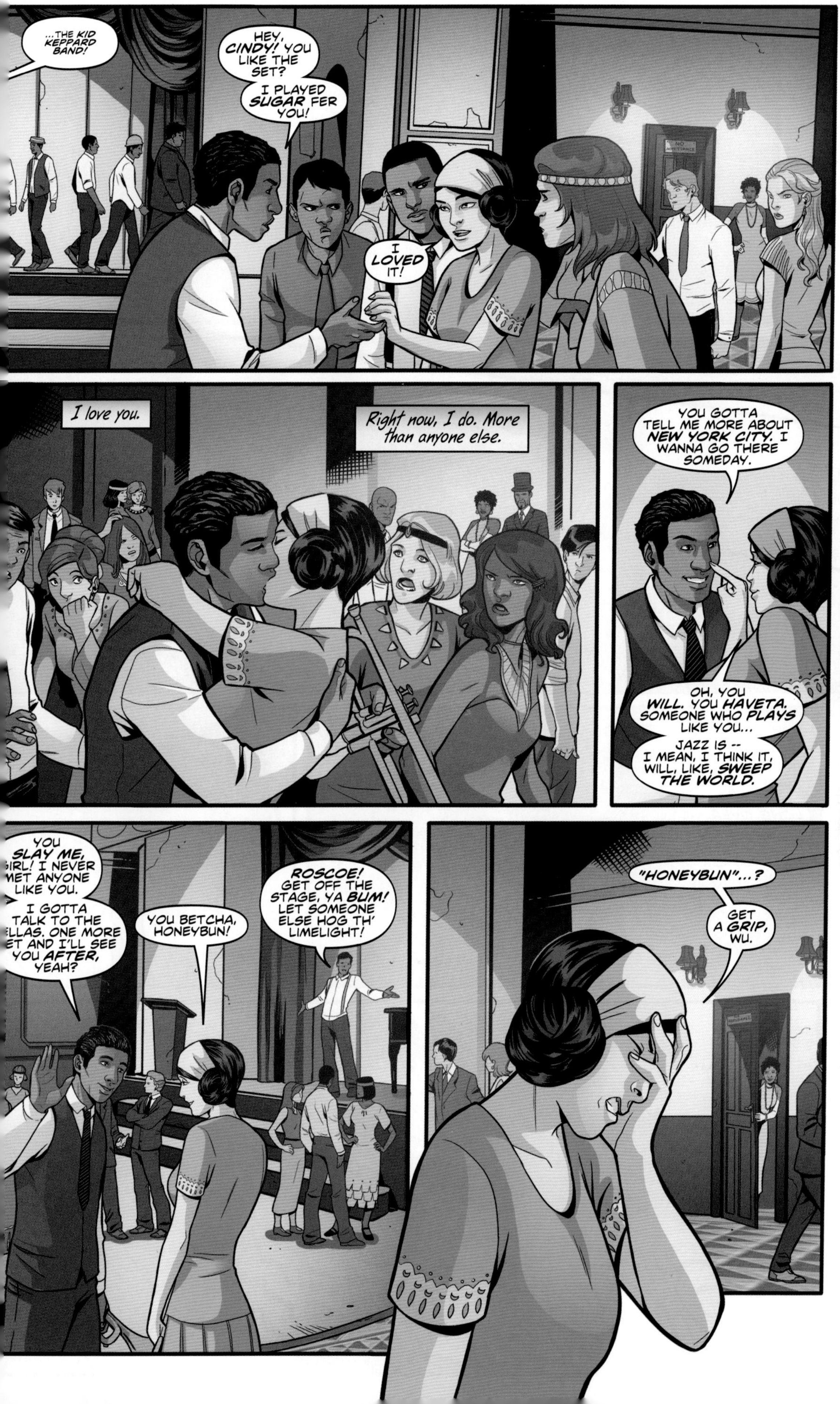

...THE KID KEPPARD BAND!
HEY, CINDY! YOU LIKE THE SET?
I PLAYED SUGAR FER YOU!
I LOVED IT!
I love you.
Right now, I do. More than anyone else.
YOU GOTTA TELL ME MORE ABOUT NEW YORK CITY. I WANNA GO THERE SOMEDAY.
OH, YOU WILL. YOU HAVETA. SOMEONE WHO PLAYS LIKE YOU...
JAZZ IS -- I MEAN, I THINK IT, WILL, LIKE, SWEEP THE WORLD.
YOU SLAY ME, GIRL! I NEVER MET ANYONE LIKE YOU.
I GOTTA TALK TO THE FELLAS. ONE MORE SET AND I'LL SEE YOU AFTER, YEAH?
YOU BETCHA, HONEYBUN!
ROSCOE! GET OFF THE STAGE, YA BUM! LET SOMEONE ELSE HOG TH' LIMELIGHT!
"HONEYBUN"...?
GET A GRIP, WU.

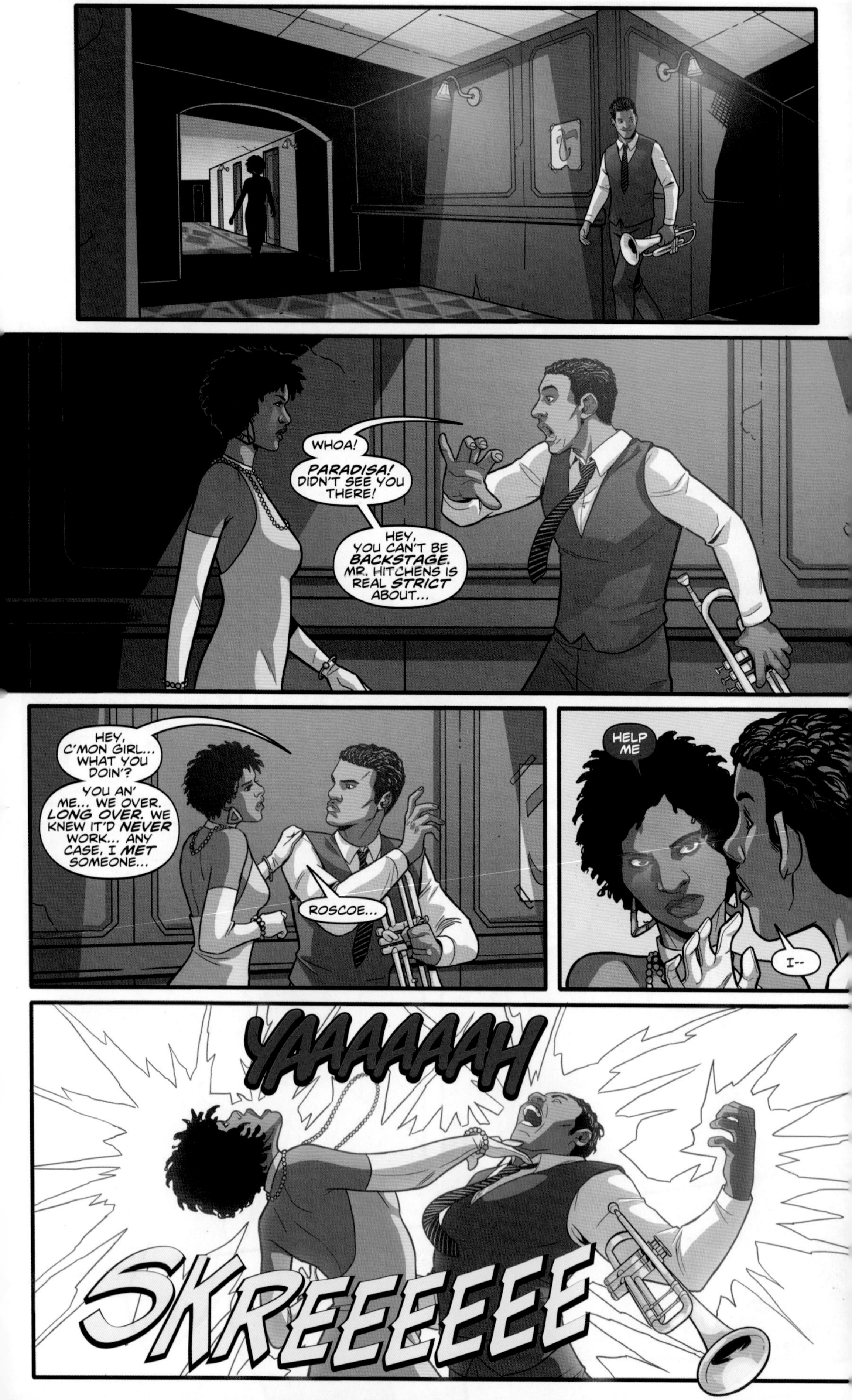
WHOA!
PARADISA! DIDN'T SEE YOU THERE!
HEY, YOU CAN'T BE BACKSTAGE. MR. HITCHENS IS REAL STRICT ABOUT...
HEY, C'MON GIRL... WHAT YOU DOIN'?
YOU AN' ME... WE OVER. LONG OVER. WE KNEW IT'D NEVER WORK... ANY CASE, I MET SOMEONE...
ROSCOE...
HELP ME
I--
YAAAAAAH
SKREEEEEEE

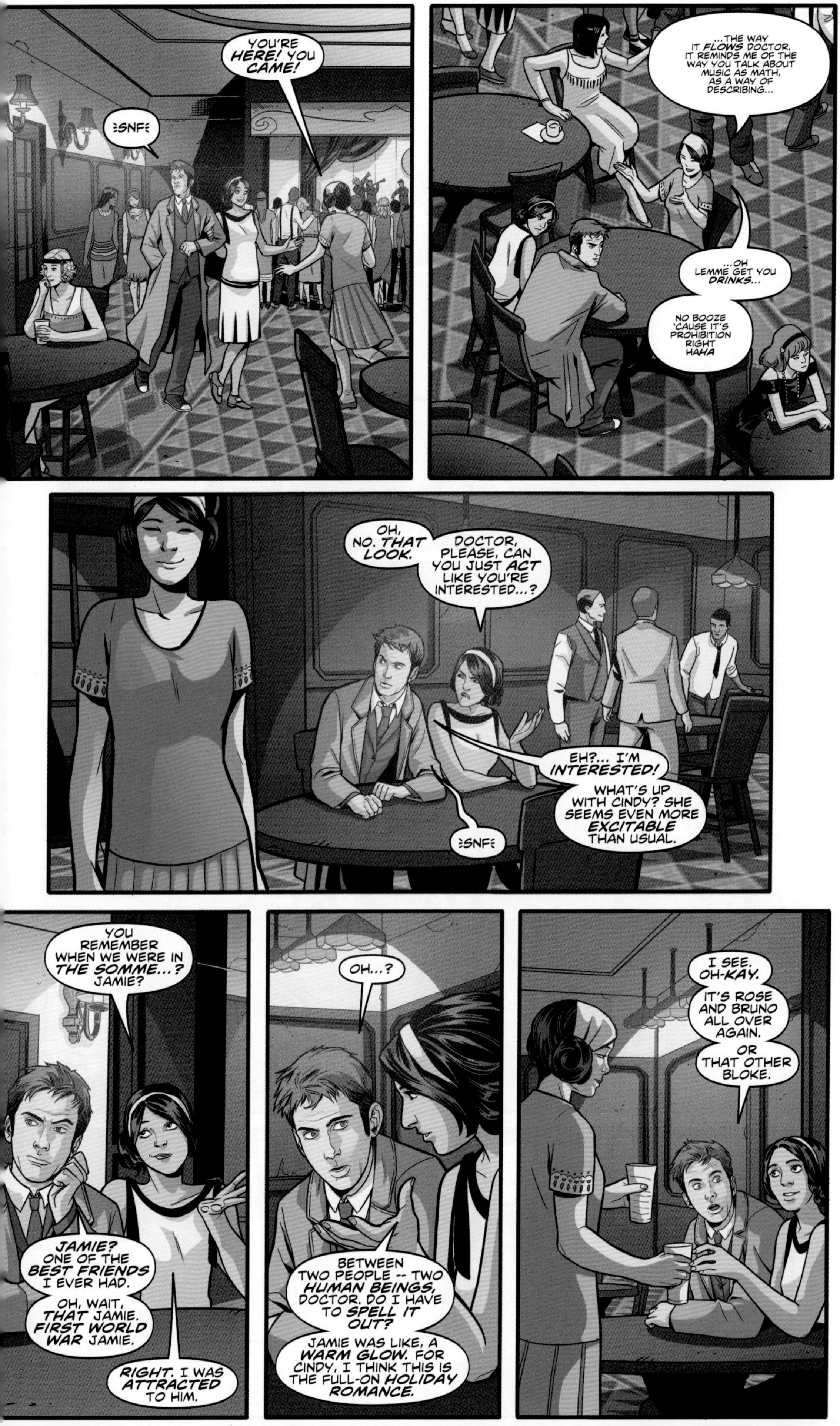
YOU'RE HERE! YOU CAME!
≥SNF≤
...THE WAY IT FLOWS DOCTOR, IT REMINDS ME OF THE WAY YOU TALK ABOUT MUSIC AS MATH, AS A WAY OF DESCRIBING...
...OH LEMME GET YOU DRINKS...
NO BOOZE 'CAUSE IT'S PROHIBITION RIGHT HAHA
OH, NO. THAT LOOK.
DOCTOR, PLEASE, CAN YOU JUST ACT LIKE YOU'RE INTERESTED...?
EH?... I'M INTERESTED!
WHAT'S UP WITH CINDY? SHE SEEMS EVEN MORE EXCITABLE THAN USUAL.
≥SNF≤
YOU REMEMBER WHEN WE WERE IN THE SOMME...? JAMIE?
JAMIE? ONE OF THE BEST FRIENDS I EVER HAD.
OH, WAIT, THAT JAMIE. FIRST WORLD WAR JAMIE.
RIGHT. I WAS ATTRACTED TO HIM.
OH...?
BETWEEN TWO PEOPLE -- TWO HUMAN BEINGS, DOCTOR. DO I HAVE TO SPELL IT OUT?
JAMIE WAS LIKE, A WARM GLOW. FOR CINDY, I THINK THIS IS THE FULL-ON HOLIDAY ROMANCE.
I SEE. OH-KAY.
IT'S ROSE AND BRUNO ALL OVER AGAIN.
OR THAT OTHER BLOKE.

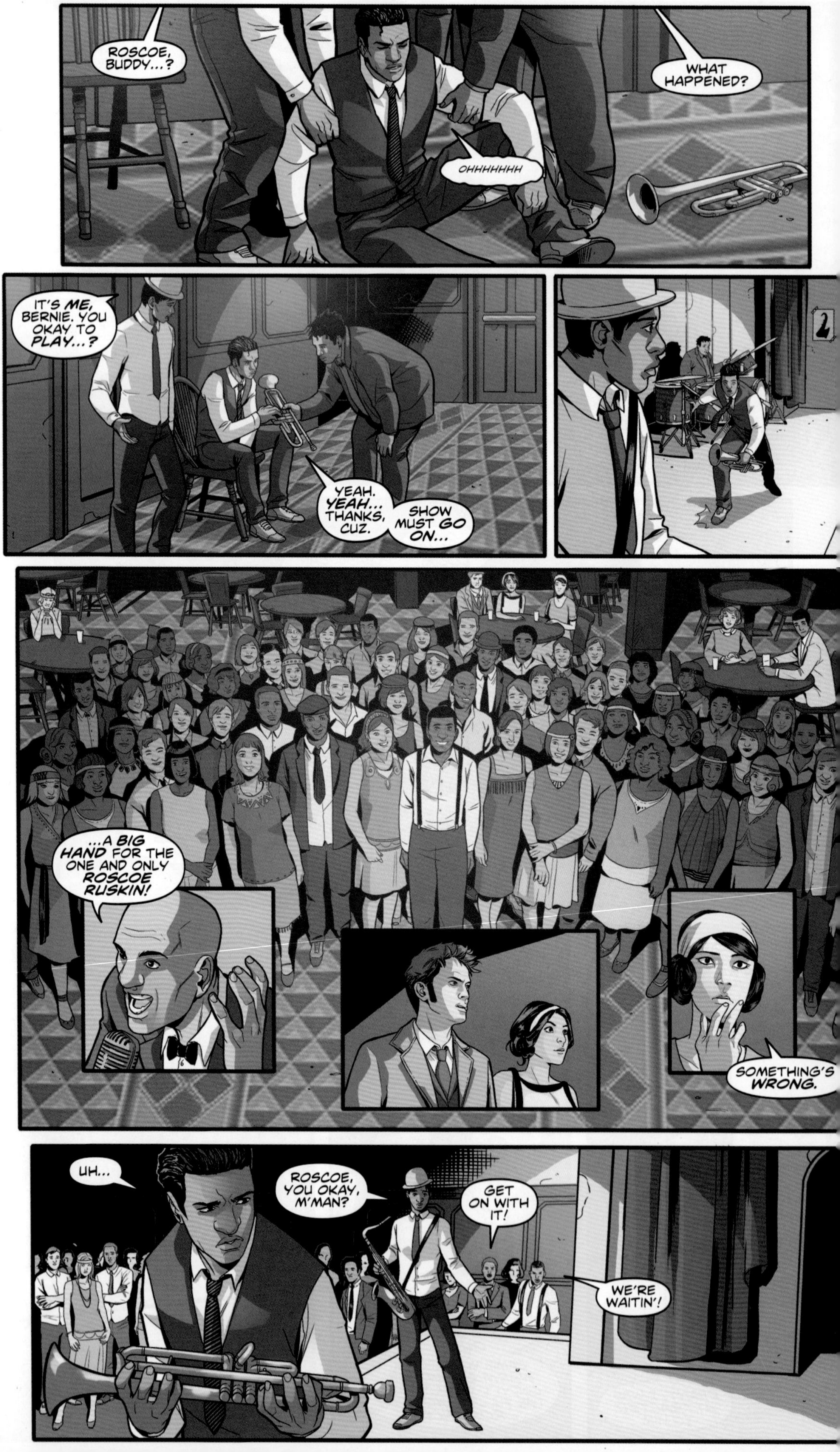
ROSCOE, BUDDY...?
WHAT HAPPENED?
OHHHHHHH
IT'S ME, BERNIE. YOU OKAY TO PLAY...?
YEAH. YEAH... THANKS, CUZ.
SHOW MUST GO ON...
2
...A BIG HAND FOR THE ONE AND ONLY ROSCOE RUSKIN!
SOMETHING'S WRONG.
UH...
ROSCOE, YOU OKAY, M'MAN?
GET ON WITH IT!
WE'RE WAITIN'!

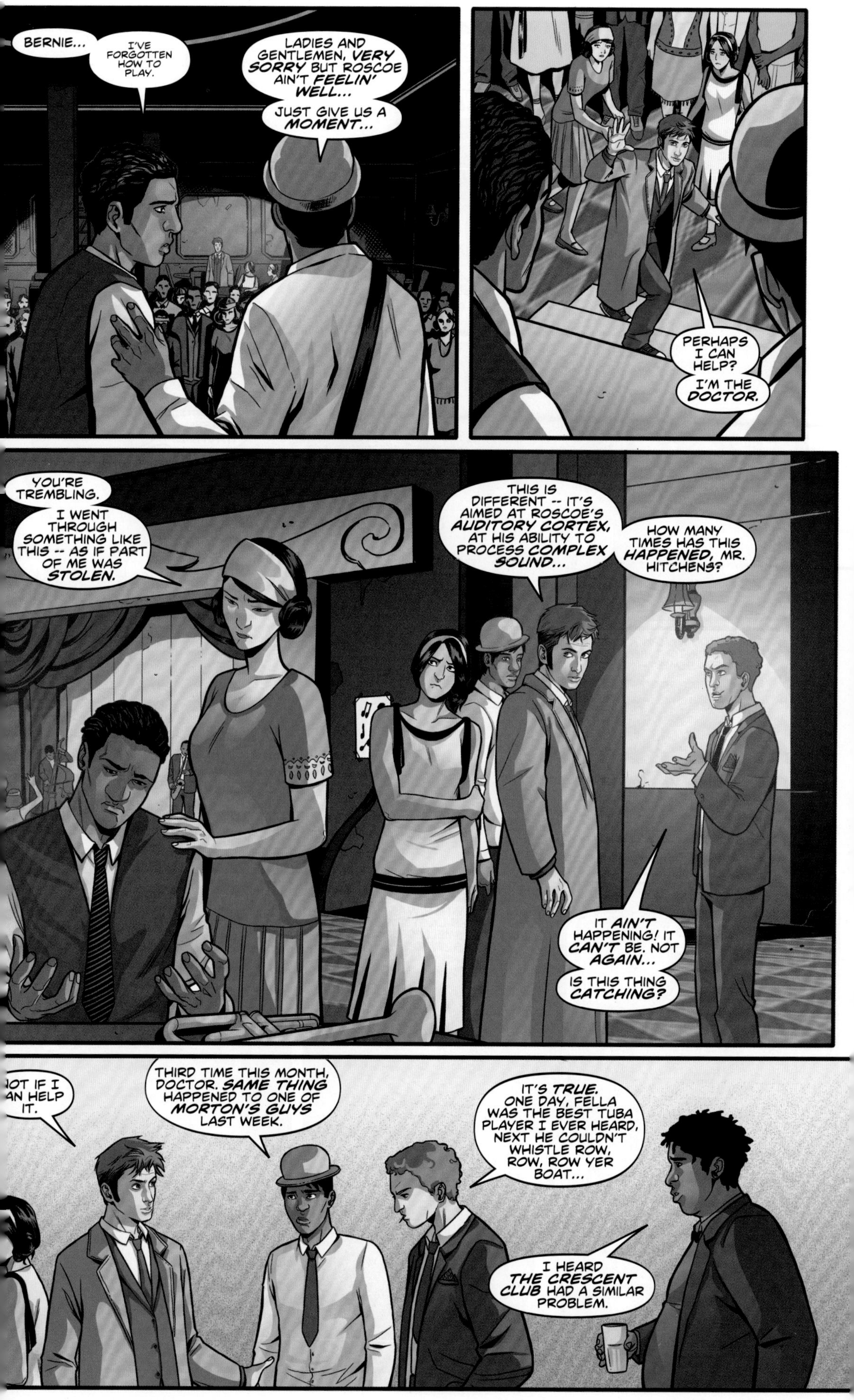
BERNIE...
I'VE FORGOTTEN HOW TO PLAY.
LADIES AND GENTLEMEN, VERY SORRY BUT ROSCOE AIN'T FEELIN' WELL...
JUST GIVE US A MOMENT...
PERHAPS I CAN HELP?
I'M THE DOCTOR.
YOU'RE TREMBLING.
I WENT THROUGH SOMETHING LIKE THIS -- AS IF PART OF ME WAS STOLEN.
THIS IS DIFFERENT -- IT'S AIMED AT ROSCOE'S AUDITORY CORTEX, AT HIS ABILITY TO PROCESS COMPLEX SOUND...
HOW MANY TIMES HAS THIS HAPPENED, MR. HITCHENS?
IT AIN'T HAPPENING! IT CAN'T BE. NOT AGAIN...
IS THIS THING CATCHING?
NOT IF I CAN HELP IT.
THIRD TIME THIS MONTH, DOCTOR. SAME THING HAPPENED TO ONE OF MORTON'S GUYS LAST WEEK.
IT'S TRUE. ONE DAY, FELLA WAS THE BEST TUBA PLAYER I EVER HEARD, NEXT HE COULDN'T WHISTLE ROW, ROW, ROW YER BOAT...
I HEARD THE CRESCENT CLUB HAD A SIMILAR PROBLEM.

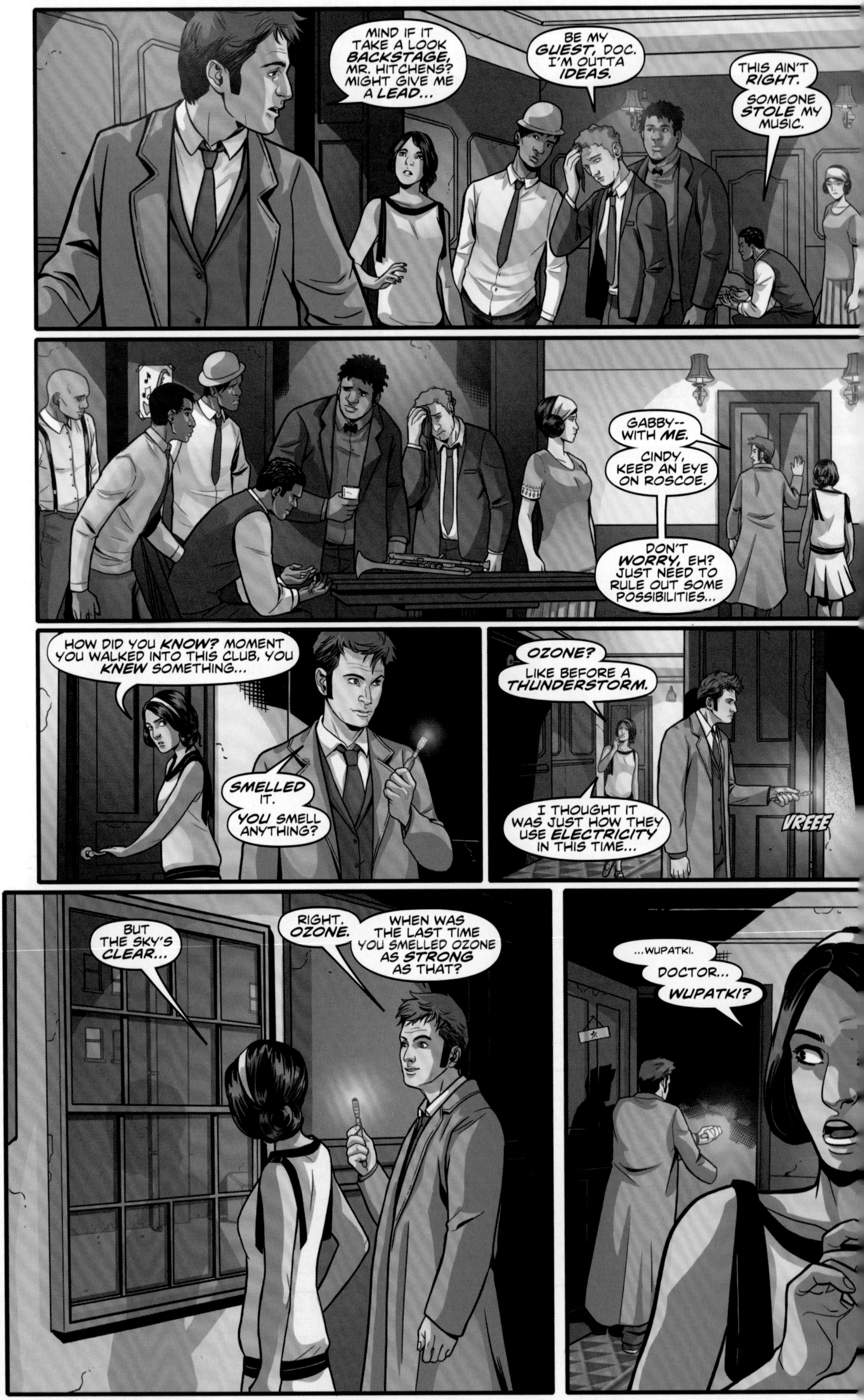
MIND IF IT TAKE A LOOK BACKSTAGE, MR. HITCHENS? MIGHT GIVE ME A LEAD...
BE MY GUEST, DOC. I'M OUTTA IDEAS.
THIS AIN'T RIGHT.
SOMEONE STOLE MY MUSIC.
GABBY-- WITH ME.
CINDY, KEEP AN EYE ON ROSCOE.
DON'T WORRY, EH? JUST NEED TO RULE OUT SOME POSSIBILITIES...
HOW DID YOU KNOW? MOMENT YOU WALKED INTO THIS CLUB, YOU KNEW SOMETHING...
SMELLED IT.
YOU SMELL ANYTHING?
OZONE?
LIKE BEFORE A THUNDERSTORM.
I THOUGHT IT WAS JUST HOW THEY USE ELECTRICITY IN THIS TIME...
VREEE
BUT THE SKY'S CLEAR...
RIGHT. OZONE.
WHEN WAS THE LAST TIME YOU SMELLED OZONE AS STRONG AS THAT?
...WUPATKI.
DOCTOR...
WUPATKI?

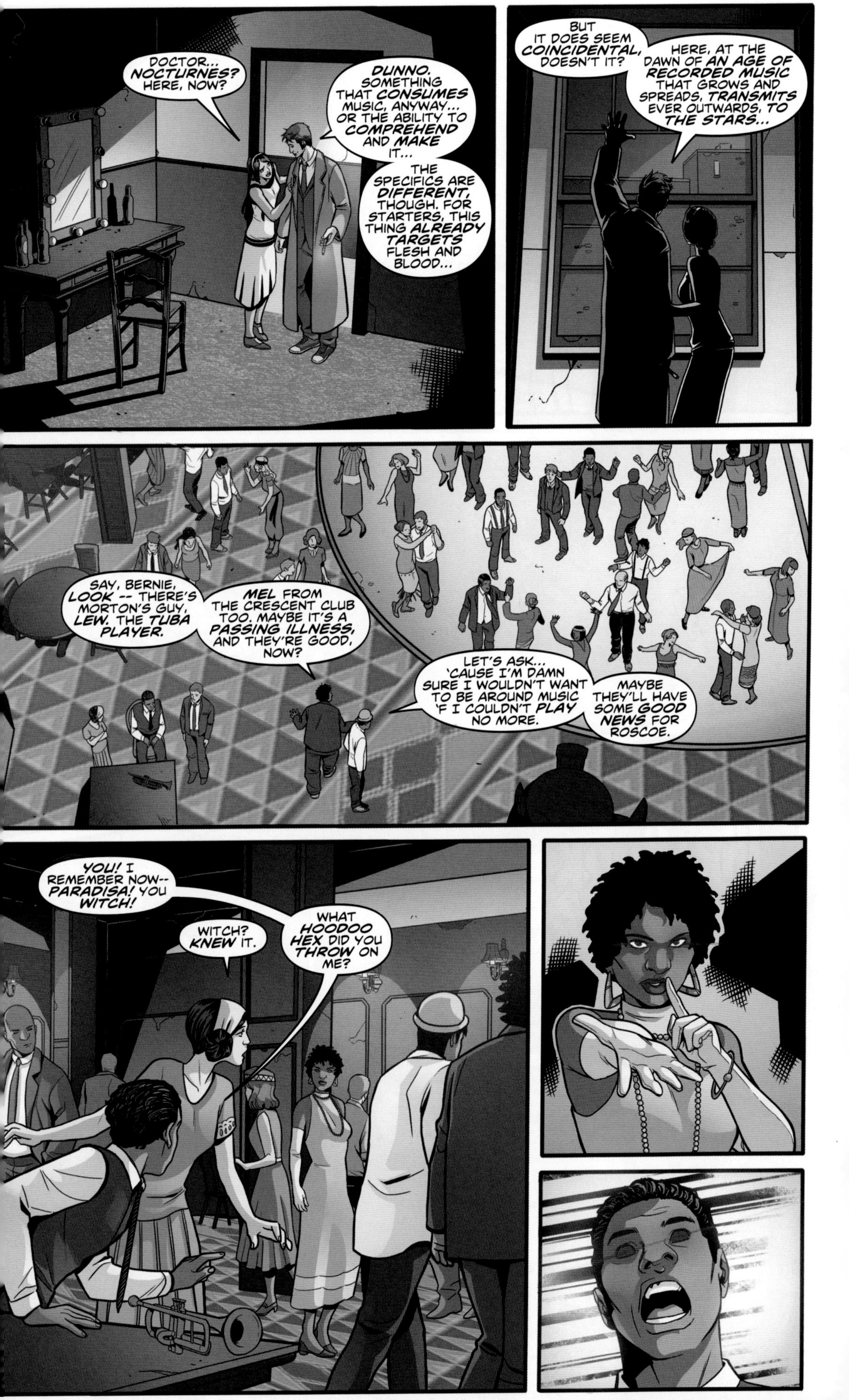
DOCTOR... NOCTURNES? HERE, NOW?
DUNNO. SOMETHING THAT CONSUMES MUSIC, ANYWAY... OR THE ABILITY TO COMPREHEND AND MAKE IT...
THE SPECIFICS ARE DIFFERENT, THOUGH. FOR STARTERS, THIS THING ALREADY TARGETS FLESH AND BLOOD...
BUT IT DOES SEEM COINCIDENTAL, DOESN'T IT?
HERE, AT THE DAWN OF AN AGE OF RECORDED MUSIC THAT GROWS AND SPREADS, TRANSMITS EVER OUTWARDS, TO THE STARS...
SAY, BERNIE, LOOK -- THERE'S MORTON'S GUY, LEW. THE TUBA PLAYER.
MEL FROM THE CRESCENT CLUB TOO. MAYBE IT'S A PASSING ILLNESS, AND THEY'RE GOOD, NOW?
LET'S ASK... 'CAUSE I'M DAMN SURE I WOULDN'T WANT TO BE AROUND MUSIC 'F I COULDN'T PLAY NO MORE.
MAYBE THEY'LL HAVE SOME GOOD NEWS FOR ROSCOE.
YOU! I REMEMBER NOW-- PARADISA! YOU WITCH!
WITCH? KNEW IT.
WHAT HOODOO HEX DID YOU THROW ON ME?

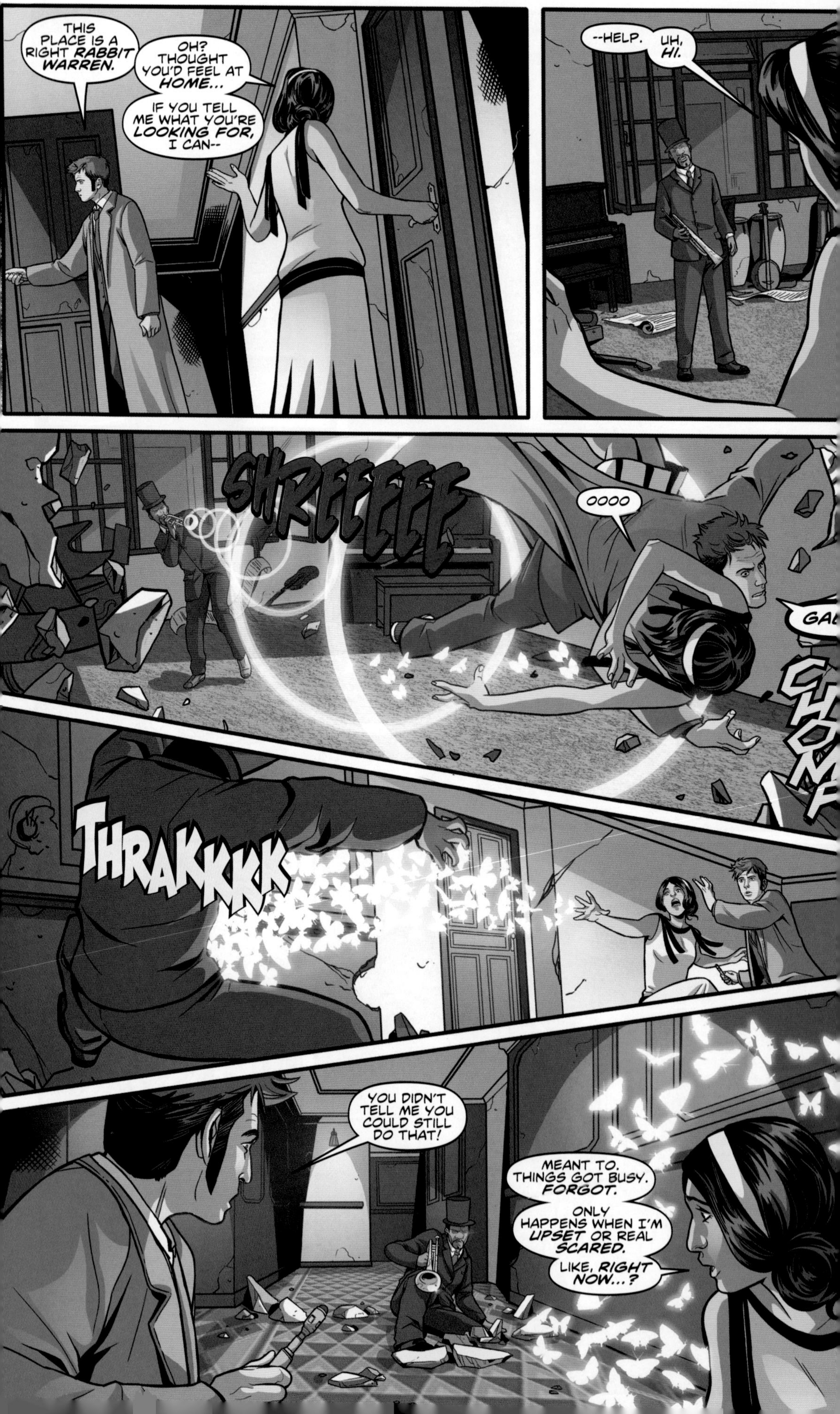
THIS PLACE IS A RIGHT RABBIT WARREN.
OH? THOUGHT YOU'D FEEL AT HOME...
IF YOU TELL ME WHAT YOU'RE LOOKING FOR, I CAN--
--HELP.
UH, HI.
SHREEEEE
OOOO
THRAKKKK
YOU DIDN'T TELL ME YOU COULD STILL DO THAT!
MEANT TO. THINGS GOT BUSY. FORGOT.
ONLY HAPPENS WHEN I'M UPSET OR REAL SCARED.
LIKE, RIGHT NOW...?

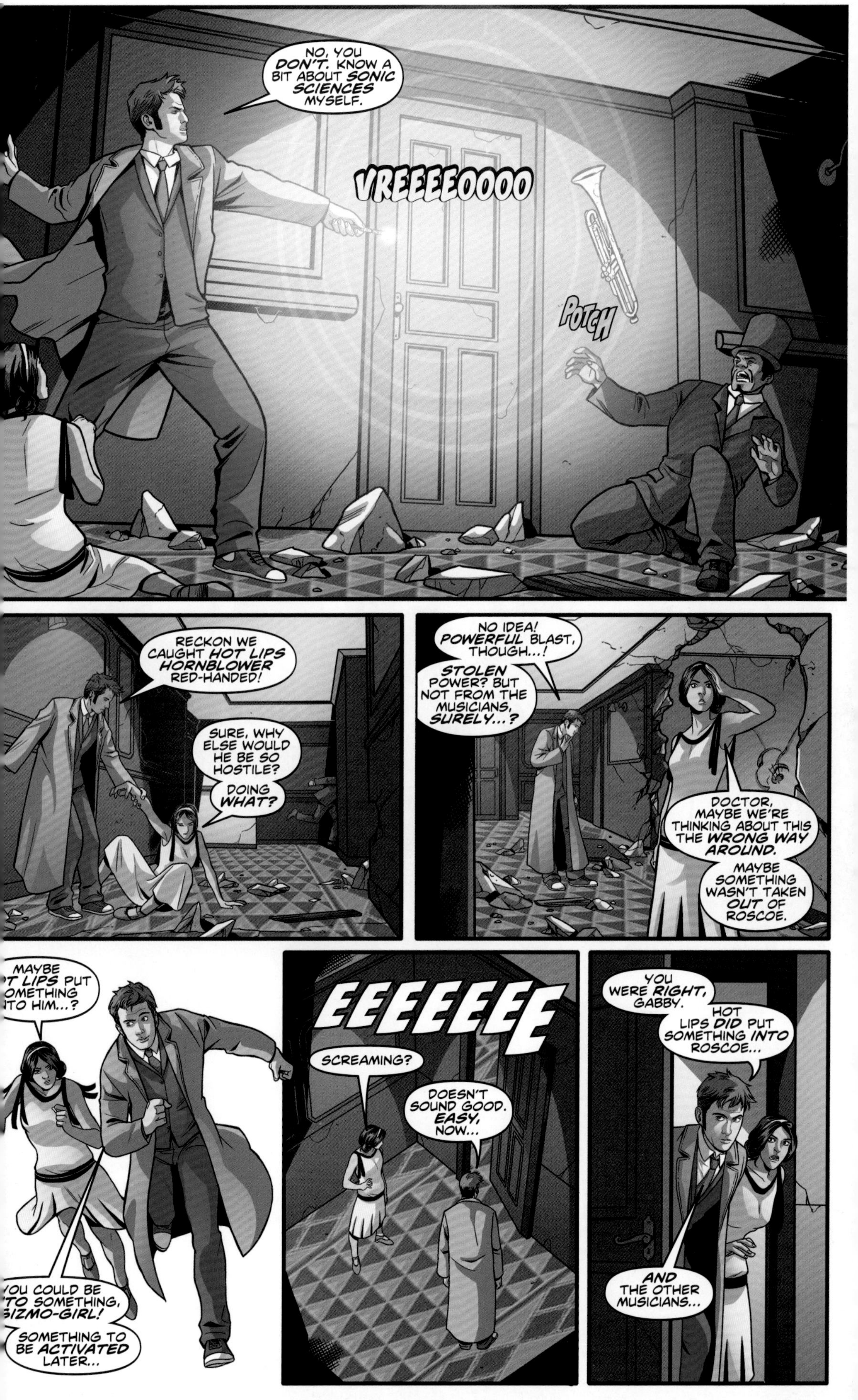
NO, YOU DON'T. KNOW A BIT ABOUT SONIC SCIENCES MYSELF.
VREEEEOOOO
POTCH
RECKON WE CAUGHT HOT LIPS HORNBLOWER RED-HANDED!
SURE, WHY ELSE WOULD HE BE SO HOSTILE?
DOING WHAT?
NO IDEA! POWERFUL BLAST, THOUGH...!
STOLEN POWER? BUT NOT FROM THE MUSICIANS, SURELY...?
DOCTOR, MAYBE WE'RE THINKING ABOUT THIS THE WRONG WAY AROUND.
MAYBE SOMETHING WASN'T TAKEN OUT OF ROSCOE.
MAYBE OT LIPS PUT OMETHING NTO HIM...?
YOU COULD BE TO SOMETHING, GIZMO-GIRL!
SOMETHING TO BE ACTIVATED LATER...
EEEEEEE
SCREAMING?
DOESN'T SOUND GOOD. EASY, NOW...
YOU WERE RIGHT, GABBY.
HOT LIPS DID PUT SOMETHING INTO ROSCOE...
AND THE OTHER MUSICIANS...

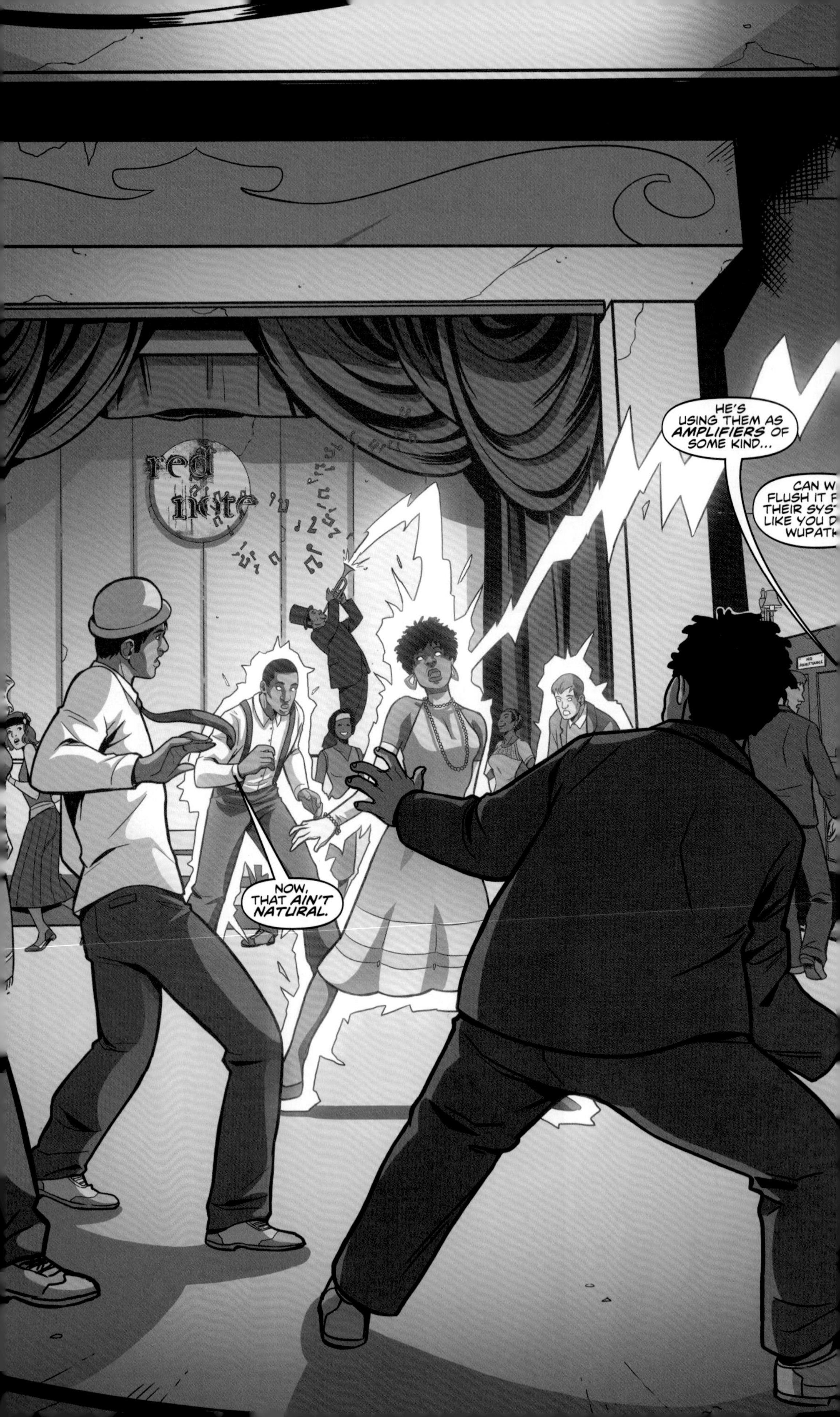
red note
NOW, THAT *AIN'T NATURAL.*
HE'S USING THEM AS *AMPLIFIERS* OF SOME KIND...
CAN W FLUSH IT F THEIR SYST LIKE YOU D WUPATK

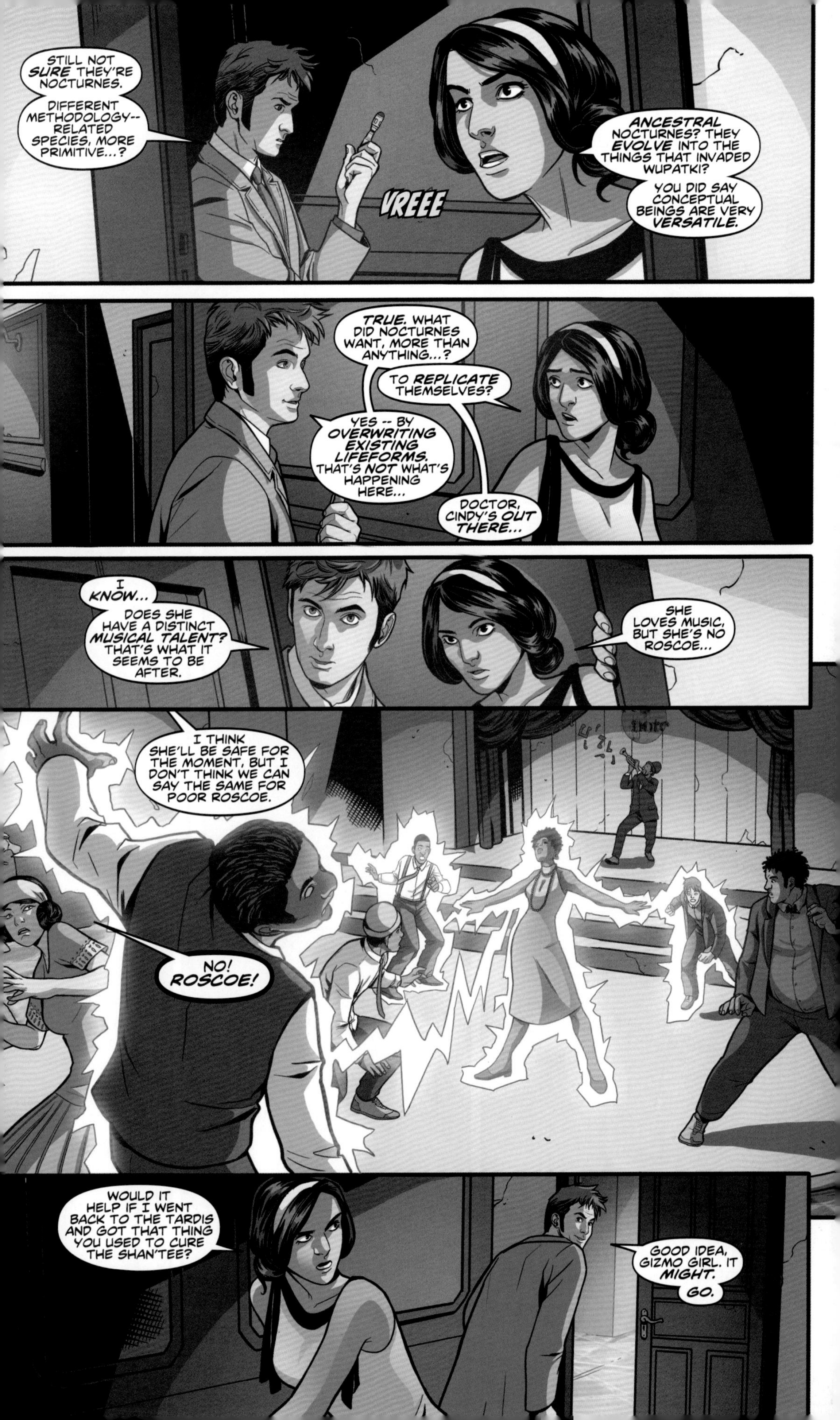
STILL NOT SURE THEY'RE NOCTURNES.
DIFFERENT METHODOLOGY-- RELATED SPECIES, MORE PRIMITIVE...?
VREEE
ANCESTRAL NOCTURNES? THEY EVOLVE INTO THE THINGS THAT INVADED WUPATKI?
YOU DID SAY CONCEPTUAL BEINGS ARE VERY VERSATILE.
TRUE. WHAT DID NOCTURNES WANT, MORE THAN ANYTHING...?
TO REPLICATE THEMSELVES?
YES -- BY OVERWRITING EXISTING LIFEFORMS. THAT'S NOT WHAT'S HAPPENING HERE...
DOCTOR, CINDY'S OUT THERE...
I KNOW...
DOES SHE HAVE A DISTINCT MUSICAL TALENT? THAT'S WHAT IT SEEMS TO BE AFTER.
SHE LOVES MUSIC, BUT SHE'S NO ROSCOE...
I THINK SHE'LL BE SAFE FOR THE MOMENT, BUT I DON'T THINK WE CAN SAY THE SAME FOR POOR ROSCOE.
NO! ROSCOE!
WOULD IT HELP IF I WENT BACK TO THE TARDIS AND GOT THAT THING YOU USED TO CURE THE SHAN'TEE?
GOOD IDEA, GIZMO GIRL. IT MIGHT.
GO.

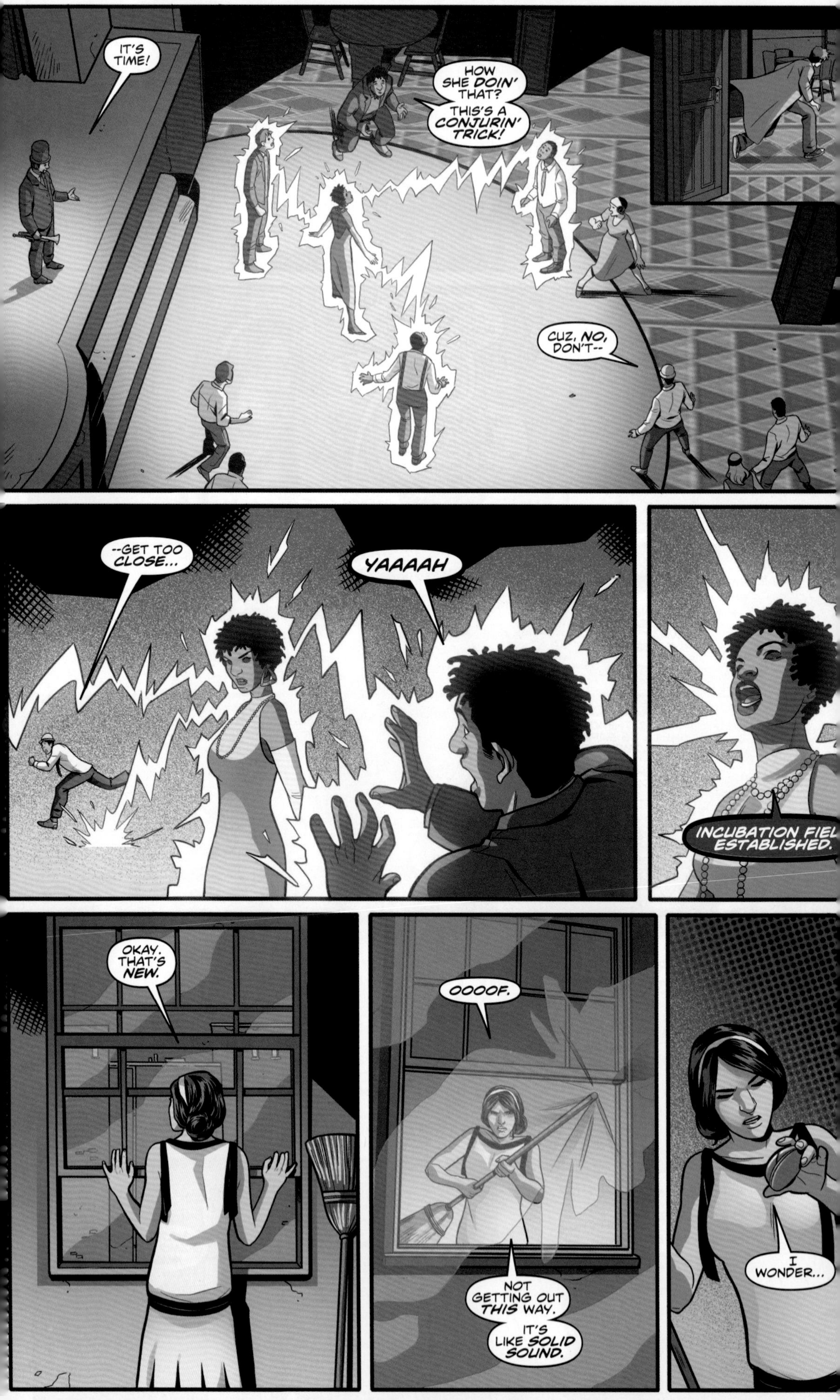
IT'S TIME!
HOW SHE DOIN' THAT?
THIS'S A CONJURIN' TRICK!
CUZ, NO, DON'T--
--GET TOO CLOSE...
YAAAAH
INCUBATION FIEL ESTABLISHED.
OKAY. THAT'S NEW.
OOOOF.
NOT GETTING OUT THIS WAY.
IT'S LIKE SOLID SOUND.
I WONDER...

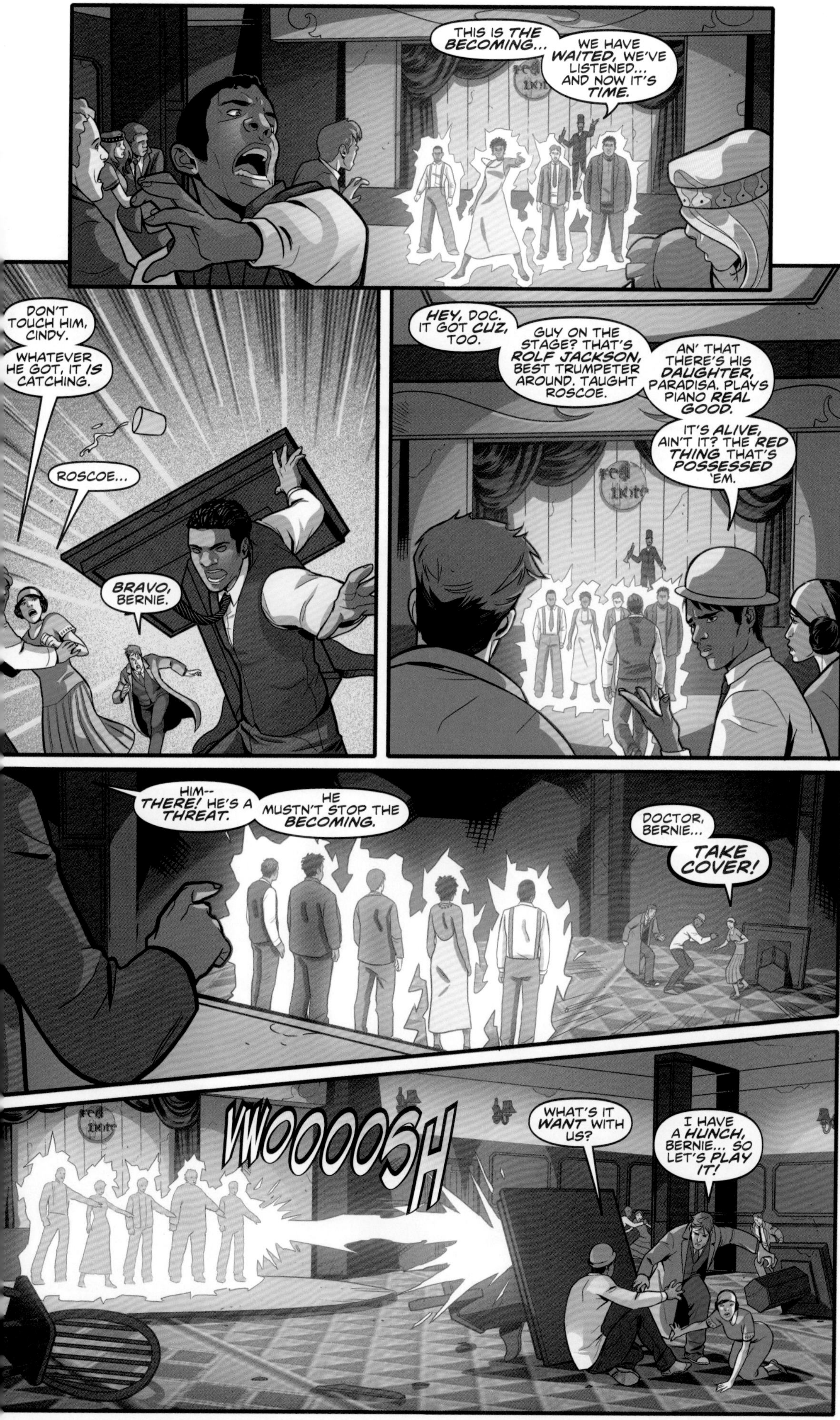
THIS IS THE BECOMING...
WE HAVE WAITED, WE'VE LISTENED... AND NOW IT'S TIME.
DON'T TOUCH HIM, CINDY.
WHATEVER HE GOT, IT IS CATCHING.
ROSCOE...
BRAVO, BERNIE.
HEY, DOC. IT GOT CUZ, TOO.
GUY ON THE STAGE? THAT'S ROLF JACKSON, BEST TRUMPETER AROUND. TAUGHT ROSCOE.
AN' THAT THERE'S HIS DAUGHTER, PARADISA. PLAYS PIANO REAL GOOD.
IT'S ALIVE, AIN'T IT? THE RED THING THAT'S POSSESSED 'EM.
HIM-- THERE! HE'S A THREAT.
HE MUSTN'T STOP THE BECOMING.
DOCTOR, BERNIE... TAKE COVER!
VWOOOOSH
WHAT'S IT WANT WITH US?
I HAVE A HUNCH, BERNIE... SO LET'S PLAY IT!

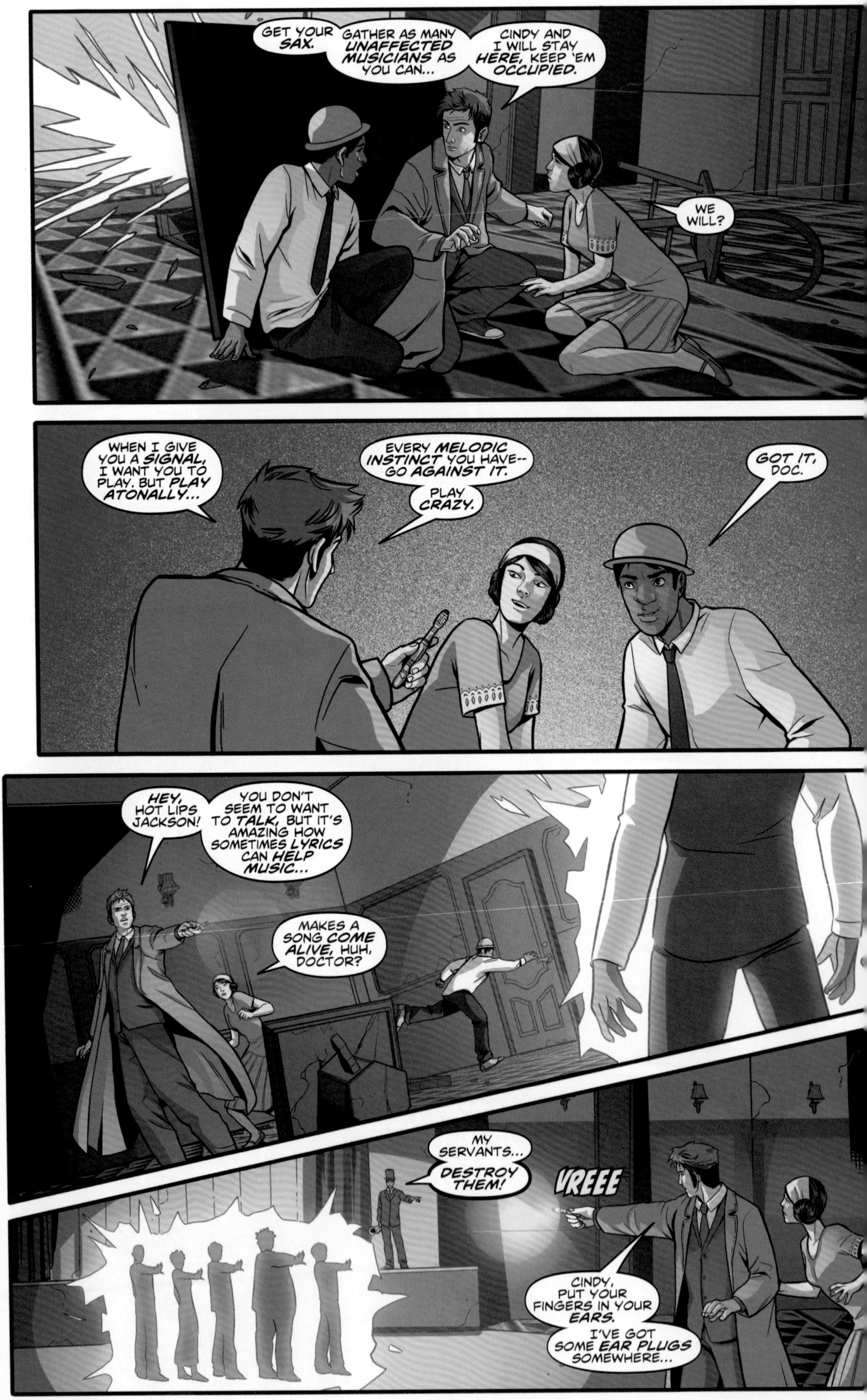
GET YOUR SAX.
GATHER AS MANY UNAFFECTED MUSICIANS AS YOU CAN...
CINDY AND I WILL STAY HERE, KEEP 'EM OCCUPIED.
WE WILL?
WHEN I GIVE YOU A SIGNAL, I WANT YOU TO PLAY. BUT PLAY ATONALLY...
EVERY MELODIC INSTINCT YOU HAVE-- GO AGAINST IT.
PLAY CRAZY.
GOT IT, DOC.
HEY, HOT LIPS JACKSON!
YOU DON'T SEEM TO WANT TO TALK, BUT IT'S AMAZING HOW SOMETIMES LYRICS CAN HELP MUSIC...
MAKES A SONG COME ALIVE, HUH, DOCTOR?
MY SERVANTS...
DESTROY THEM!
VREEE
CINDY, PUT YOUR FINGERS IN YOUR EARS.
I'VE GOT SOME EAR PLUGS SOMEWHERE...

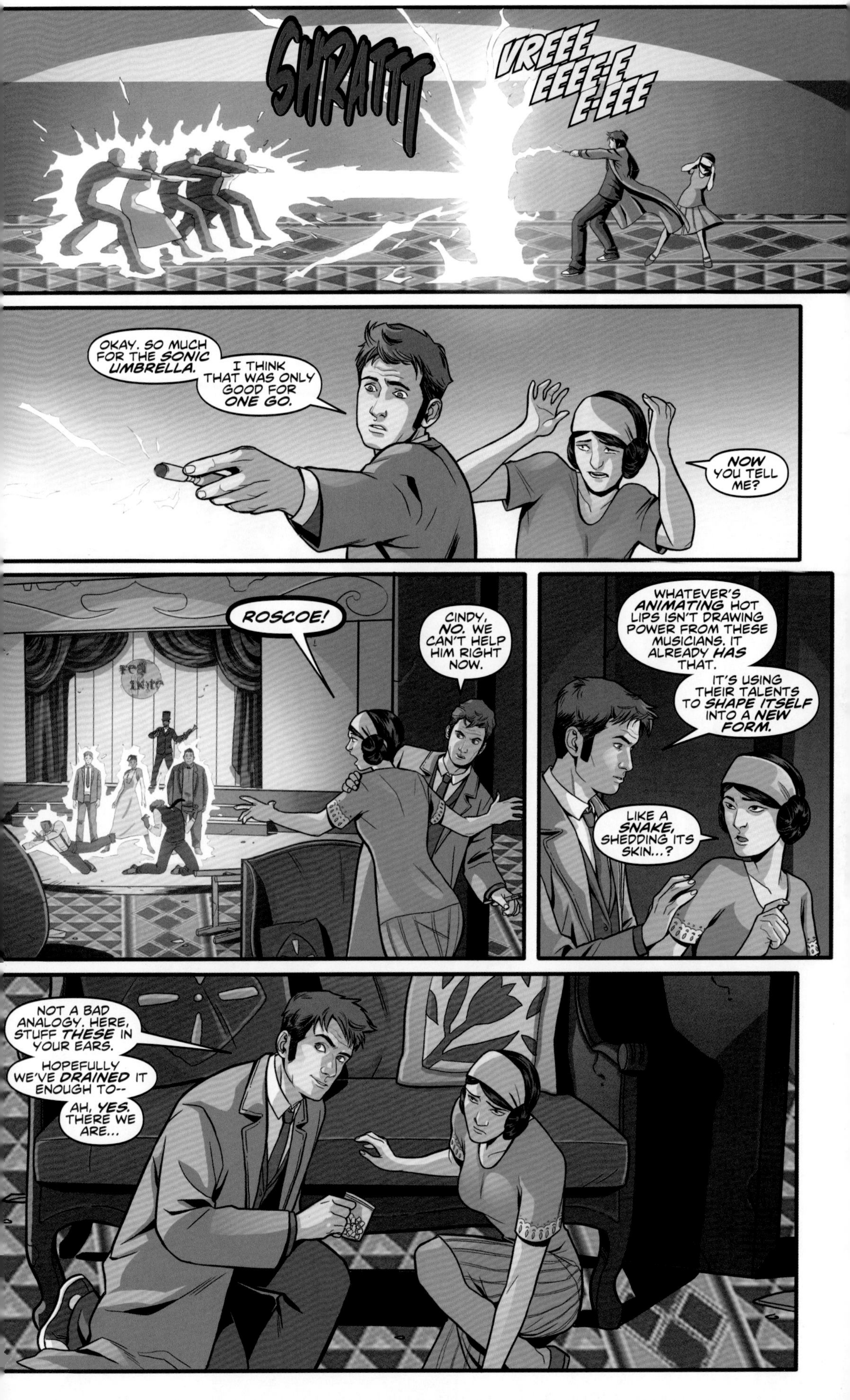
SHRATTT
VREEE EEEE-E E-EEE
OKAY. SO MUCH FOR THE SONIC UMBRELLA.
I THINK THAT WAS ONLY GOOD FOR ONE GO.
NOW YOU TELL ME?
ROSCOE!
CINDY, NO. WE CAN'T HELP HIM RIGHT NOW.
WHATEVER'S ANIMATING HOT LIPS ISN'T DRAWING POWER FROM THESE MUSICIANS. IT ALREADY HAS THAT.
IT'S USING THEIR TALENTS TO SHAPE ITSELF INTO A NEW FORM.
LIKE A SNAKE, SHEDDING ITS SKIN...?
NOT A BAD ANALOGY. HERE, STUFF THESE IN YOUR EARS.
HOPEFULLY WE'VE DRAINED IT ENOUGH TO--
AH, YES. THERE WE ARE...

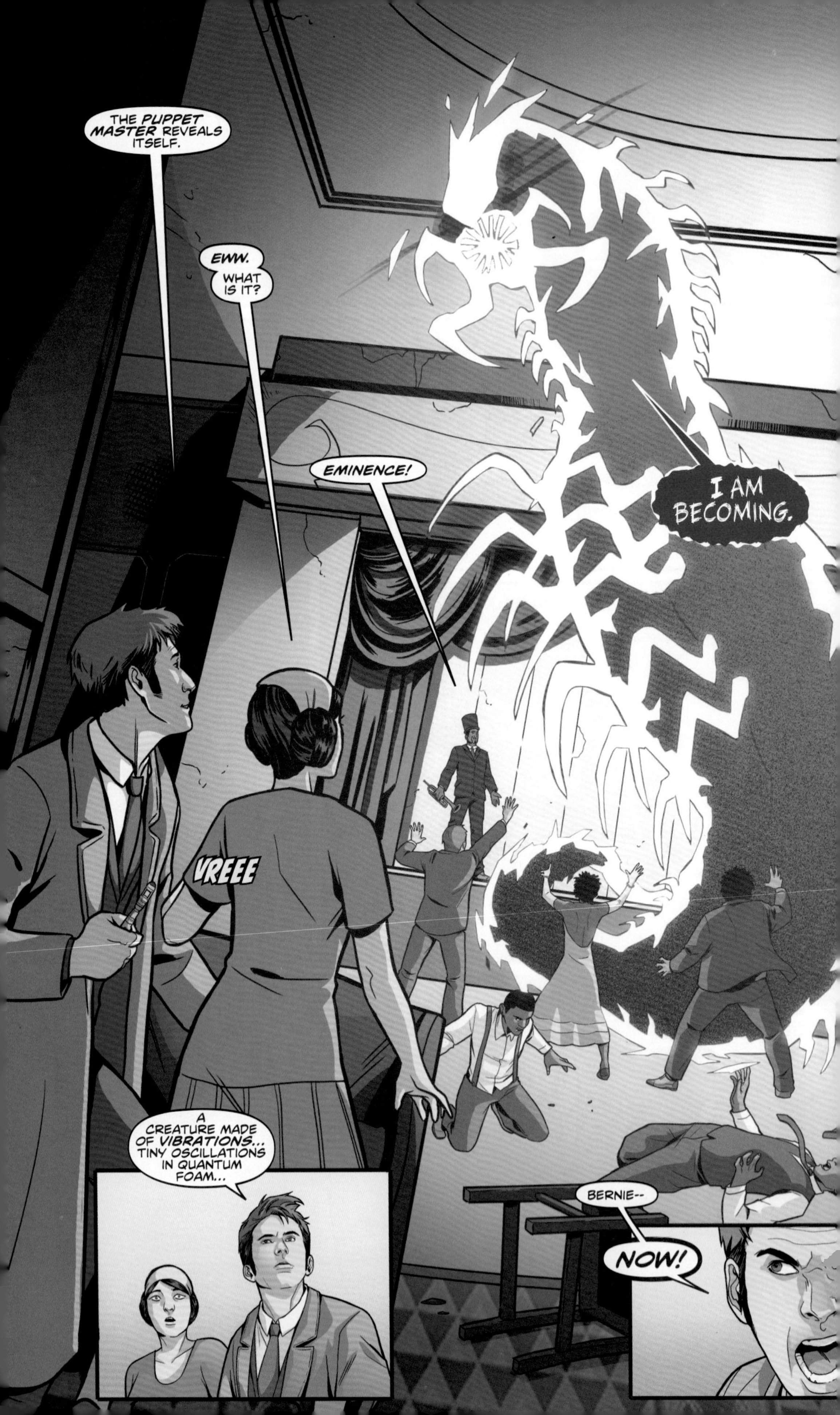
THE *PUPPET MASTER* REVEALS ITSELF.
EWW. WHAT IS IT?
EMINENCE!
I AM BECOMING.
VREEE
A CREATURE MADE OF *VIBRATIONS*... TINY OSCILLATIONS IN QUANTUM FOAM...
BERNIE--
NOW!

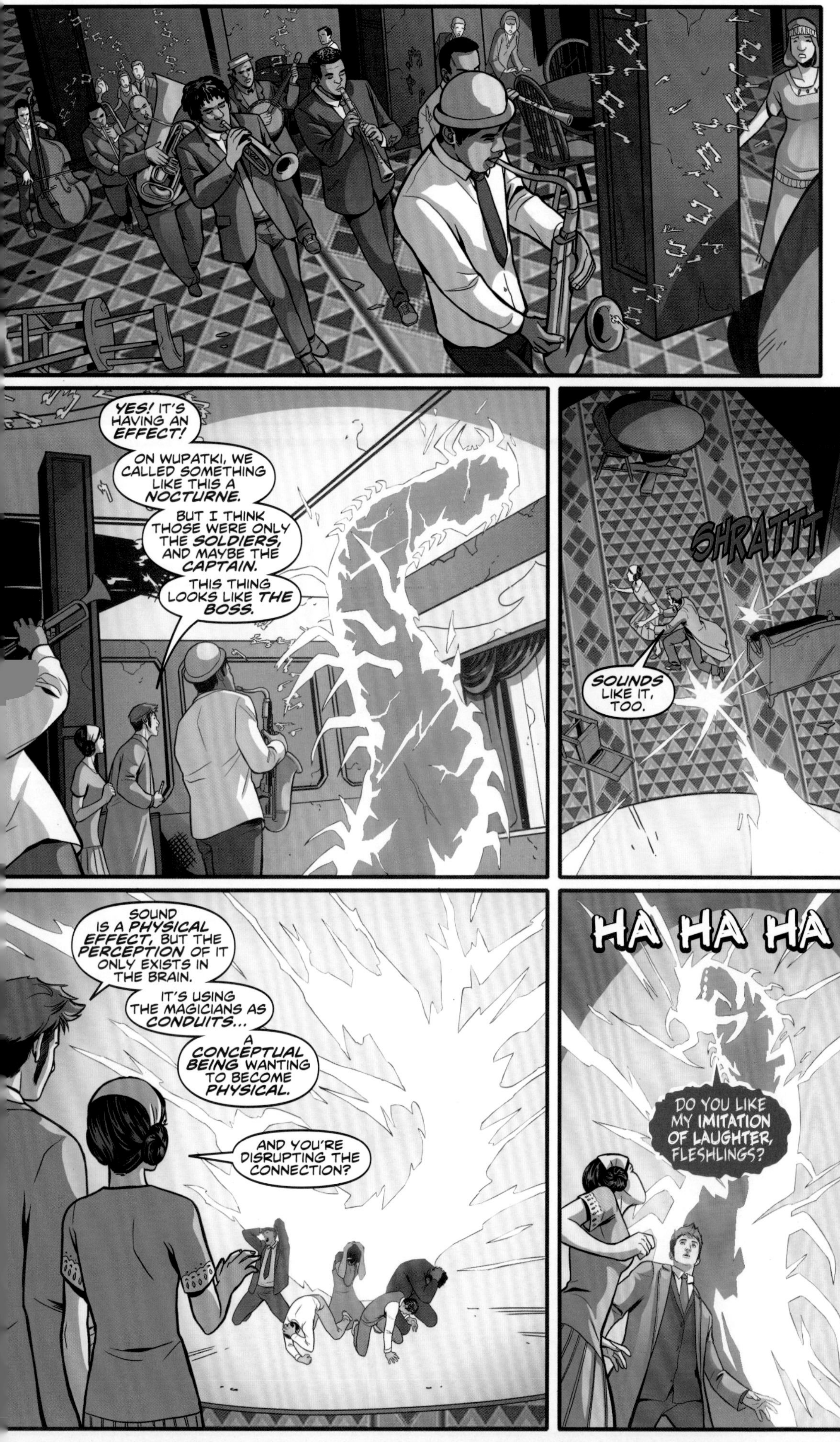

YES! IT'S HAVING AN EFFECT!
ON WUPATKI, WE CALLED SOMETHING LIKE THIS A NOCTURNE.
BUT I THINK THOSE WERE ONLY THE SOLDIERS, AND MAYBE THE CAPTAIN.
THIS THING LOOKS LIKE THE BOSS.
SHRATTT
SOUNDS LIKE IT, TOO.
SOUND IS A PHYSICAL EFFECT, BUT THE PERCEPTION OF IT ONLY EXISTS IN THE BRAIN.
IT'S USING THE MAGICIANS AS CONDUITS...
A CONCEPTUAL BEING WANTING TO BECOME PHYSICAL.
AND YOU'RE DISRUPTING THE CONNECTION?
HA HA HA
DO YOU LIKE MY IMITATION OF LAUGHTER, FLESHLINGS?

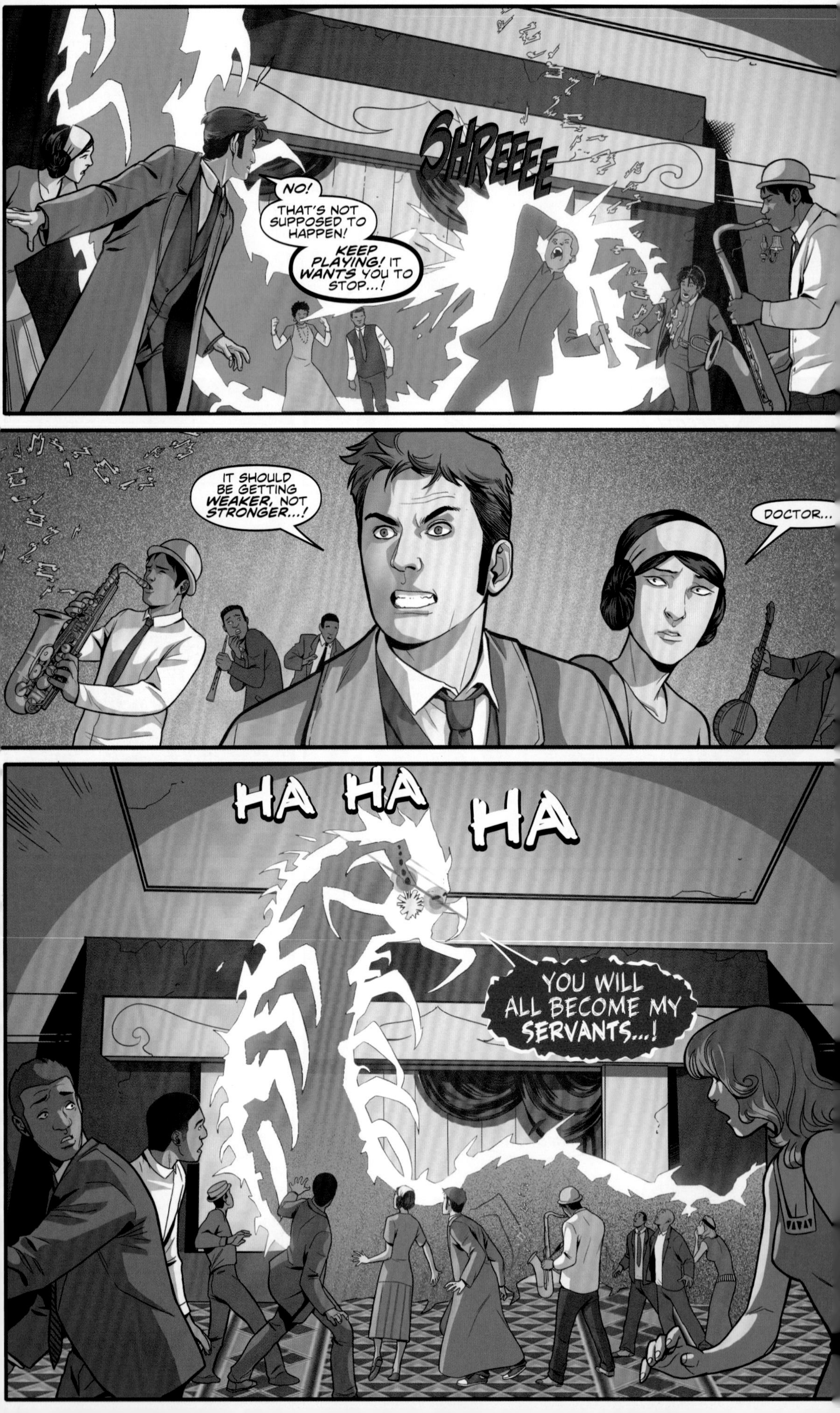
SHREEEE
NO!
THAT'S NOT SUPPOSED TO HAPPEN!
KEEP PLAYING! IT WANTS YOU TO STOP...!
IT SHOULD BE GETTING WEAKER, NOT STRONGER...!
DOCTOR...
HA HA HA
YOU WILL ALL BECOME MY SERVANTS...!

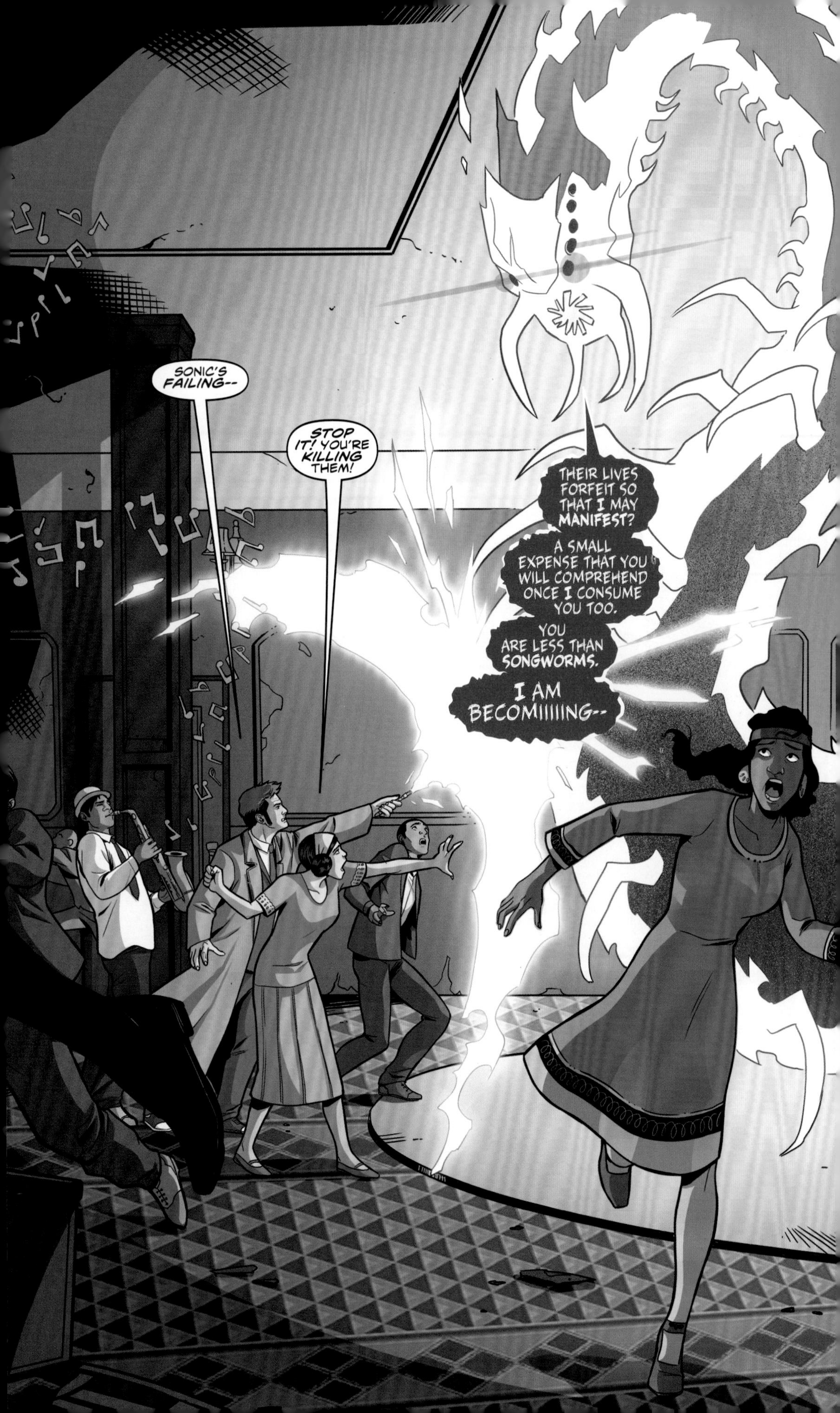
SONIC'S FAILING--
STOP IT! YOU'RE KILLING THEM!
THEIR LIVES FORFEIT SO THAT I MAY MANIFEST?
A SMALL EXPENSE THAT YOU WILL COMPREHEND ONCE I CONSUME YOU TOO.
YOU ARE LESS THAN SONGWORMS.
I AM BECOMIIIIING--

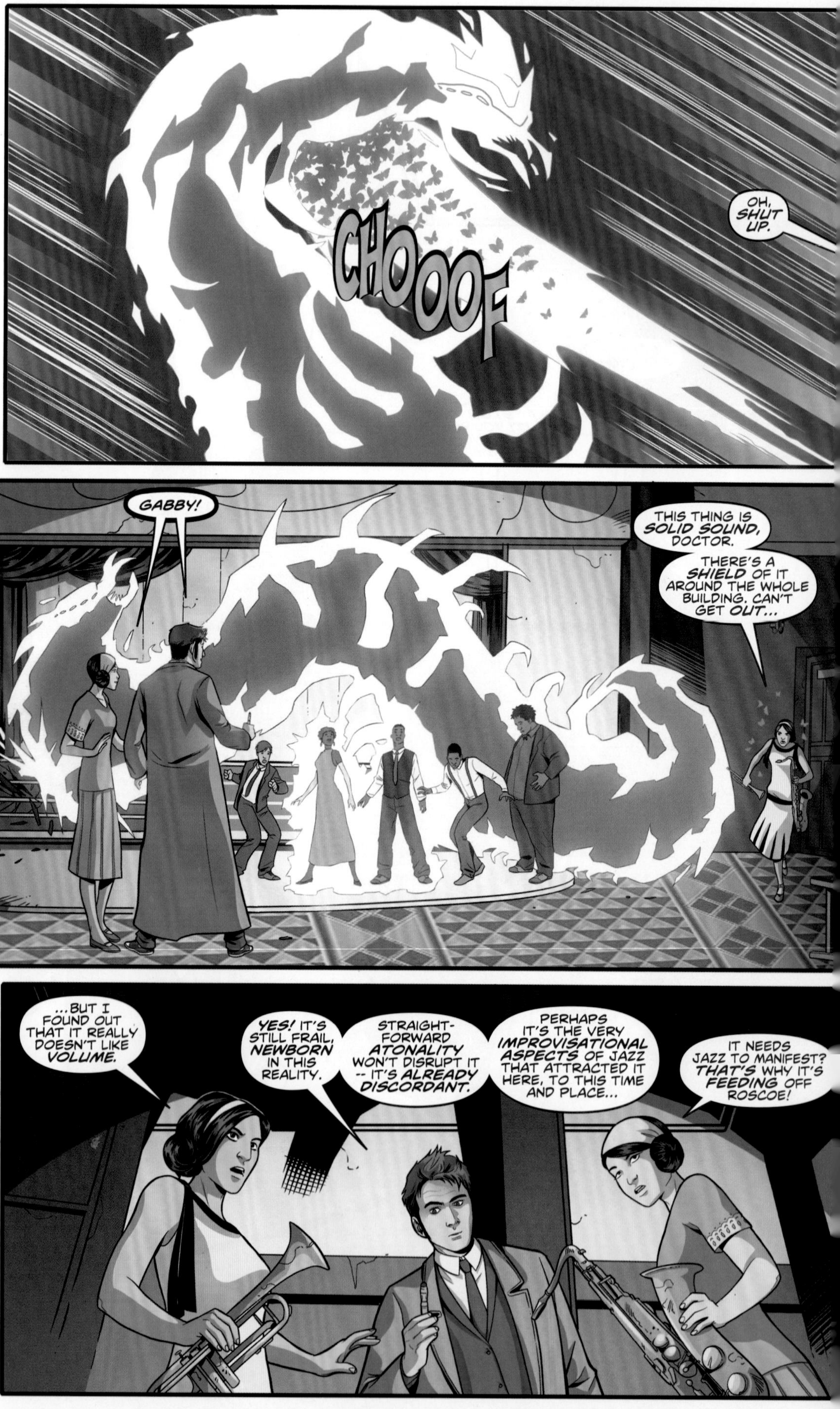
CHOOOF
OH, SHUT UP.
GABBY!
THIS THING IS SOLID SOUND, DOCTOR.
THERE'S A SHIELD OF IT AROUND THE WHOLE BUILDING. CAN'T GET OUT...
...BUT I FOUND OUT THAT IT REALLY DOESN'T LIKE VOLUME.
YES! IT'S STILL FRAIL, NEWBORN IN THIS REALITY.
STRAIGHT-FORWARD ATONALITY WON'T DISRUPT IT -- IT'S ALREADY DISCORDANT.
PERHAPS IT'S THE VERY IMPROVISATIONAL ASPECTS OF JAZZ THAT ATTRACTED IT HERE, TO THIS TIME AND PLACE...
IT NEEDS JAZZ TO MANIFEST? THAT'S WHY IT'S FEEDING OFF ROSCOE!

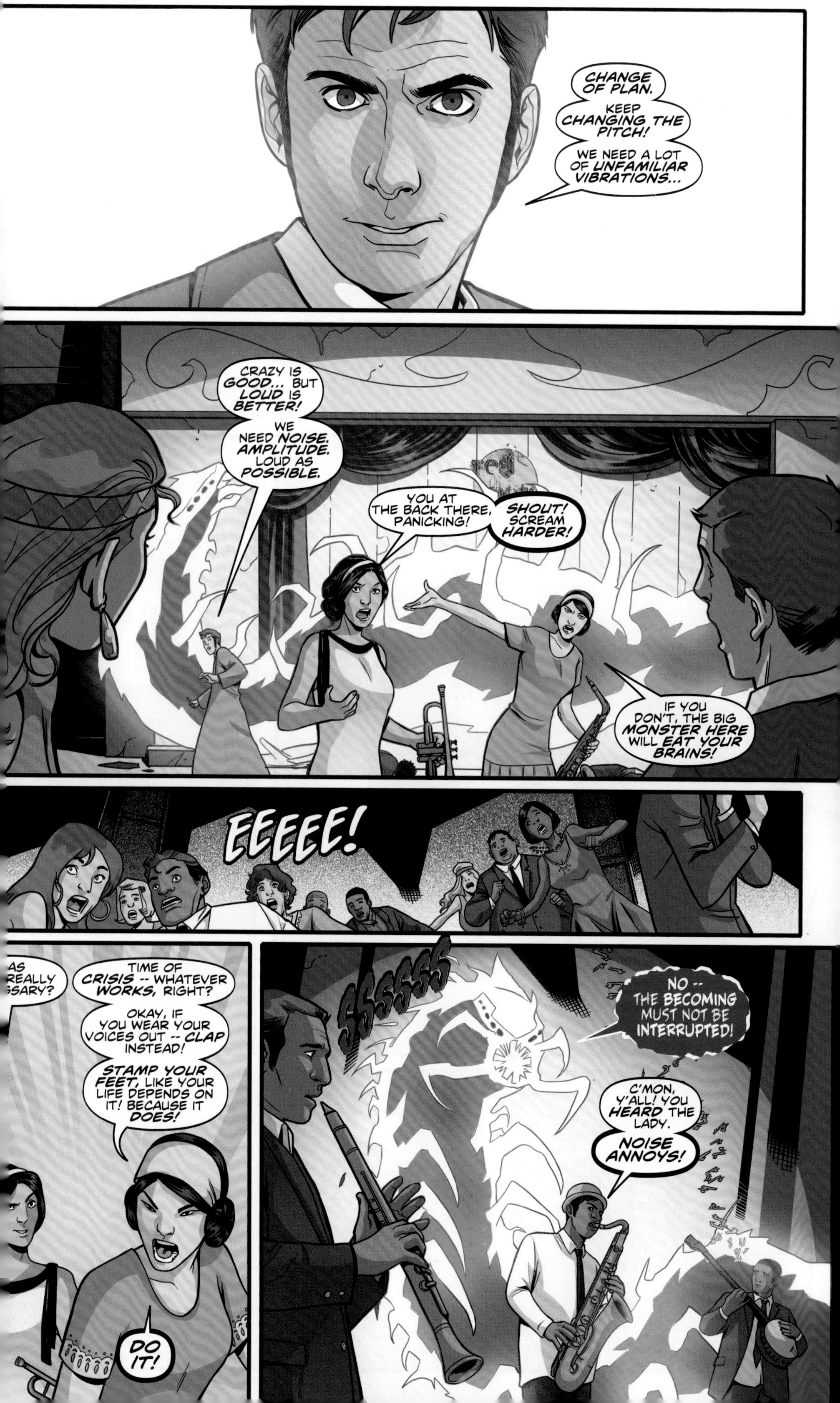
CHANGE OF PLAN.
KEEP CHANGING THE PITCH!
WE NEED A LOT OF UNFAMILIAR VIBRATIONS...
CRAZY IS GOOD... BUT LOUD IS BETTER!
WE NEED NOISE. AMPLITUDE. LOUD AS POSSIBLE.
YOU AT THE BACK THERE, PANICKING!
SHOUT! SCREAM HARDER!
IF YOU DON'T, THE BIG MONSTER HERE WILL EAT YOUR BRAINS!
EEEEE!
AS REALLY SSARY?
TIME OF CRISIS -- WHATEVER WORKS, RIGHT?
OKAY, IF YOU WEAR YOUR VOICES OUT -- CLAP INSTEAD!
STAMP YOUR FEET, LIKE YOUR LIFE DEPENDS ON IT! BECAUSE IT DOES!
DO IT!
SSSSSS
NO -- THE BECOMING MUST NOT BE INTERRUPTED!
C'MON, Y'ALL! YOU HEARD THE LADY.
NOISE ANNOYS!

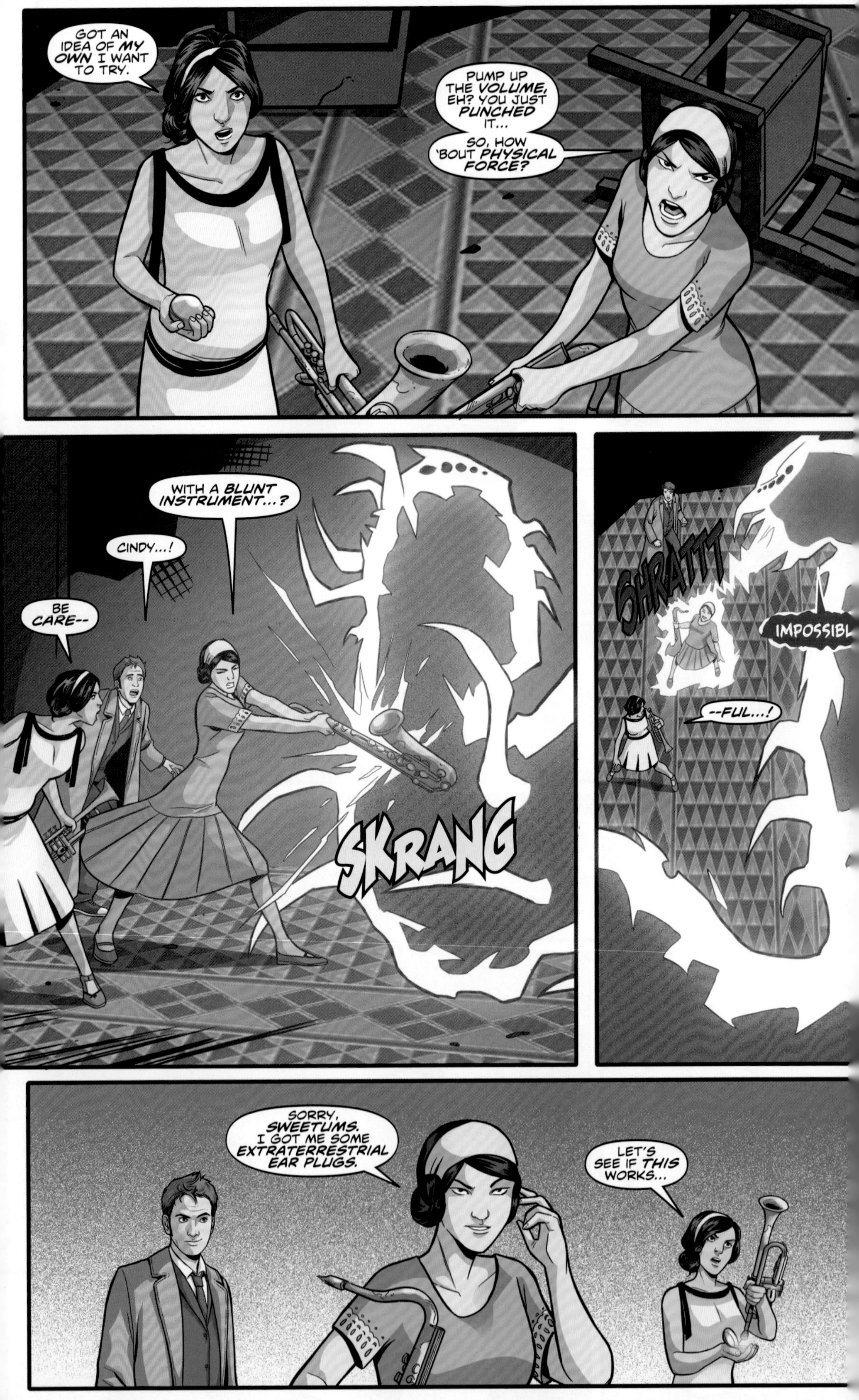
GOT AN IDEA OF MY OWN I WANT TO TRY.
PUMP UP THE VOLUME, EH? YOU JUST PUNCHED IT...
SO, HOW 'BOUT PHYSICAL FORCE?
WITH A BLUNT INSTRUMENT...?
CINDY...!
BE CARE--
SKRANG
SHRATTT
--FUL...!
IMPOSSIBL
SORRY, SWEETUMS. I GOT ME SOME EXTRATERRESTRIAL EAR PLUGS.
LET'S SEE IF THIS WORKS...

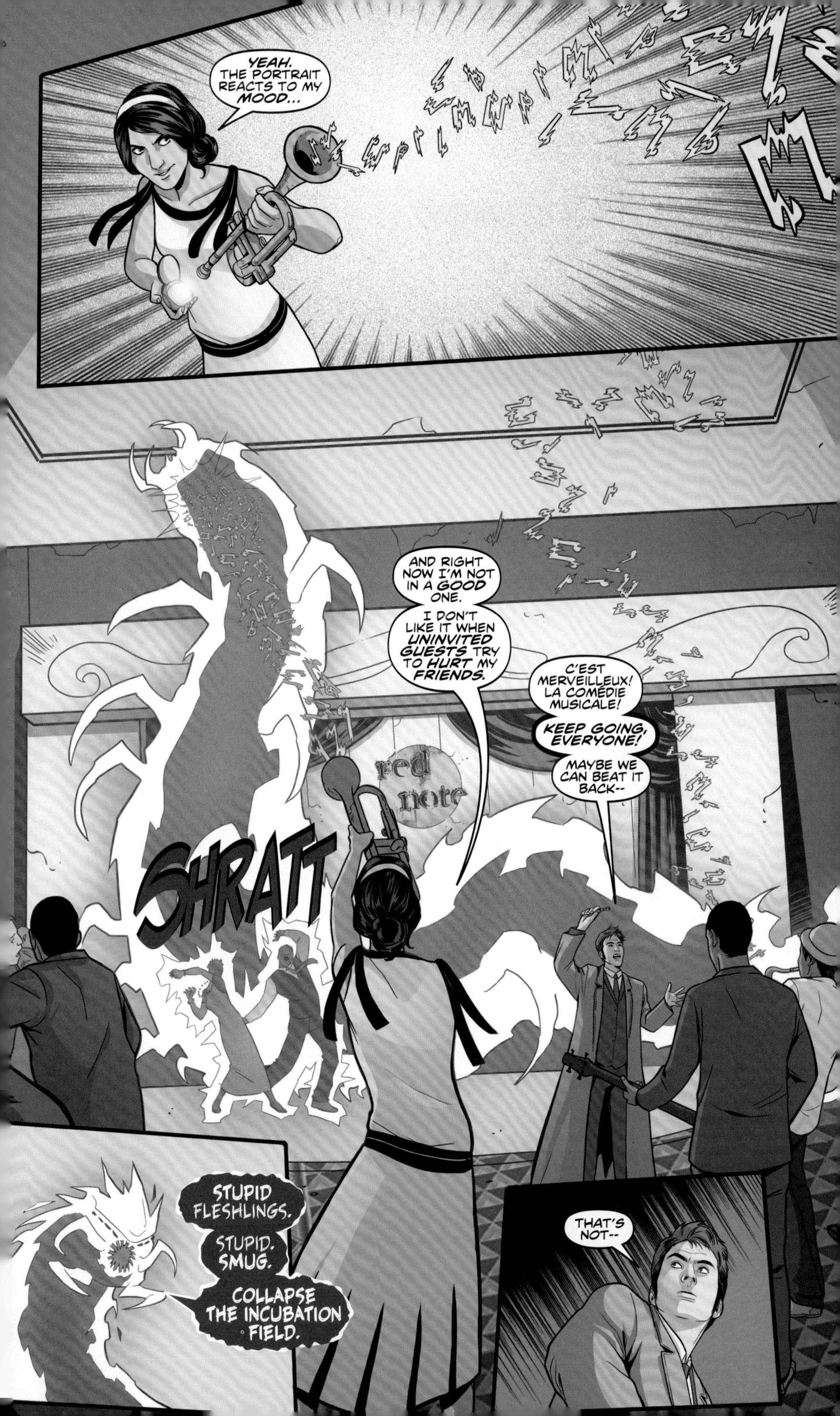

YEAH. THE PORTRAIT REACTS TO MY MOOD...
AND RIGHT NOW I'M NOT IN A GOOD ONE.
I DON'T LIKE IT WHEN UNINVITED GUESTS TRY TO HURT MY FRIENDS.
C'EST MERVEILLEUX! LA COMÉDIE MUSICALE!
KEEP GOING, EVERYONE!
MAYBE WE CAN BEAT IT BACK--
red note
SHRATT
STUPID FLESHLINGS.
STUPID. SMUG.
COLLAPSE THE INCUBATION FIELD.
THAT'S NOT--

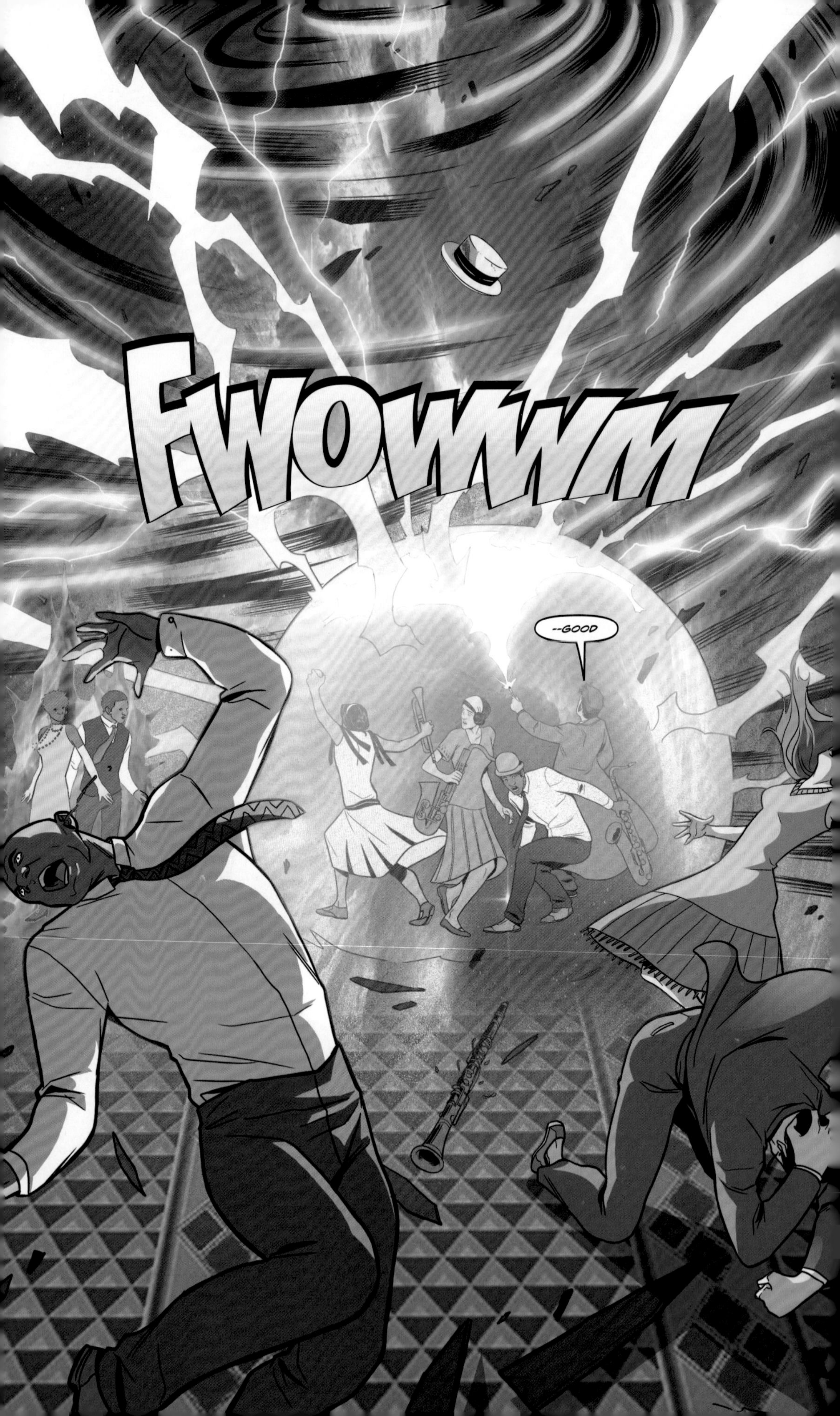
FWOWWM
--GOOD

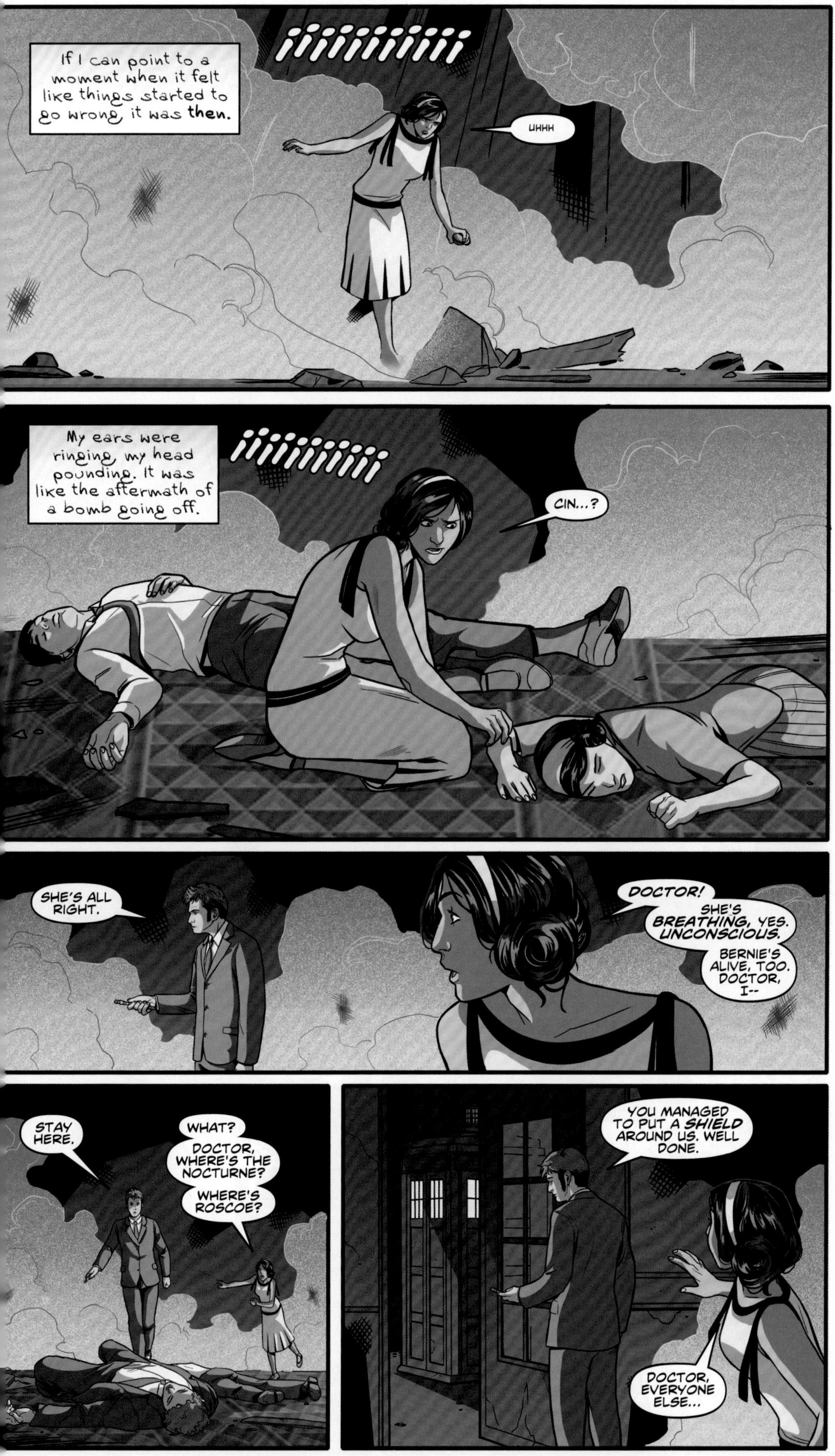
If I can point to a moment when it felt like things started to go wrong, it was then.
iiiiiiiiiii
UHHH
My ears were ringing, my head pounding. It was like the aftermath of a bomb going off.
iiiiiiiiiii
CIN...?
SHE'S ALL RIGHT.
DOCTOR!
SHE'S BREATHING, YES. UNCONSCIOUS.
BERNIE'S ALIVE, TOO. DOCTOR, I--
STAY HERE.
WHAT?
DOCTOR, WHERE'S THE NOCTURNE?
WHERE'S ROSCOE?
YOU MANAGED TO PUT A SHIELD AROUND US. WELL DONE.
DOCTOR, EVERYONE ELSE...

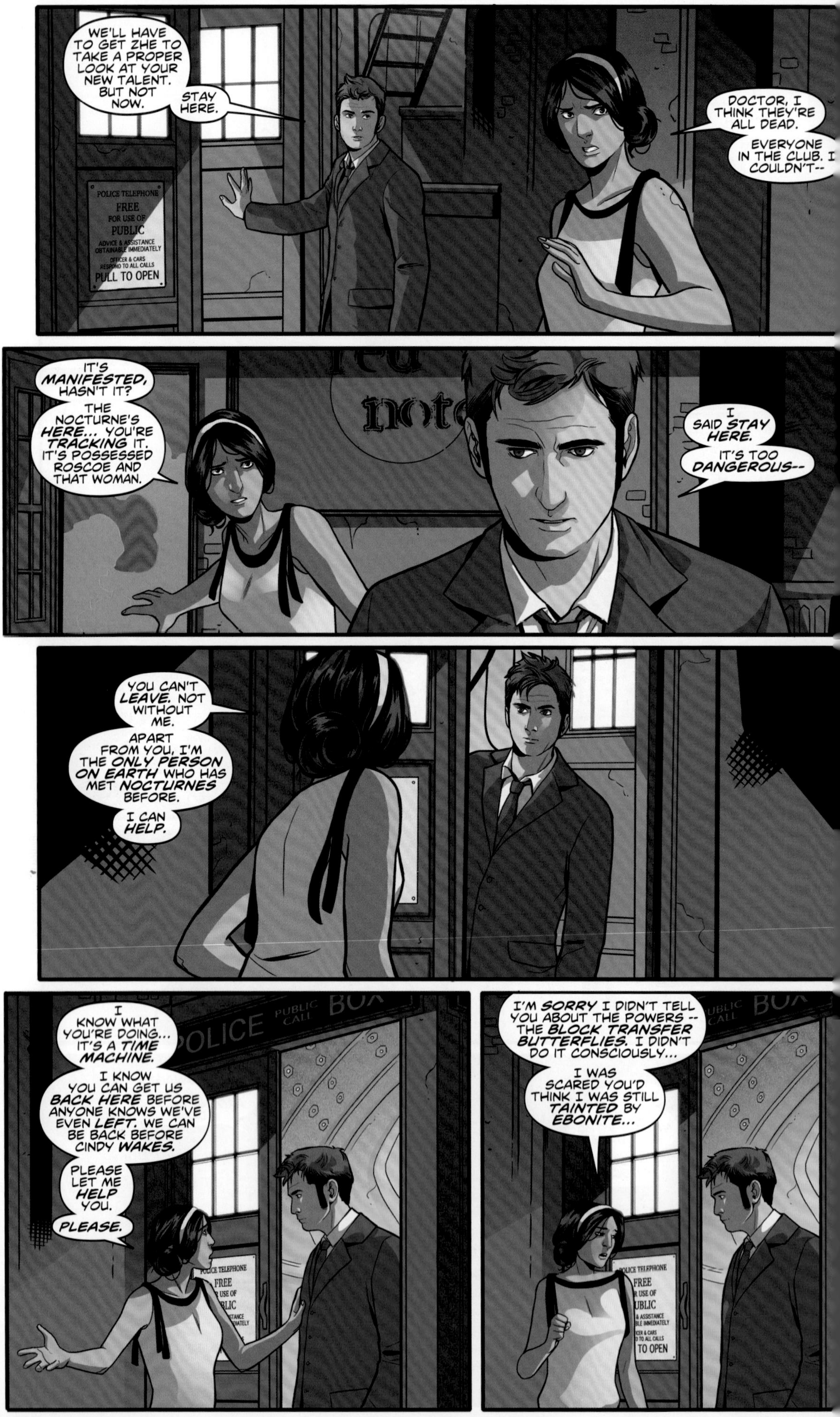
WE'LL HAVE TO GET ZHE TO TAKE A PROPER LOOK AT YOUR NEW TALENT. BUT NOT NOW.
STAY HERE.
DOCTOR, I THINK THEY'RE ALL DEAD.
EVERYONE IN THE CLUB. I COULDN'T--
POLICE TELEPHONE FREE FOR USE OF PUBLIC ADVICE & ASSISTANCE OBTAINABLE IMMEDIATELY OFFICER & CARS RESPOND TO ALL CALLS PULL TO OPEN
IT'S MANIFESTED, HASN'T IT?
THE NOCTURNE'S HERE... YOU'RE TRACKING IT. IT'S POSSESSED ROSCOE AND THAT WOMAN.
I SAID STAY HERE.
IT'S TOO DANGEROUS--
YOU CAN'T LEAVE. NOT WITHOUT ME.
APART FROM YOU, I'M THE ONLY PERSON ON EARTH WHO HAS MET NOCTURNES BEFORE.
I CAN HELP.
I KNOW WHAT YOU'RE DOING... IT'S A TIME MACHINE.
I KNOW YOU CAN GET US BACK HERE BEFORE ANYONE KNOWS WE'VE EVEN LEFT. WE CAN BE BACK BEFORE CINDY WAKES.
PLEASE LET ME HELP YOU.
PLEASE.
POLICE PUBLIC CALL BOX
I'M SORRY I DIDN'T TELL YOU ABOUT THE POWERS -- THE BLOCK TRANSFER BUTTERFLIES. I DIDN'T DO IT CONSCIOUSLY...
I WAS SCARED YOU'D THINK I WAS STILL TAINTED BY EBONITE...

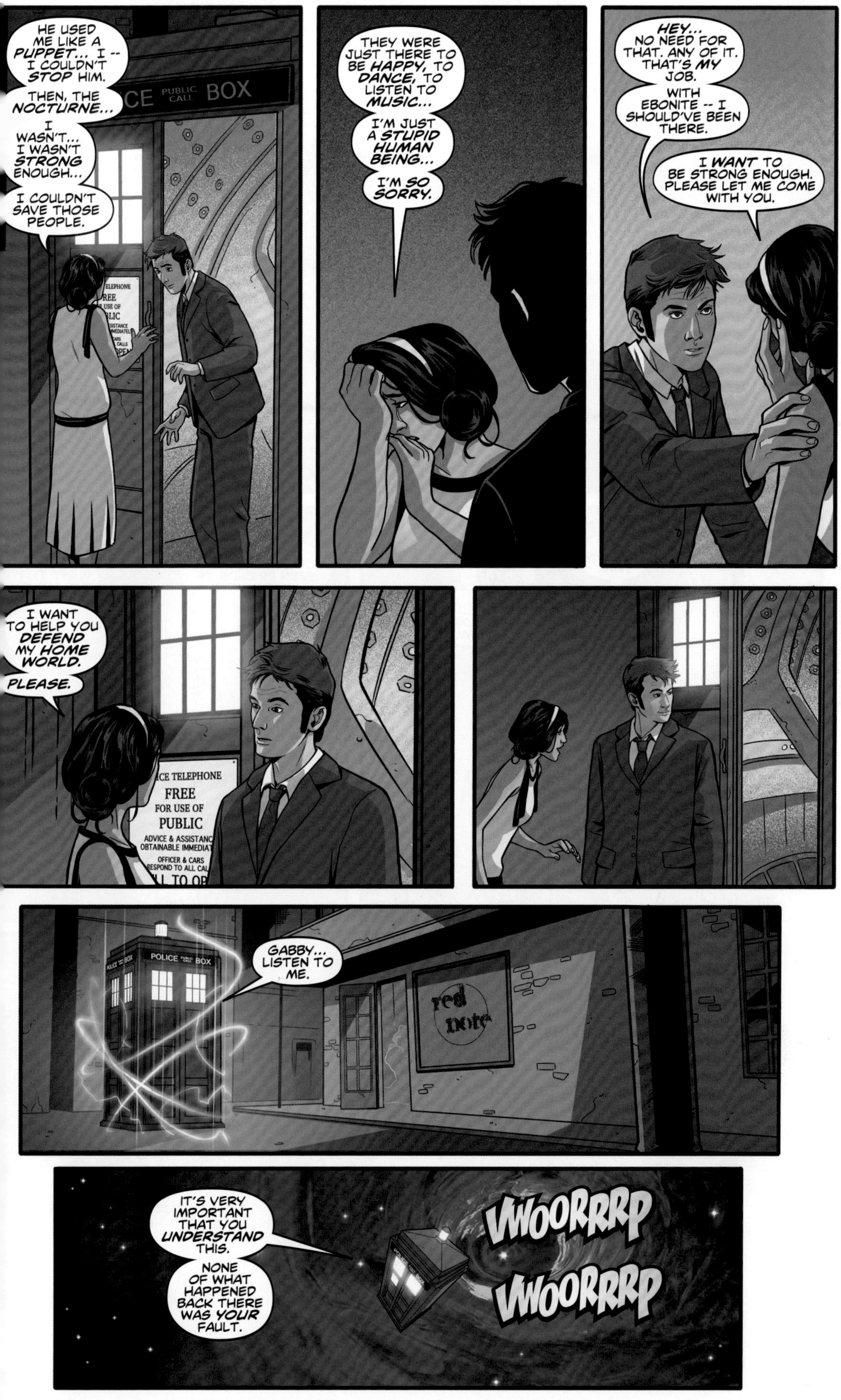
HE USED ME LIKE A PUPPET... I -- I COULDN'T STOP HIM.
THEN, THE NOCTURNE...
I WASN'T... I WASN'T STRONG ENOUGH...
I COULDN'T SAVE THOSE PEOPLE.
POLICE PUBLIC CALL BOX
THEY WERE JUST THERE TO BE HAPPY, TO DANCE, TO LISTEN TO MUSIC...
I'M JUST A STUPID HUMAN BEING...
I'M SO SORRY.
HEY... NO NEED FOR THAT. ANY OF IT. THAT'S MY JOB.
WITH EBONITE -- I SHOULD'VE BEEN THERE.
I WANT TO BE STRONG ENOUGH. PLEASE LET ME COME WITH YOU.
I WANT TO HELP YOU DEFEND MY HOME WORLD.
PLEASE.
FREE
FOR USE OF
PUBLIC
ADVICE & ASSISTANC
OBTAINABLE IMMEDIAT
OFFICER & CARS
RESPOND TO ALL CAL
POLICE PUBLIC CALL BOX
GABBY... LISTEN TO ME.
red note
IT'S VERY IMPORTANT THAT YOU UNDERSTAND THIS.
NONE OF WHAT HAPPENED BACK THERE WAS YOUR FAULT.
VWOORRRP
VWOORRRP

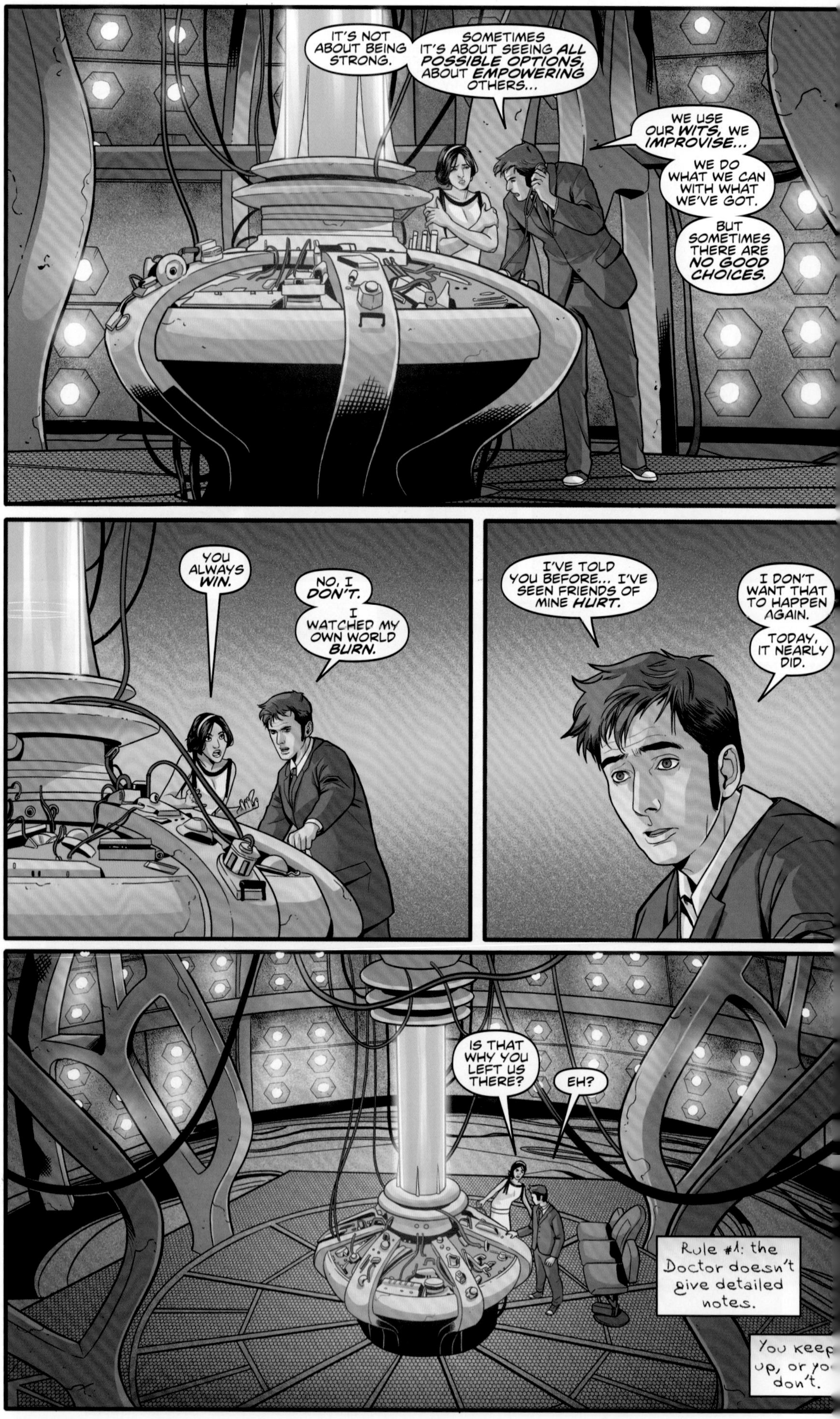
IT'S NOT ABOUT BEING STRONG.
SOMETIMES IT'S ABOUT SEEING ALL POSSIBLE OPTIONS, ABOUT EMPOWERING OTHERS...
WE USE OUR WITS, WE IMPROVISE...
WE DO WHAT WE CAN WITH WHAT WE'VE GOT.
BUT SOMETIMES THERE ARE NO GOOD CHOICES.
YOU ALWAYS WIN.
NO, I DON'T.
I WATCHED MY OWN WORLD BURN.
I'VE TOLD YOU BEFORE... I'VE SEEN FRIENDS OF MINE HURT.
I DON'T WANT THAT TO HAPPEN AGAIN.
TODAY, IT NEARLY DID.
IS THAT WHY YOU LEFT US THERE?
EH?
Rule #1: the Doctor doesn't give detailed notes.
You keep up, or yo don't.

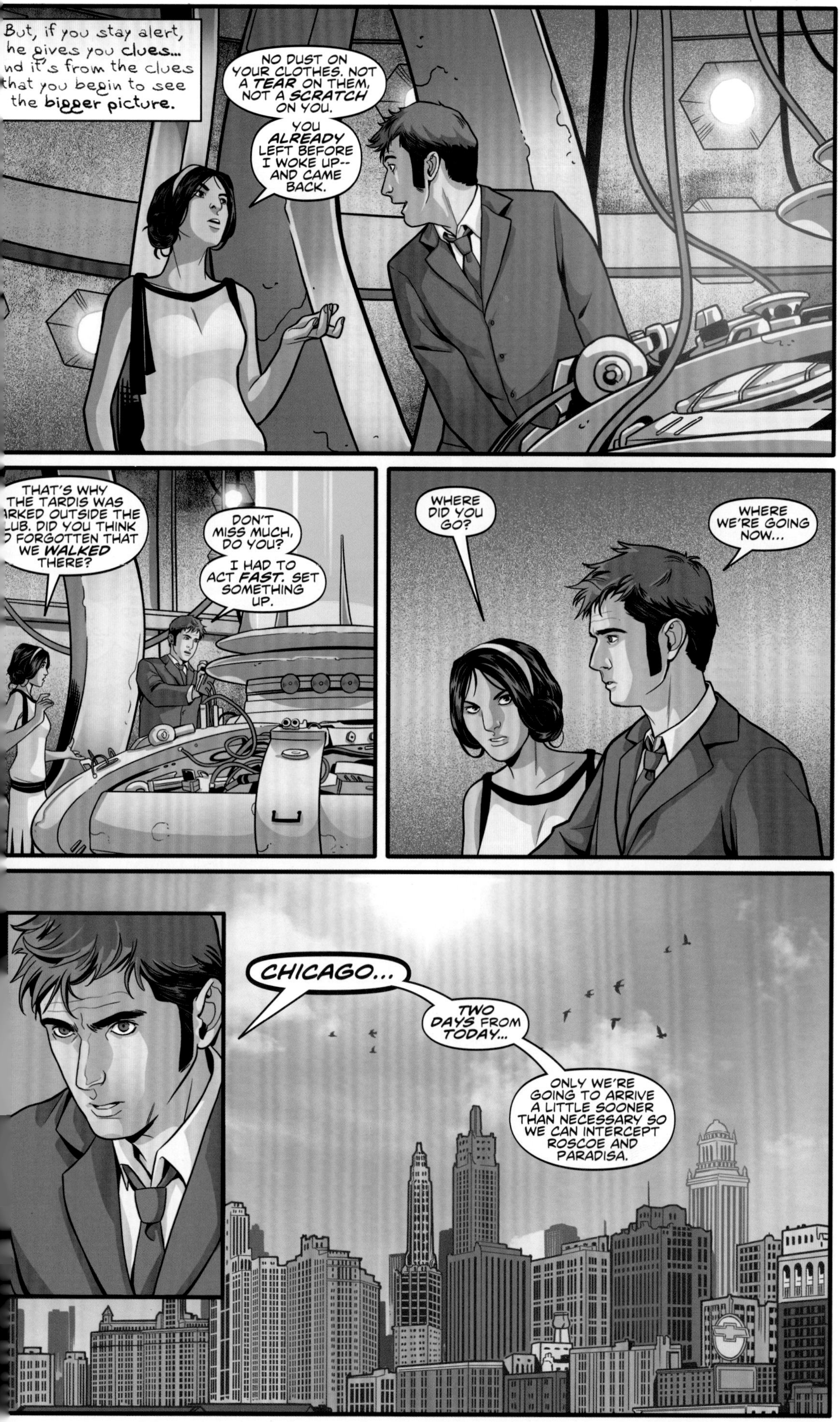
But, if you stay alert, he gives you **clues...** nd it's from the clues that you begin to see the **bigger picture.**
NO DUST ON YOUR CLOTHES. NOT A *TEAR* ON THEM, NOT A *SCRATCH* ON YOU.
YOU *ALREADY* LEFT BEFORE I WOKE UP-- AND CAME BACK.
THAT'S WHY THE TARDIS WAS ARKED OUTSIDE THE LUB. DID YOU THINK D FORGOTTEN THAT WE *WALKED* THERE?
DON'T MISS MUCH, DO YOU?
I HAD TO ACT *FAST.* SET SOMETHING UP.
WHERE DID YOU GO?
WHERE WE'RE GOING NOW...
CHICAGO...
TWO DAYS FROM *TODAY...*
ONLY WE'RE GOING TO ARRIVE A LITTLE SOONER THAN NECESSARY SO WE CAN INTERCEPT ROSCOE AND PARADISA.

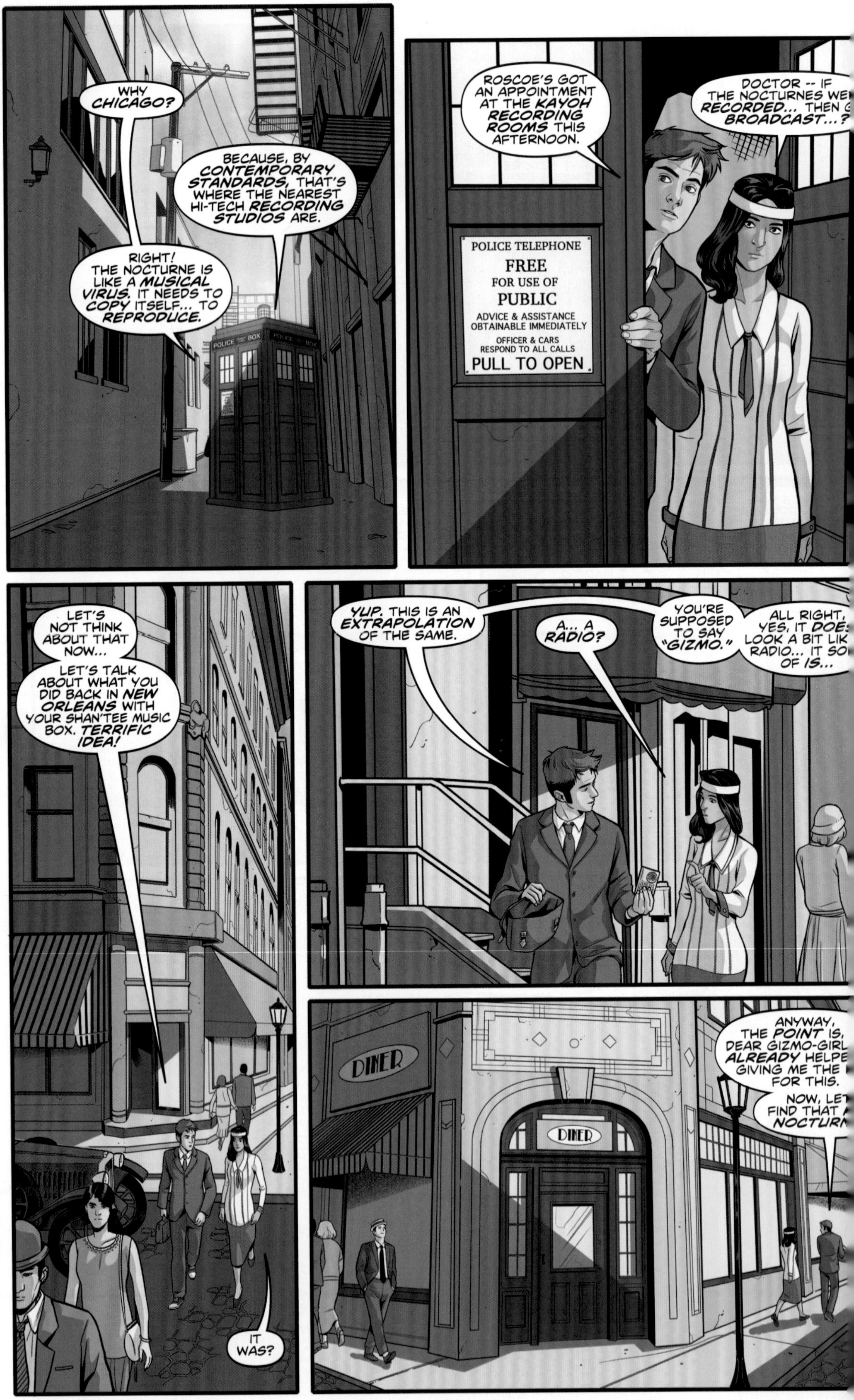
WHY CHICAGO?
BECAUSE, BY CONTEMPORARY STANDARDS, THAT'S WHERE THE NEAREST HI-TECH RECORDING STUDIOS ARE.
RIGHT! THE NOCTURNE IS LIKE A MUSICAL VIRUS. IT NEEDS TO COPY ITSELF... TO REPRODUCE.
POLICE BOX
ROSCOE'S GOT AN APPOINTMENT AT THE KAYOH RECORDING ROOMS THIS AFTERNOON.
POLICE TELEPHONE FREE FOR USE OF PUBLIC ADVICE & ASSISTANCE OBTAINABLE IMMEDIATELY OFFICER & CARS RESPOND TO ALL CALLS PULL TO OPEN
DOCTOR -- IF THE NOCTURNES WE RECORDED... THEN BROADCAST...?
LET'S NOT THINK ABOUT THAT NOW...
LET'S TALK ABOUT WHAT YOU DID BACK IN NEW ORLEANS WITH YOUR SHAN'TEE MUSIC BOX. TERRIFIC IDEA!
IT WAS?
YUP. THIS IS AN EXTRAPOLATION OF THE SAME.
A... A RADIO?
YOU'RE SUPPOSED TO SAY "GIZMO."
ALL RIGHT, YES, IT DOE LOOK A BIT LIK RADIO... IT SO OF IS...
DINER
DINER
ANYWAY, THE POINT IS, DEAR GIZMO-GIRL ALREADY HELPE GIVING ME THE FOR THIS.
NOW, LET FIND THAT NOCTURN

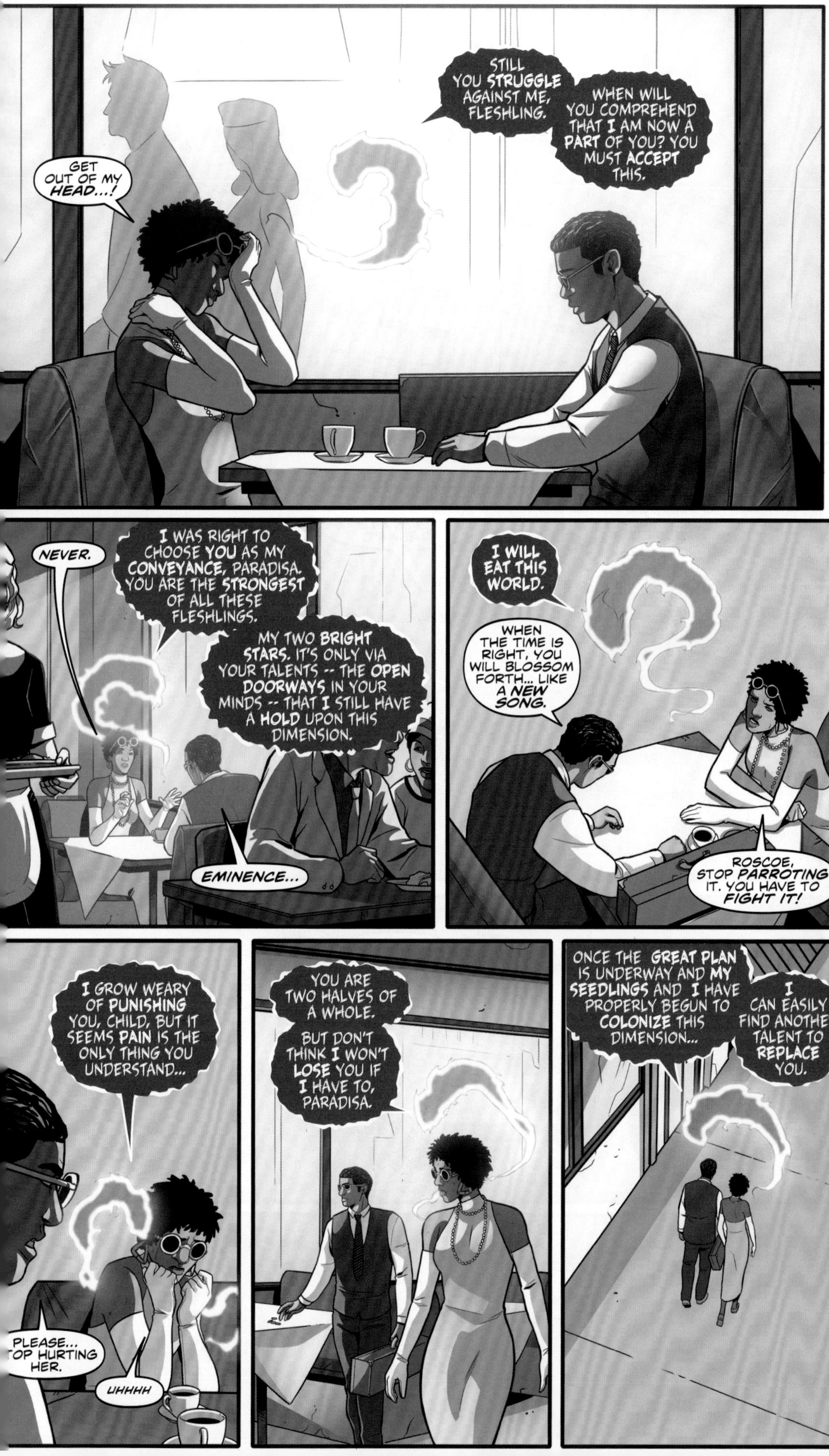
GET OUT OF MY HEAD...!
STILL YOU STRUGGLE AGAINST ME, FLESHLING.
WHEN WILL YOU COMPREHEND THAT I AM NOW A PART OF YOU? YOU MUST ACCEPT THIS.
NEVER.
I WAS RIGHT TO CHOOSE YOU AS MY CONVEYANCE, PARADISA. YOU ARE THE STRONGEST OF ALL THESE FLESHLINGS.
MY TWO BRIGHT STARS. IT'S ONLY VIA YOUR TALENTS -- THE OPEN DOORWAYS IN YOUR MINDS -- THAT I STILL HAVE A HOLD UPON THIS DIMENSION.
EMINENCE...
I WILL EAT THIS WORLD.
WHEN THE TIME IS RIGHT, YOU WILL BLOSSOM FORTH... LIKE A NEW SONG.
ROSCOE, STOP PARROTING IT. YOU HAVE TO FIGHT IT!
I GROW WEARY OF PUNISHING YOU, CHILD, BUT IT SEEMS PAIN IS THE ONLY THING YOU UNDERSTAND...
PLEASE... TOP HURTING HER.
UHHHH
YOU ARE TWO HALVES OF A WHOLE.
BUT DON'T THINK I WON'T LOSE YOU IF I HAVE TO, PARADISA.
ONCE THE GREAT PLAN IS UNDERWAY AND MY SEEDLINGS AND I HAVE PROPERLY BEGUN TO COLONIZE THIS DIMENSION...
I CAN EASILY FIND ANOTHER TALENT TO REPLACE YOU.

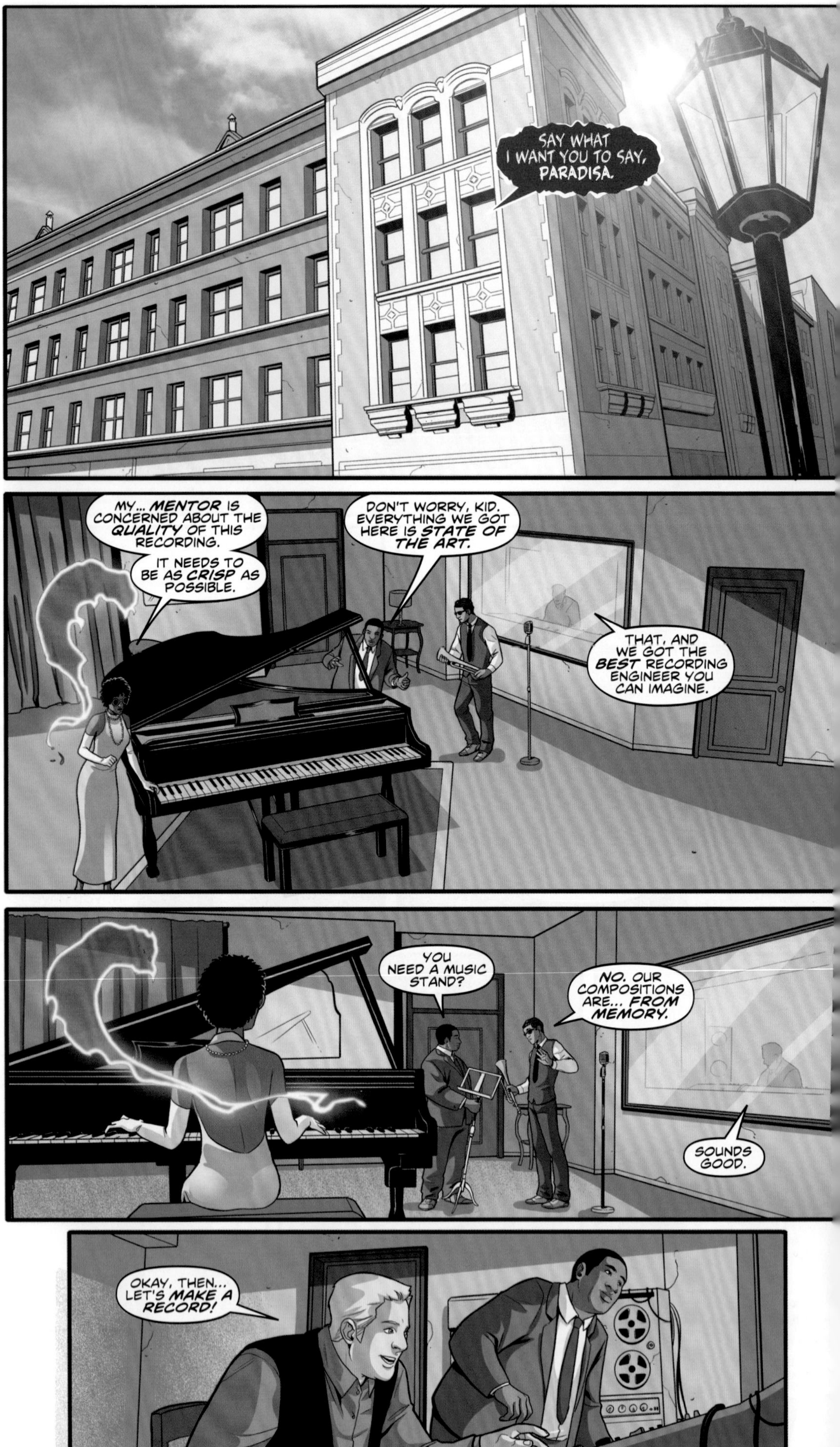
SAY WHAT I WANT YOU TO SAY, PARADISA.
MY... MENTOR IS CONCERNED ABOUT THE QUALITY OF THIS RECORDING.
IT NEEDS TO BE AS CRISP AS POSSIBLE.
DON'T WORRY, KID. EVERYTHING WE GOT HERE IS STATE OF THE ART.
THAT, AND WE GOT THE BEST RECORDING ENGINEER YOU CAN IMAGINE.
YOU NEED A MUSIC STAND?
NO. OUR COMPOSITIONS ARE... FROM MEMORY.
SOUNDS GOOD.
OKAY, THEN... LET'S MAKE A RECORD!

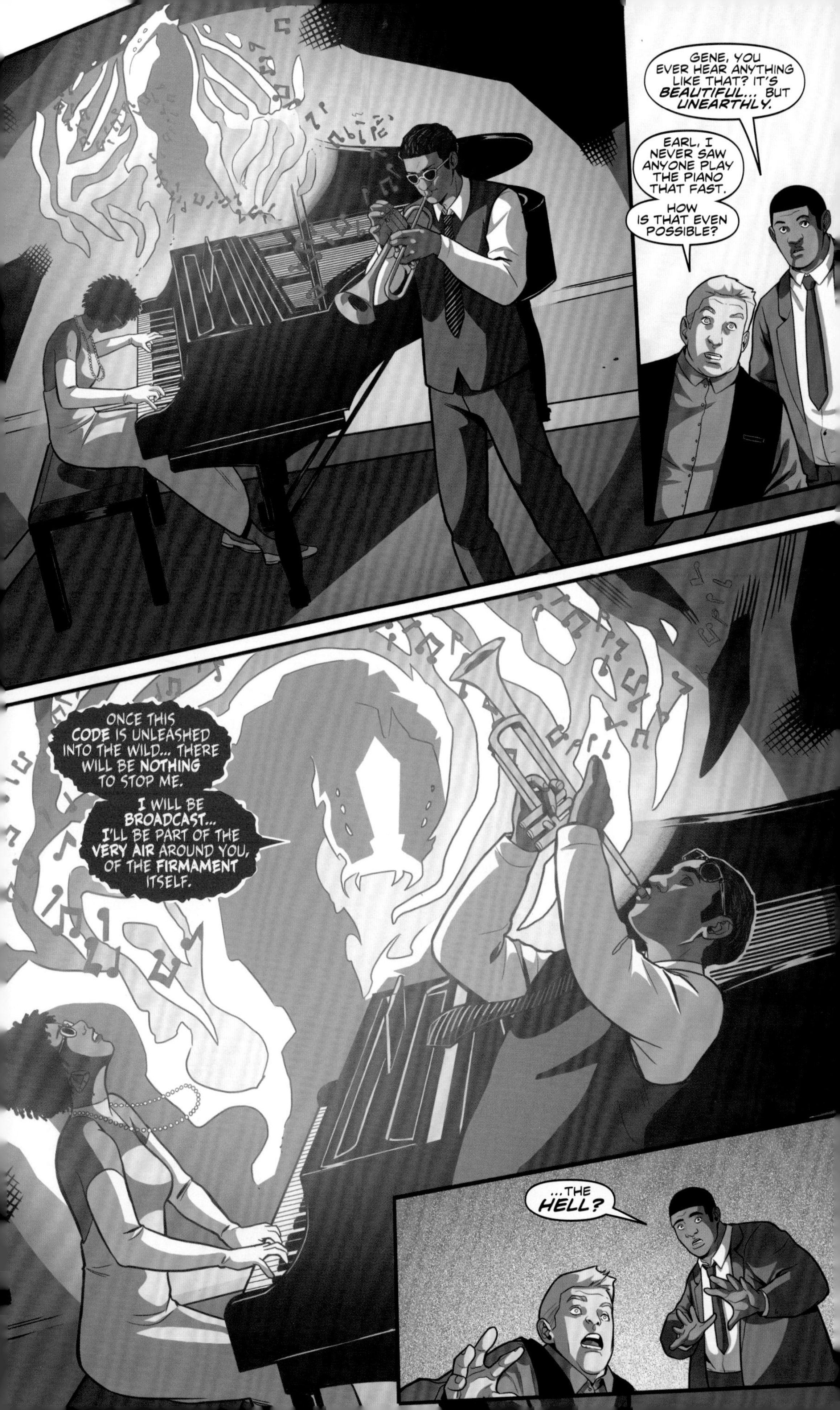

GENE, YOU EVER HEAR ANYTHING LIKE THAT? IT'S *BEAUTIFUL*... BUT *UNEARTHLY*.
EARL, I NEVER SAW ANYONE PLAY THE PIANO THAT FAST.
HOW IS THAT EVEN POSSIBLE?
ONCE THIS **CODE** IS UNLEASHED INTO THE WILD... THERE WILL BE **NOTHING** TO STOP ME.
I WILL BE **BROADCAST...** **I'LL** BE PART OF THE **VERY AIR** AROUND YOU, OF THE **FIRMAMENT** ITSELF.
...THE *HELL?*

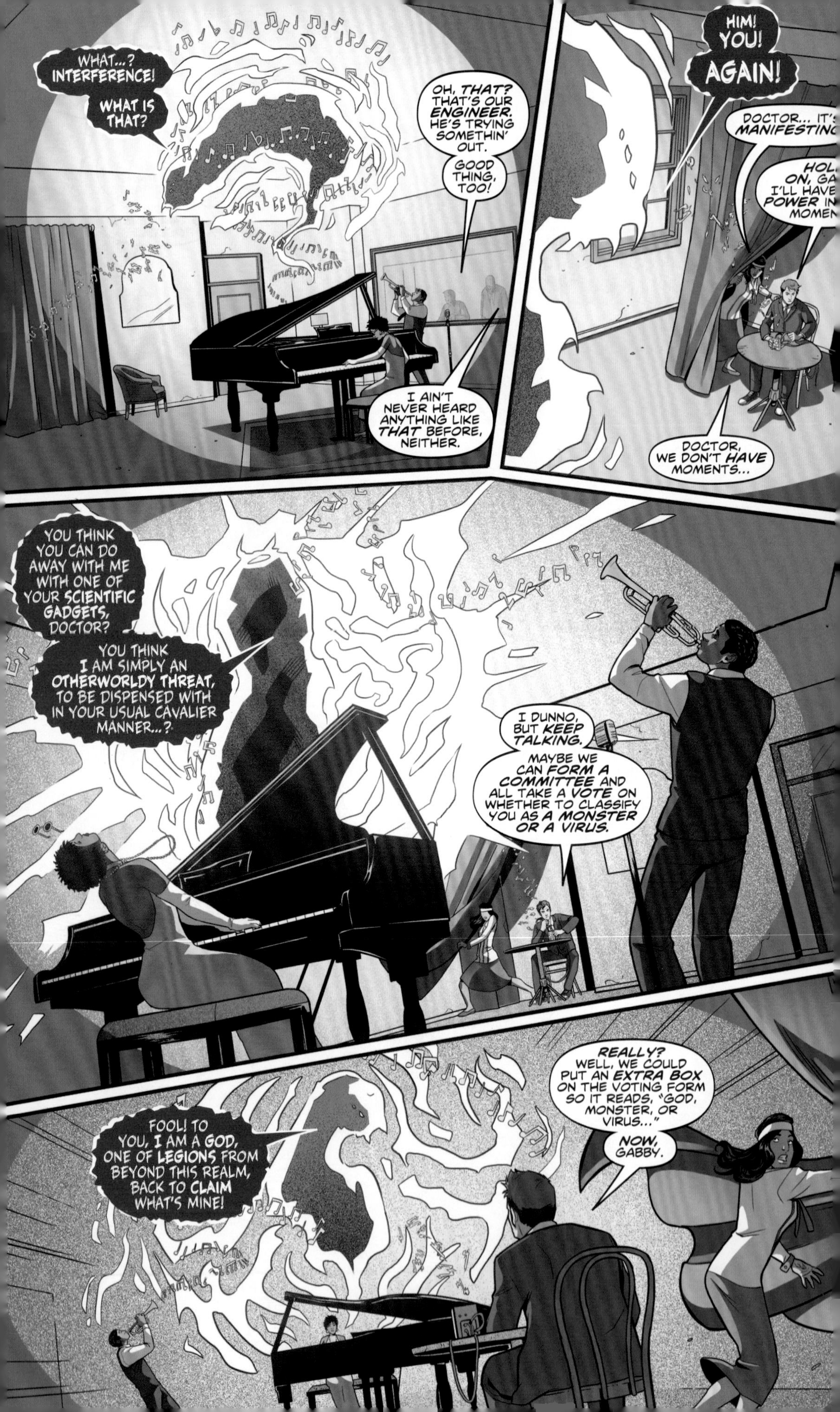
WHAT...? INTERFERENCE!
WHAT IS THAT?
OH, THAT? THAT'S OUR ENGINEER. HE'S TRYING SOMETHIN' OUT.
GOOD THING, TOO!
I AIN'T NEVER HEARD ANYTHING LIKE THAT BEFORE, NEITHER.
HIM! YOU! AGAIN!
DOCTOR... IT'S MANIFESTING
HOL ON, GA I'LL HAVE POWER IN MOMEN
DOCTOR, WE DON'T HAVE MOMENTS...
YOU THINK YOU CAN DO AWAY WITH ME WITH ONE OF YOUR SCIENTIFIC GADGETS, DOCTOR?
YOU THINK I AM SIMPLY AN OTHERWORLDY THREAT, TO BE DISPENSED WITH IN YOUR USUAL CAVALIER MANNER...?
I DUNNO, BUT KEEP TALKING.
MAYBE WE CAN FORM A COMMITTEE AND ALL TAKE A VOTE ON WHETHER TO CLASSIFY YOU AS A MONSTER OR A VIRUS.
FOOL! TO YOU, I AM A GOD, ONE OF LEGIONS FROM BEYOND THIS REALM, BACK TO CLAIM WHAT'S MINE!
REALLY? WELL, WE COULD PUT AN EXTRA BOX ON THE VOTING FORM SO IT READS, "GOD, MONSTER, OR VIRUS..."
NOW, GABBY.

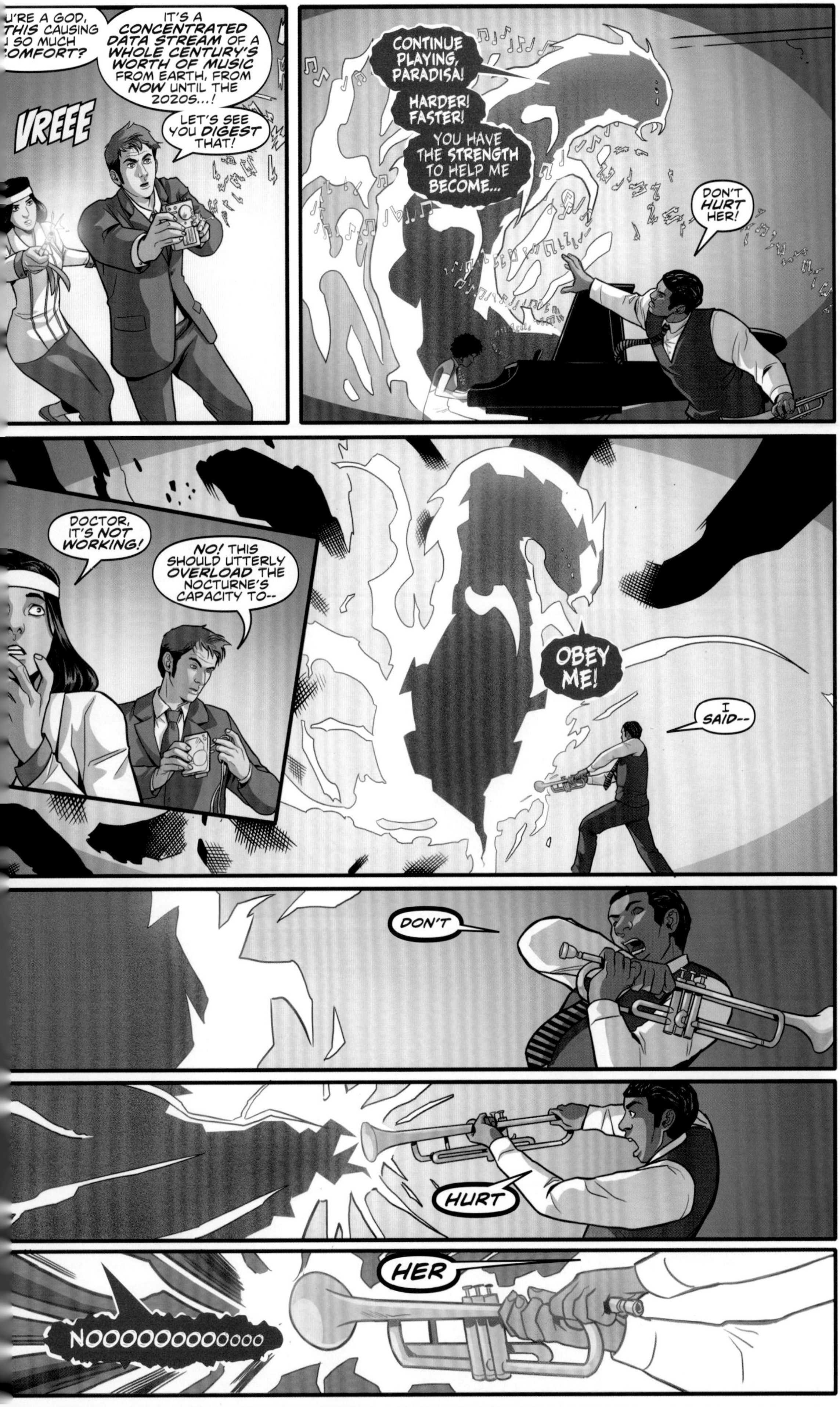
U'RE A GOD, THIS CAUSING U SO MUCH COMFORT?
IT'S A CONCENTRATED DATA STREAM OF A WHOLE CENTURY'S WORTH OF MUSIC FROM EARTH, FROM NOW UNTIL THE 2020S...!
VREEE
LET'S SEE YOU DIGEST THAT!
CONTINUE PLAYING, PARADISA!
HARDER! FASTER!
YOU HAVE THE STRENGTH TO HELP ME BECOME...
DON'T HURT HER!
DOCTOR, IT'S NOT WORKING!
NO! THIS SHOULD UTTERLY OVERLOAD THE NOCTURNE'S CAPACITY TO--
OBEY ME!
I SAID--
DON'T
HURT
HER
NOOOOOOOOOooo

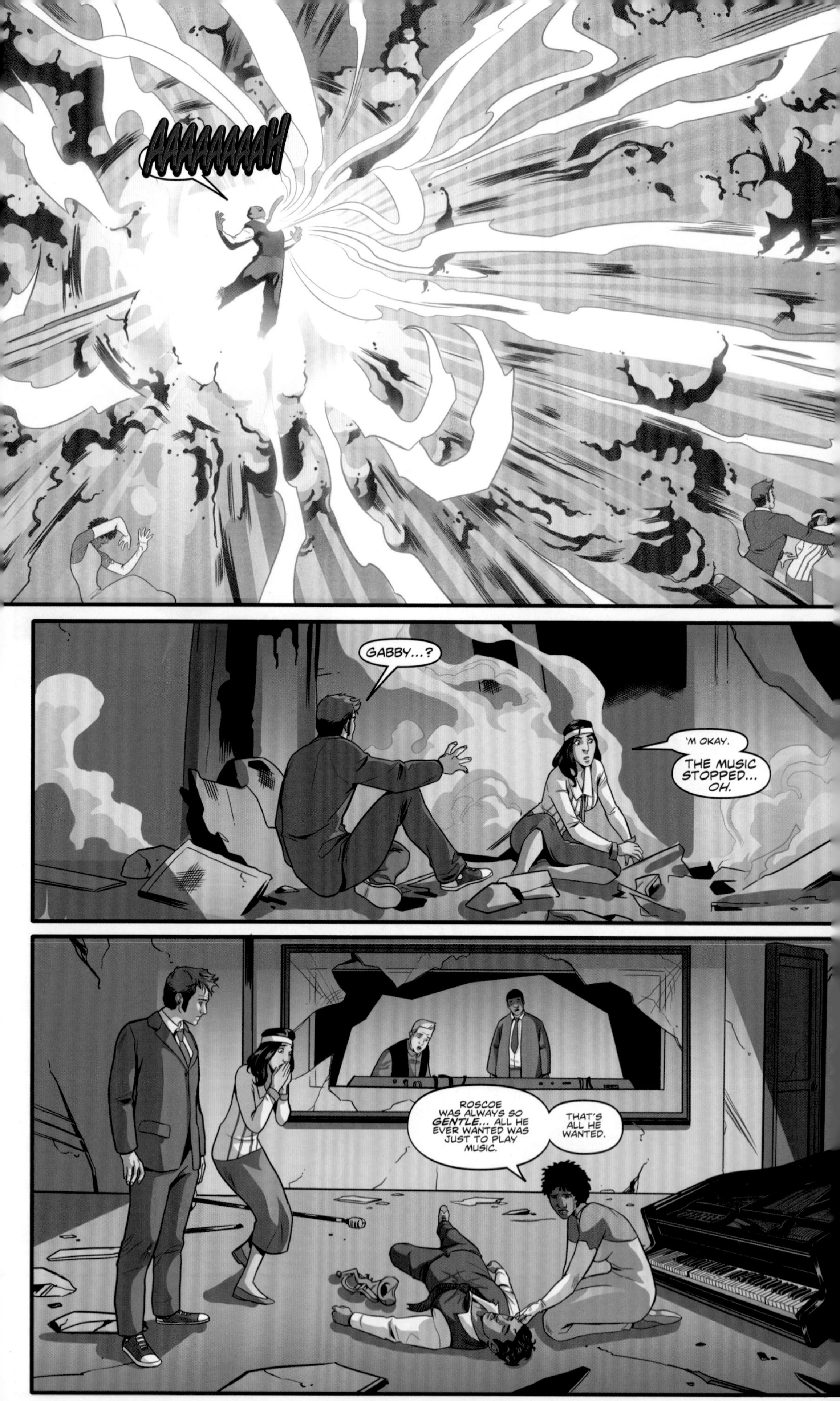
AAAAAAAAH
GABBY...?
'M OKAY.
THE MUSIC STOPPED... OH.
ROSCOE WAS ALWAYS SO GENTLE... ALL HE EVER WANTED WAS JUST TO PLAY MUSIC.
THAT'S ALL HE WANTED.

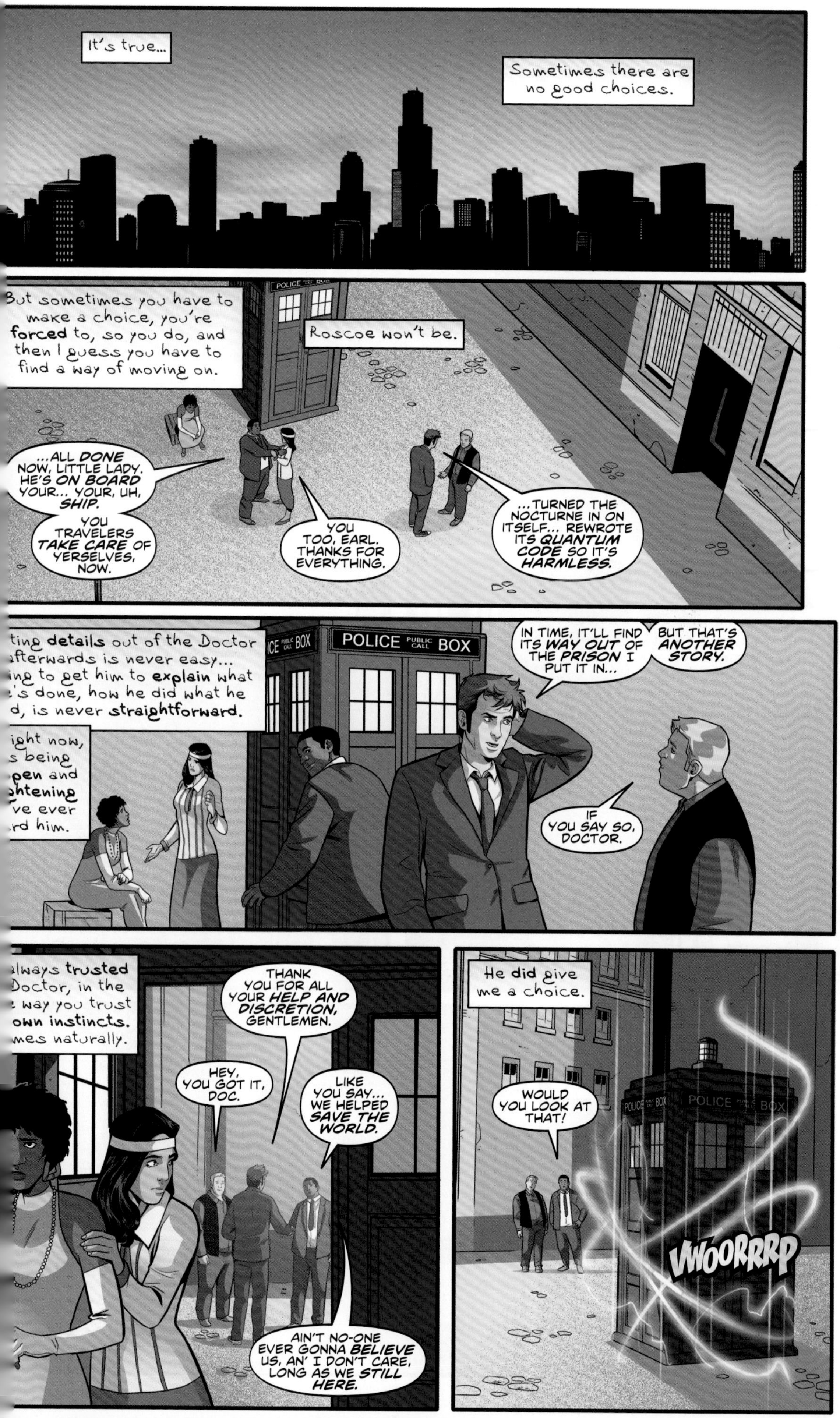

It's true...
Sometimes there are no good choices.
But sometimes you have to make a choice, you're **forced** to, so you do, and then I guess you have to find a way of moving on.
Roscoe won't be.
POLICE PUBLIC CALL BOX
...ALL **DONE** NOW, LITTLE LADY. HE'S **ON BOARD** YOUR... YOUR, UH, **SHIP.**
YOU TRAVELERS ***TAKE CARE*** OF YERSELVES, NOW.
YOU TOO, EARL. THANKS FOR EVERYTHING.
...TURNED THE NOCTURNE IN ON ITSELF... REWROTE ITS ***QUANTUM CODE*** SO IT'S ***HARMLESS.***
...ting **details** out of the Doctor afterwards is never easy... ...ing to get him to **explain** what ...'s done, how he did what he ...d, is never **straightforward.**
...ight now, ...s being ...**pen** and ...**htening** ...ve ever ...rd him.
POLICE PUBLIC CALL BOX
IN TIME, IT'LL FIND ITS ***WAY OUT*** OF THE ***PRISON*** I PUT IT IN...
BUT THAT'S ***ANOTHER STORY.***
IF YOU SAY SO, DOCTOR.
...always **trusted** ...Doctor, in the ... way you trust ...**own instincts.** ...mes naturally.
THANK YOU FOR ALL YOUR ***HELP AND DISCRETION,*** GENTLEMEN.
HEY, YOU GOT IT, DOC.
LIKE YOU SAY... WE HELPED ***SAVE THE WORLD.***
AIN'T NO-ONE EVER GONNA ***BELIEVE*** US, AN' I DON'T CARE, LONG AS WE ***STILL HERE.***
He **did** give me a choice.
WOULD YOU LOOK AT THAT!
POLICE PUBLIC CALL BOX
VWOORRRP

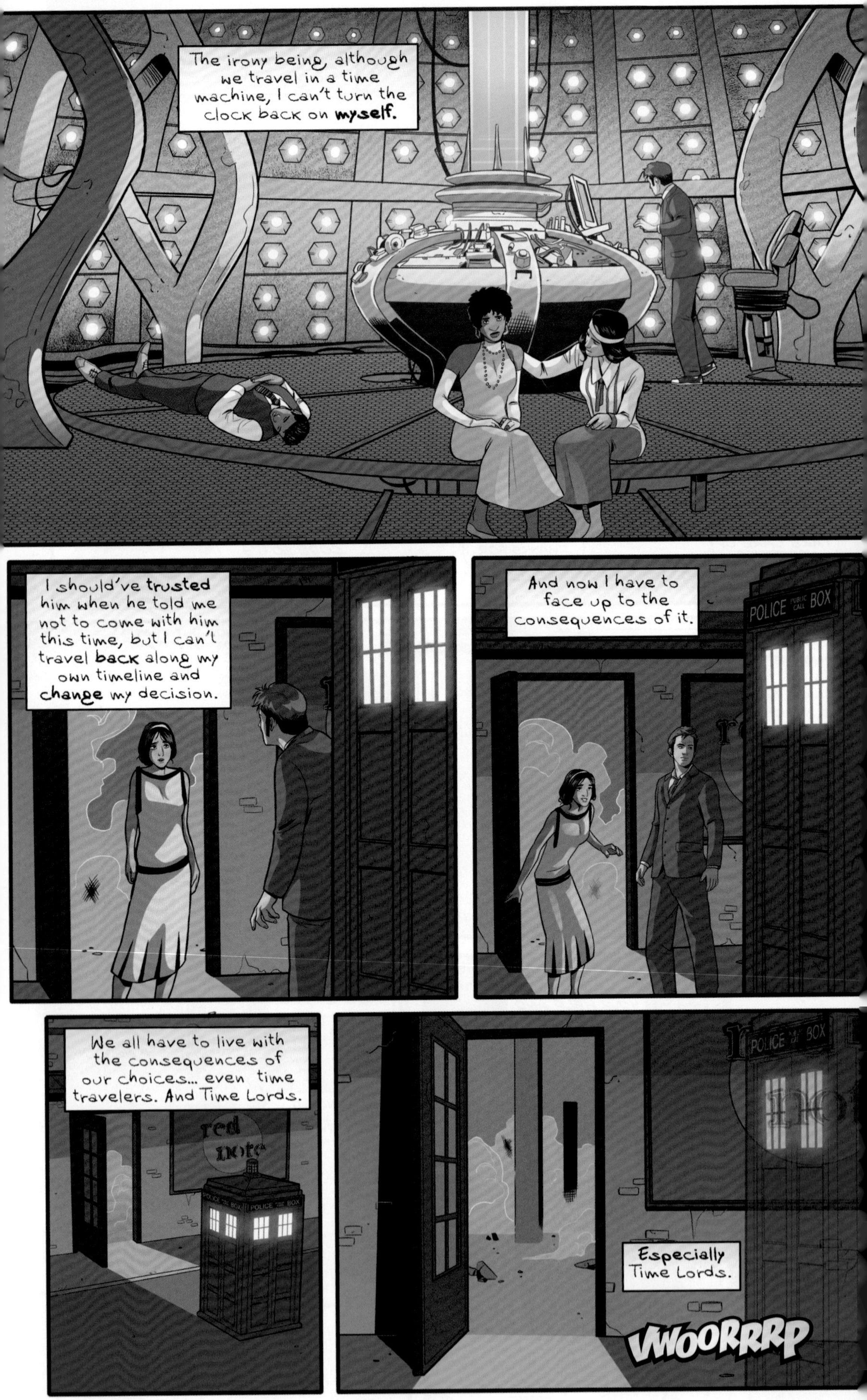
The irony being, although we travel in a time machine, I can't turn the clock back on myself.
I should've trusted him when he told me not to come with him this time, but I can't travel back along my own timeline and change my decision.
And now I have to face up to the consequences of it.
POLICE PUBLIC CALL BOX
We all have to live with the consequences of our choices... even time travelers. And Time Lords.
red note
POLICE BOX
Especially Time Lords.
VWOORRRP

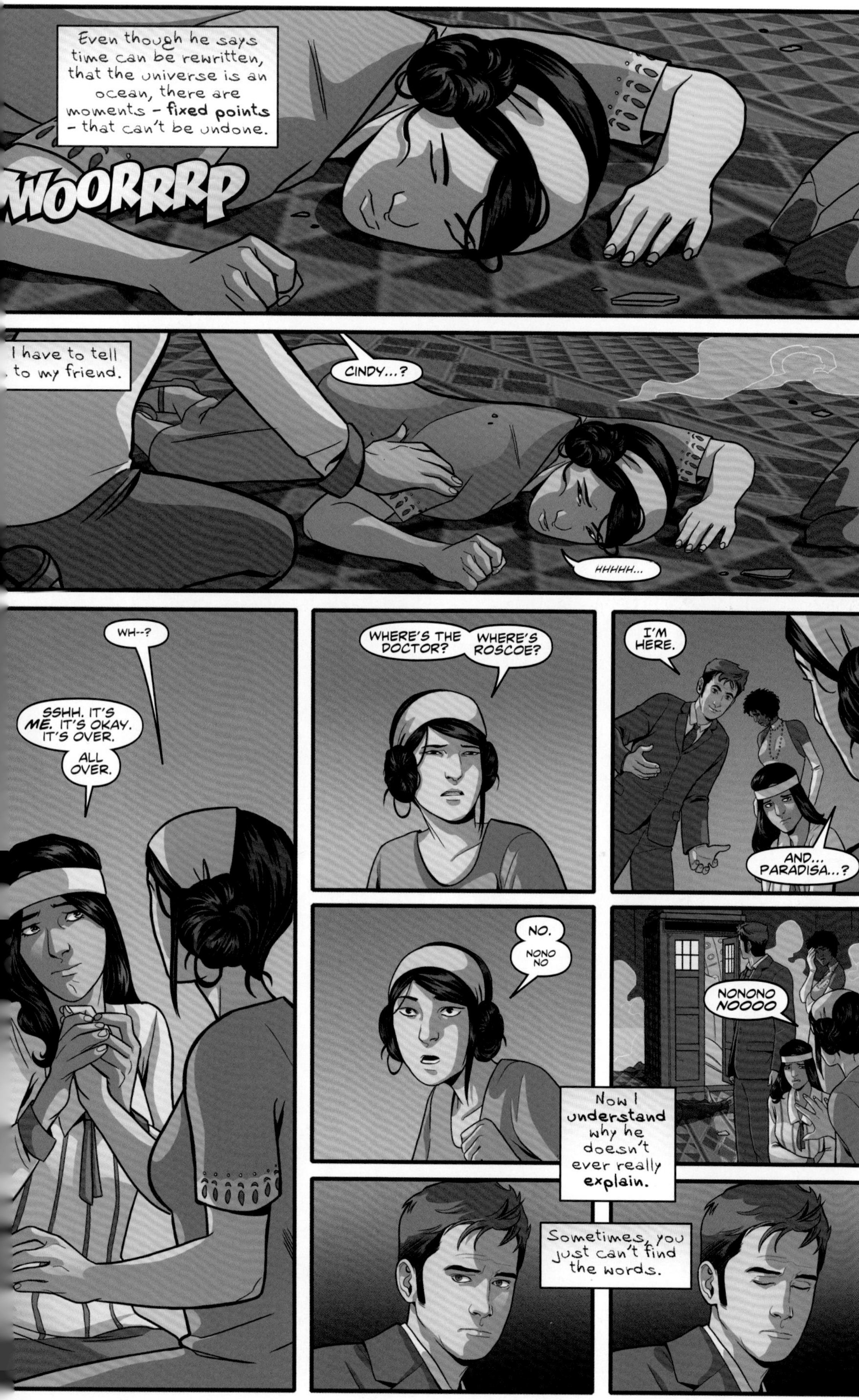

Even though he says time can be rewritten, that the universe is an ocean, there are moments – **fixed points** – that can't be undone.
WOORRRP
I have to tell
to my friend.
CINDY...?
HHHHH...
WH--?
SSHH. IT'S *ME*. IT'S OKAY. IT'S OVER.
ALL OVER.
WHERE'S THE DOCTOR?
WHERE'S ROSCOE?
I'M HERE.
AND... PARADISA...?
NO.
NONO NO
NONONO NOOOO
Now I **understand** why he doesn't ever really **explain**.
Sometimes, you just can't find the words.

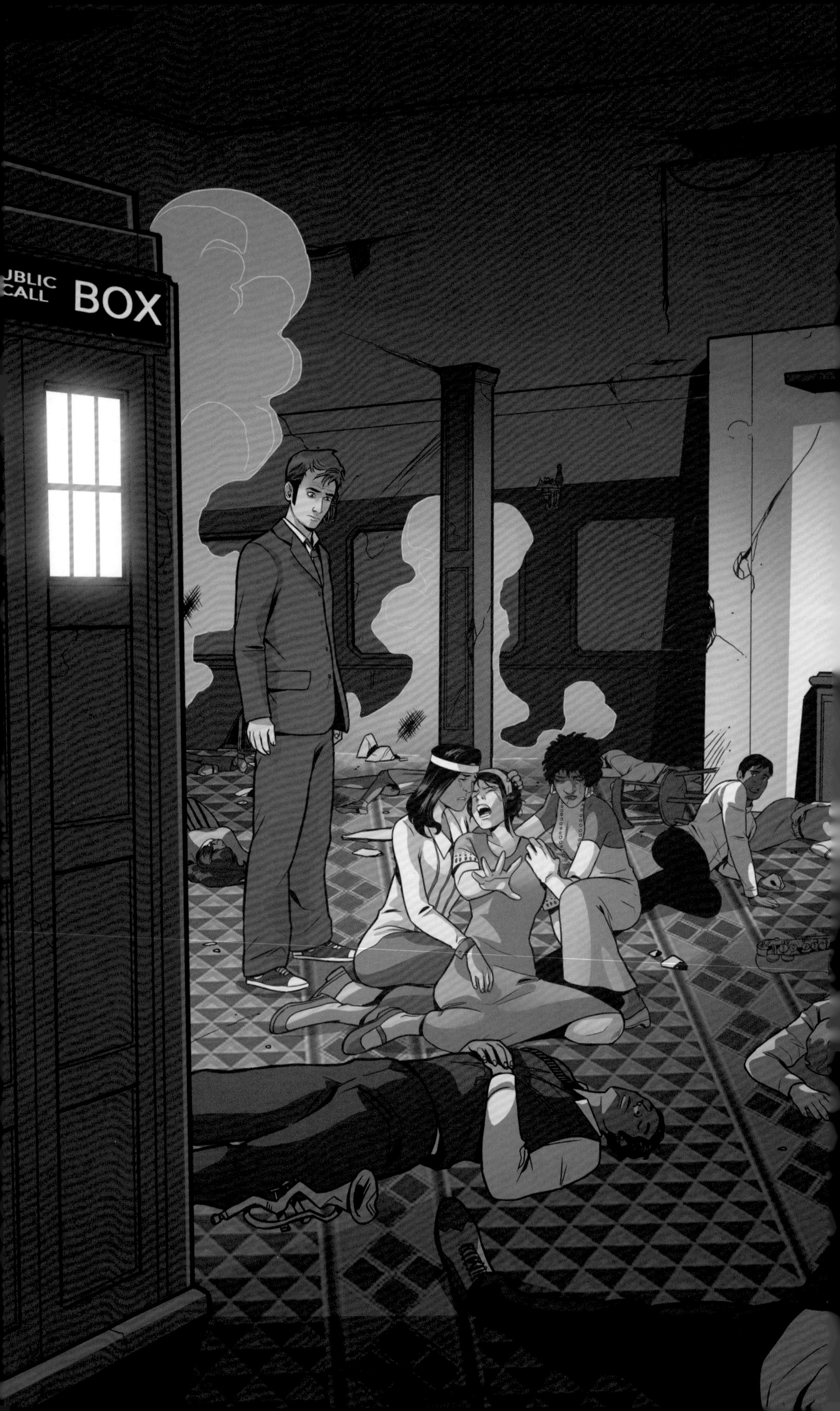
UBLIC
CALL
BOX

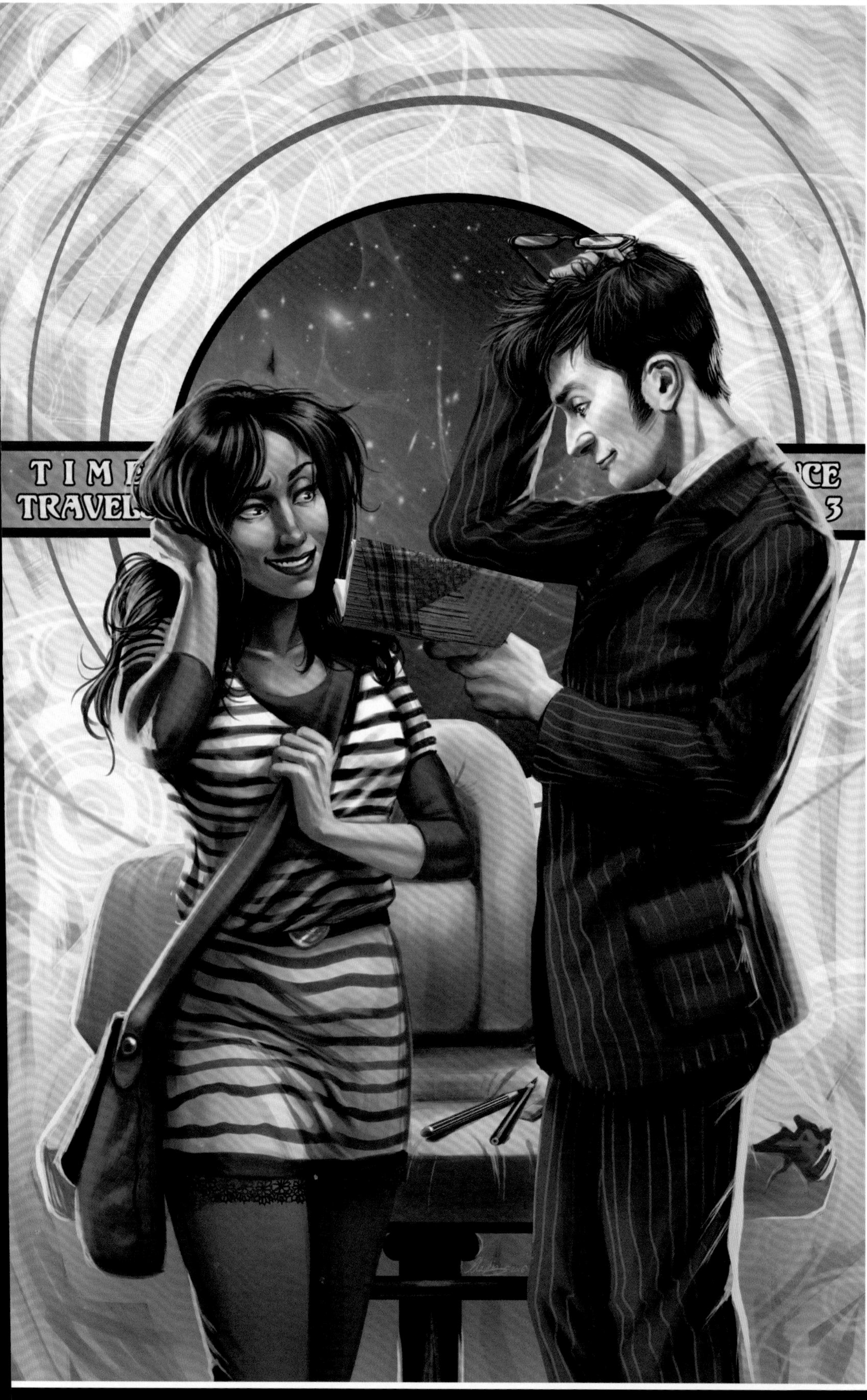

10D #2.12 Cover A: CLAUDIA IANNICIELO

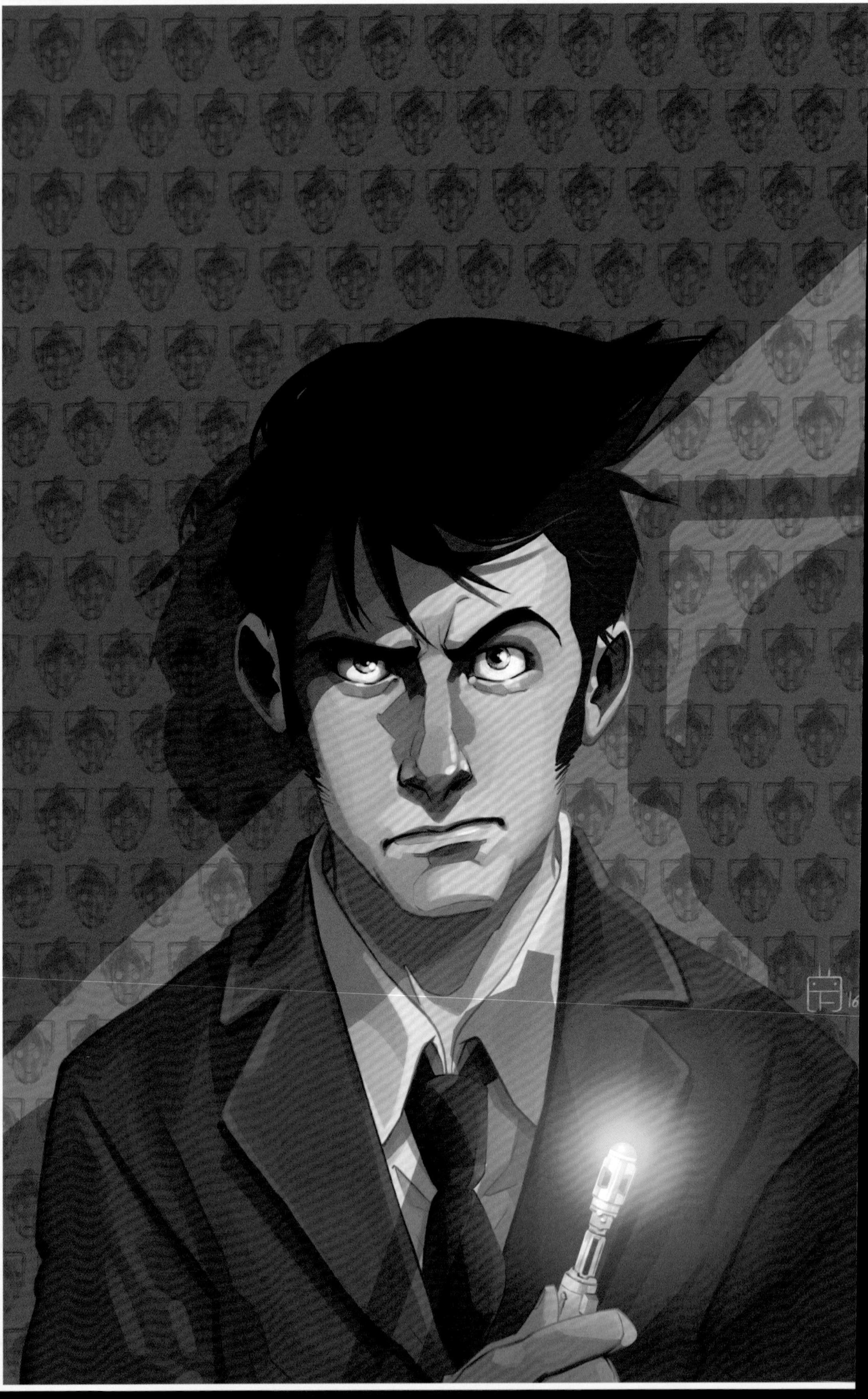

10D #2.14 Cover A: ARIANNA FLOREAN

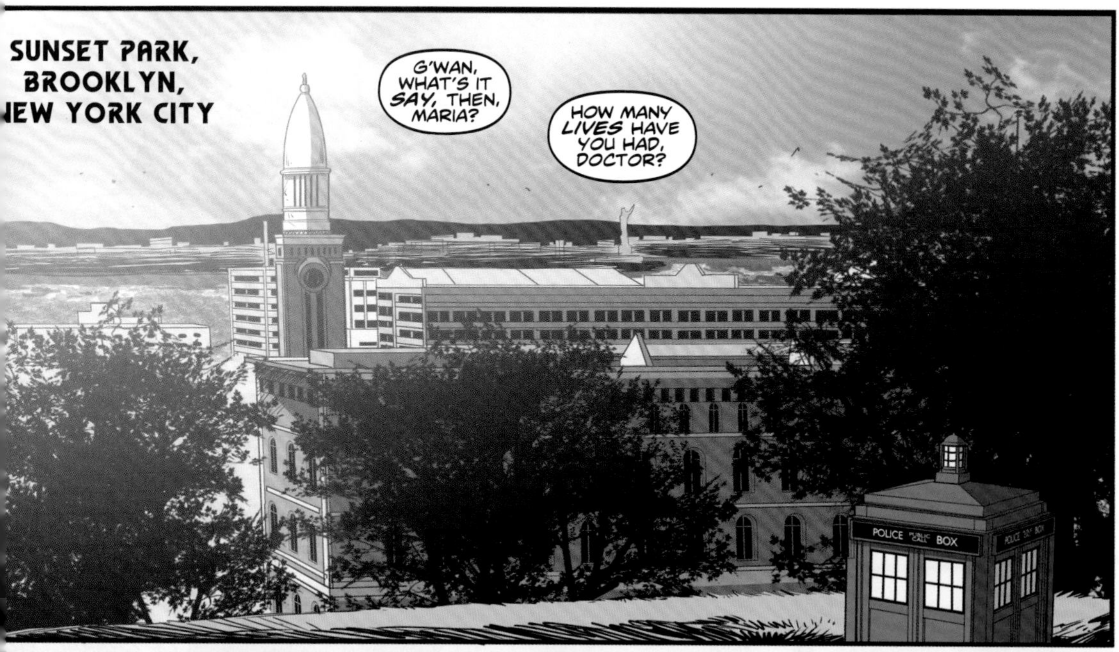
SUNSET PARK, BROOKLYN, NEW YORK CITY
G'WAN, WHAT'S IT SAY, THEN, MARIA?
HOW MANY LIVES HAVE YOU HAD, DOCTOR?
POLICE PUBLIC CALL BOX

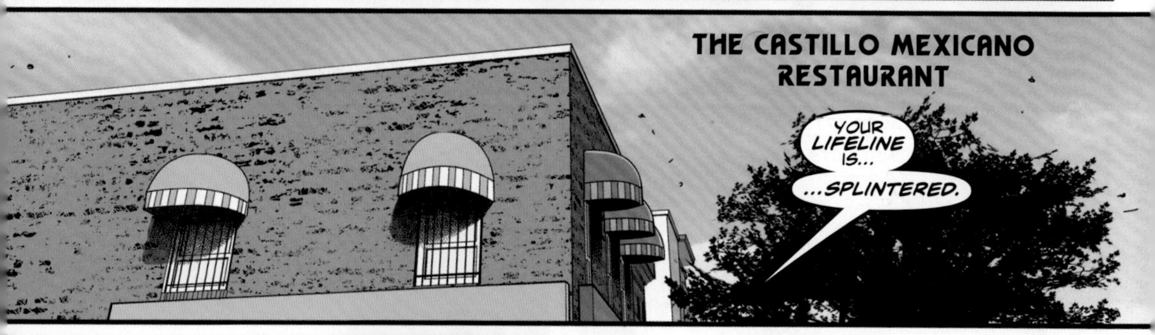
THE CASTILLO MEXICANO RESTAURANT
YOUR LIFELINE IS...
...SPLINTERED.

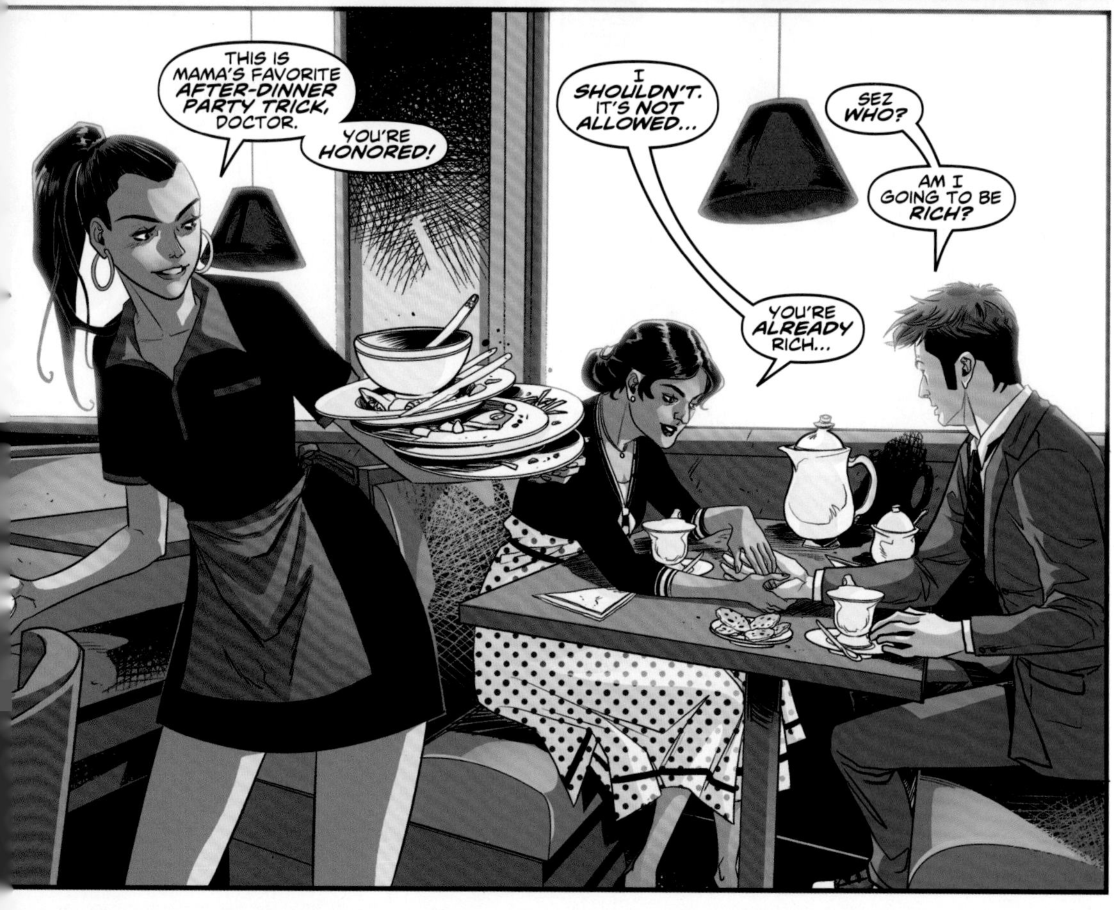
THIS IS MAMA'S FAVORITE AFTER-DINNER PARTY TRICK, DOCTOR.
YOU'RE HONORED!
I SHOULDN'T. IT'S NOT ALLOWED...
SEZ WHO?
AM I GOING TO BE RICH?
YOU'RE ALREADY RICH...

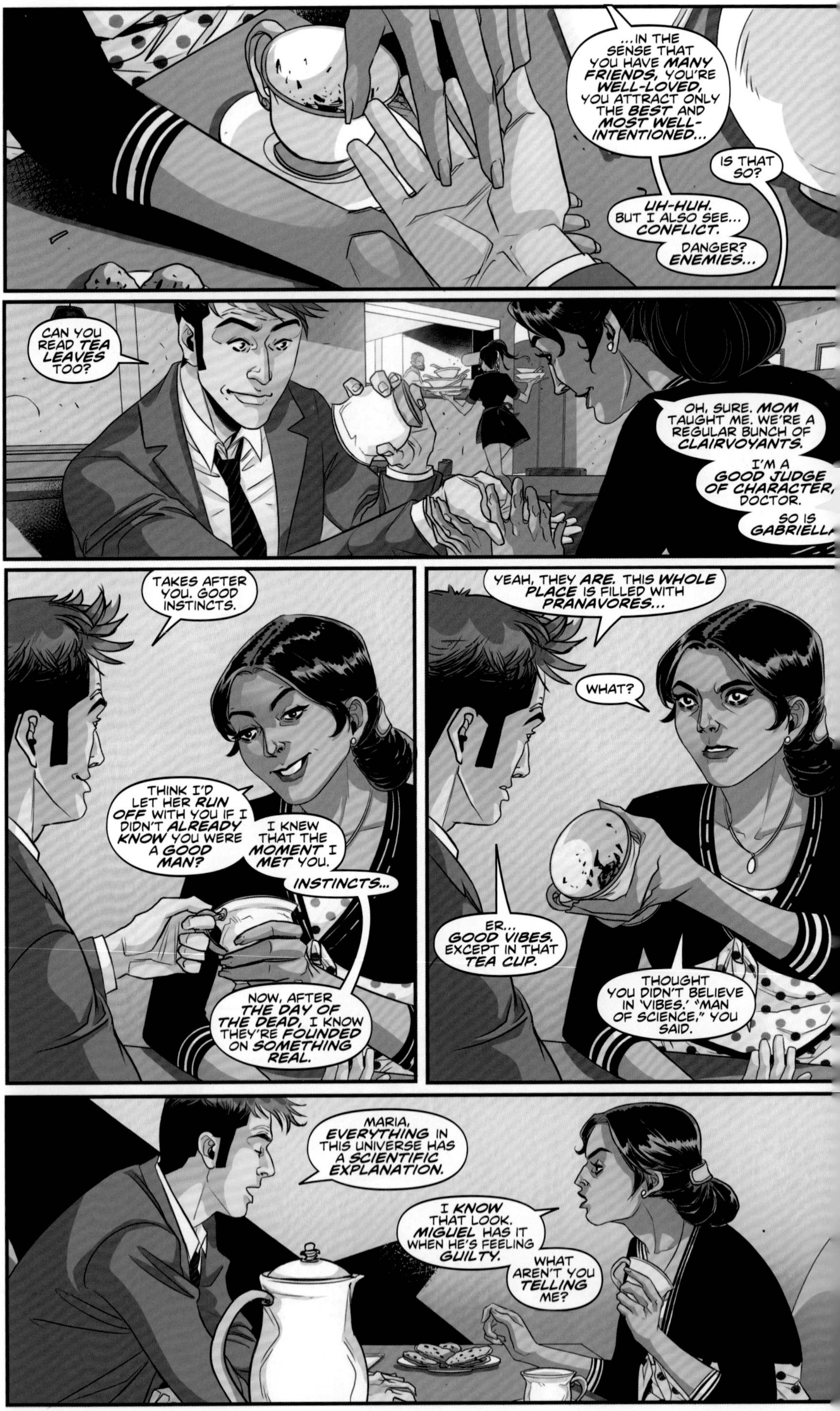
...IN THE SENSE THAT YOU HAVE MANY FRIENDS, YOU'RE WELL-LOVED, YOU ATTRACT ONLY THE BEST AND MOST WELL-INTENTIONED...
IS THAT SO?
UH-HUH. BUT I ALSO SEE... CONFLICT.
DANGER? ENEMIES...
CAN YOU READ TEA LEAVES TOO?
OH, SURE. MOM TAUGHT ME. WE'RE A REGULAR BUNCH OF CLAIRVOYANTS.
I'M A GOOD JUDGE OF CHARACTER, DOCTOR.
SO IS GABRIELL
TAKES AFTER YOU. GOOD INSTINCTS.
THINK I'D LET HER RUN OFF WITH YOU IF I DIDN'T ALREADY KNOW YOU WERE A GOOD MAN?
I KNEW THAT THE MOMENT I MET YOU.
INSTINCTS...
NOW, AFTER THE DAY OF THE DEAD, I KNOW THEY'RE FOUNDED ON SOMETHING REAL.
YEAH, THEY ARE. THIS WHOLE PLACE IS FILLED WITH PRANAVORES...
WHAT?
ER... GOOD VIBES. EXCEPT IN THAT TEA CUP.
THOUGHT YOU DIDN'T BELIEVE IN 'VIBES.' "MAN OF SCIENCE," YOU SAID.
MARIA, EVERYTHING IN THIS UNIVERSE HAS A SCIENTIFIC EXPLANATION.
I KNOW THAT LOOK. MIGUEL HAS IT WHEN HE'S FEELING GUILTY.
WHAT AREN'T YOU TELLING ME?

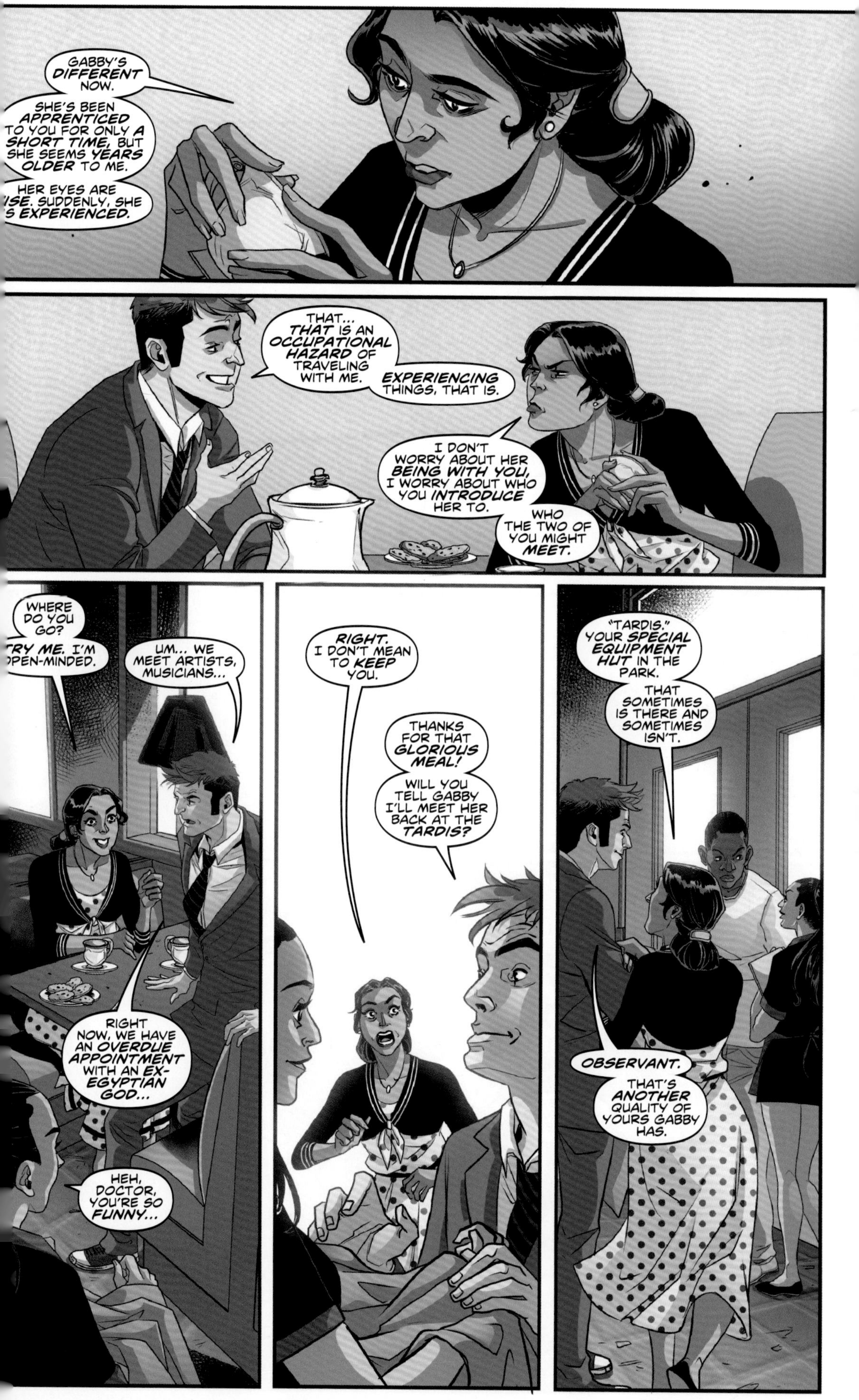
GABBY'S DIFFERENT NOW.
SHE'S BEEN APPRENTICED TO YOU FOR ONLY A SHORT TIME, BUT SHE SEEMS YEARS OLDER TO ME.
HER EYES ARE ...ISE. SUDDENLY, SHE ...S EXPERIENCED.
THAT... THAT IS AN OCCUPATIONAL HAZARD OF TRAVELING WITH ME.
EXPERIENCING THINGS, THAT IS.
I DON'T WORRY ABOUT HER BEING WITH YOU, I WORRY ABOUT WHO YOU INTRODUCE HER TO.
WHO THE TWO OF YOU MIGHT MEET.
WHERE DO YOU GO?
...RY ME. I'M ...PEN-MINDED.
UM... WE MEET ARTISTS, MUSICIANS...
RIGHT NOW, WE HAVE AN OVERDUE APPOINTMENT WITH AN EX-EGYPTIAN GOD...
HEH, DOCTOR, YOU'RE SO FUNNY...
RIGHT. I DON'T MEAN TO KEEP YOU.
THANKS FOR THAT GLORIOUS MEAL!
WILL YOU TELL GABBY I'LL MEET HER BACK AT THE TARDIS?
"TARDIS." YOUR SPECIAL EQUIPMENT HUT IN THE PARK.
THAT SOMETIMES IS THERE AND SOMETIMES ISN'T.
OBSERVANT.
THAT'S ANOTHER QUALITY OF YOURS GABBY HAS.

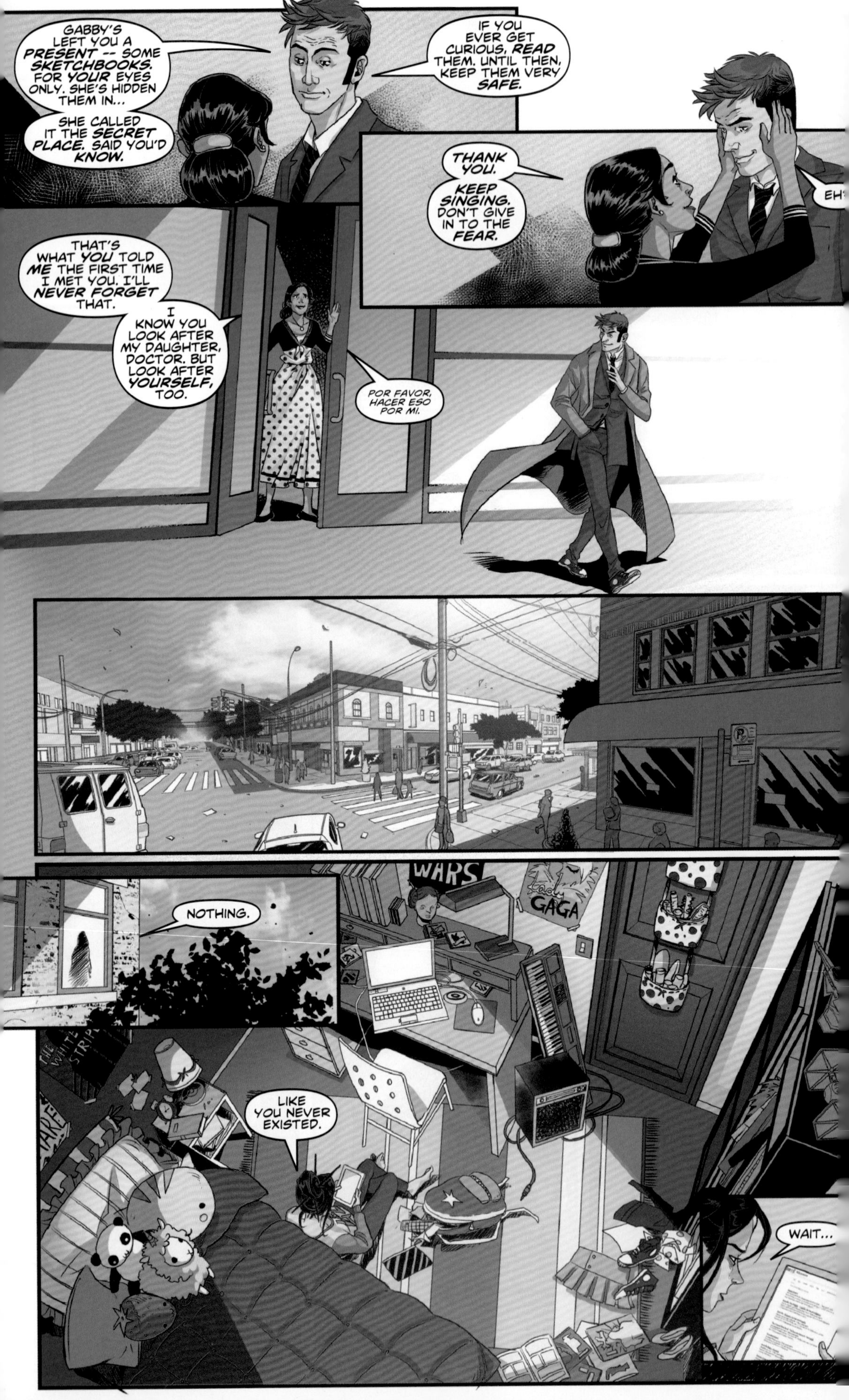
GABBY'S LEFT YOU A PRESENT -- SOME SKETCHBOOKS. FOR YOUR EYES ONLY. SHE'S HIDDEN THEM IN...
SHE CALLED IT THE SECRET PLACE. SAID YOU'D KNOW.
IF YOU EVER GET CURIOUS, READ THEM. UNTIL THEN, KEEP THEM VERY SAFE.
THANK YOU.
KEEP SINGING. DON'T GIVE IN TO THE FEAR.
EH?
THAT'S WHAT YOU TOLD ME THE FIRST TIME I MET YOU. I'LL NEVER FORGET THAT.
I KNOW YOU LOOK AFTER MY DAUGHTER, DOCTOR. BUT LOOK AFTER YOURSELF, TOO.
POR FAVOR, HACER ESO POR MI.
NOTHING.
WARS
GAGA
LIKE YOU NEVER EXISTED.
WAIT...

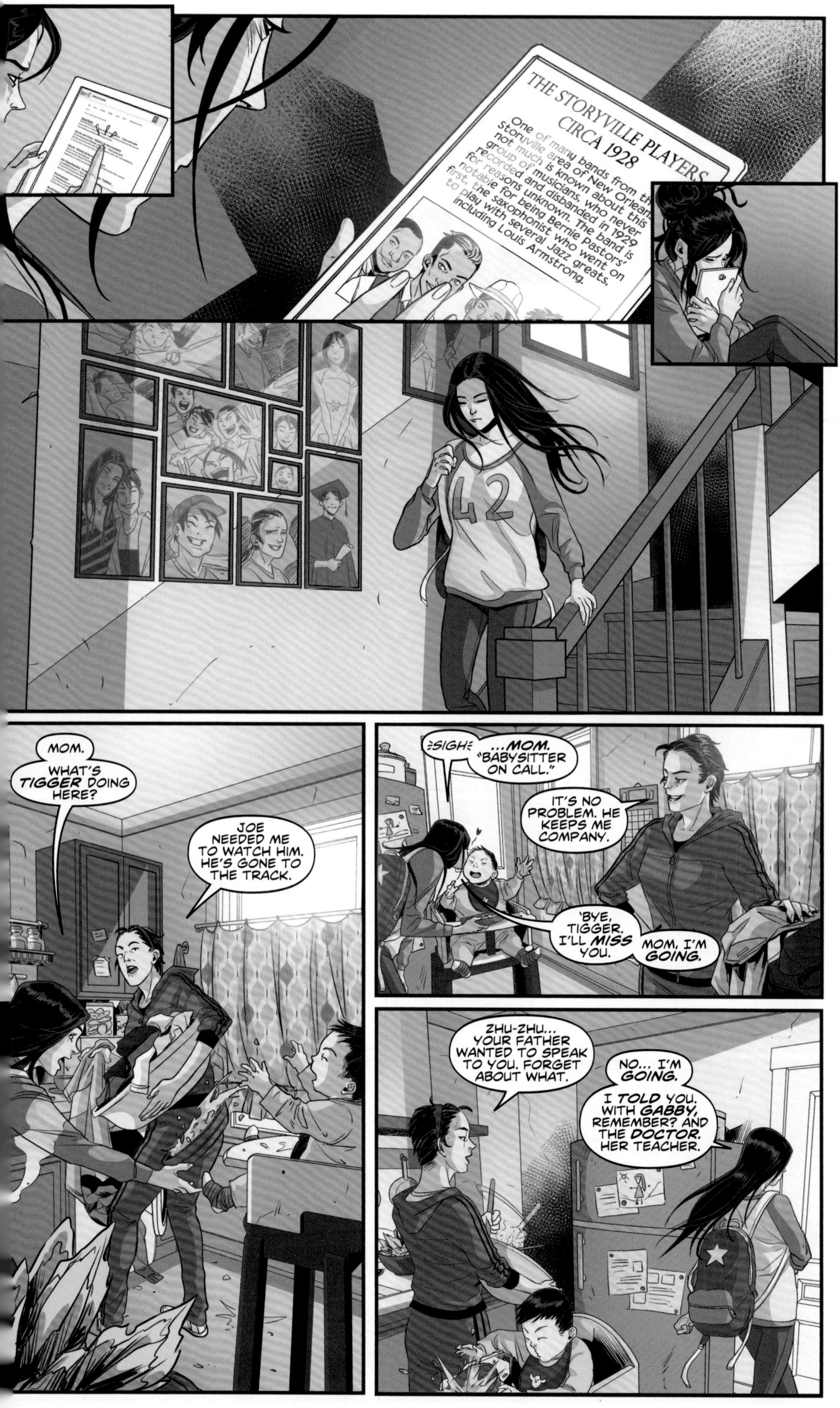

THE STORYVILLE PLAYERS CIRCA 1928
One of many bands from the Storyville area of New Orleans not much is known about this group of musicians, who never recorded and disbanded in 1929 for reasons unknown. The band is notable for being Bernie Pastors' first, the saxophonist who went on to play with several Jazz greats, including Louis Armstrong.
42
MOM. WHAT'S TIGGER DOING HERE?
JOE NEEDED ME TO WATCH HIM. HE'S GONE TO THE TRACK.
SIGH
...MOM. "BABYSITTER ON CALL."
IT'S NO PROBLEM. HE KEEPS ME COMPANY.
'BYE, TIGGER. I'LL MISS YOU.
MOM, I'M GOING.
ZHU-ZHU... YOUR FATHER WANTED TO SPEAK TO YOU. FORGET ABOUT WHAT.
NO... I'M GOING.
I TOLD YOU. WITH GABBY, REMEMBER? AND THE DOCTOR. HER TEACHER.

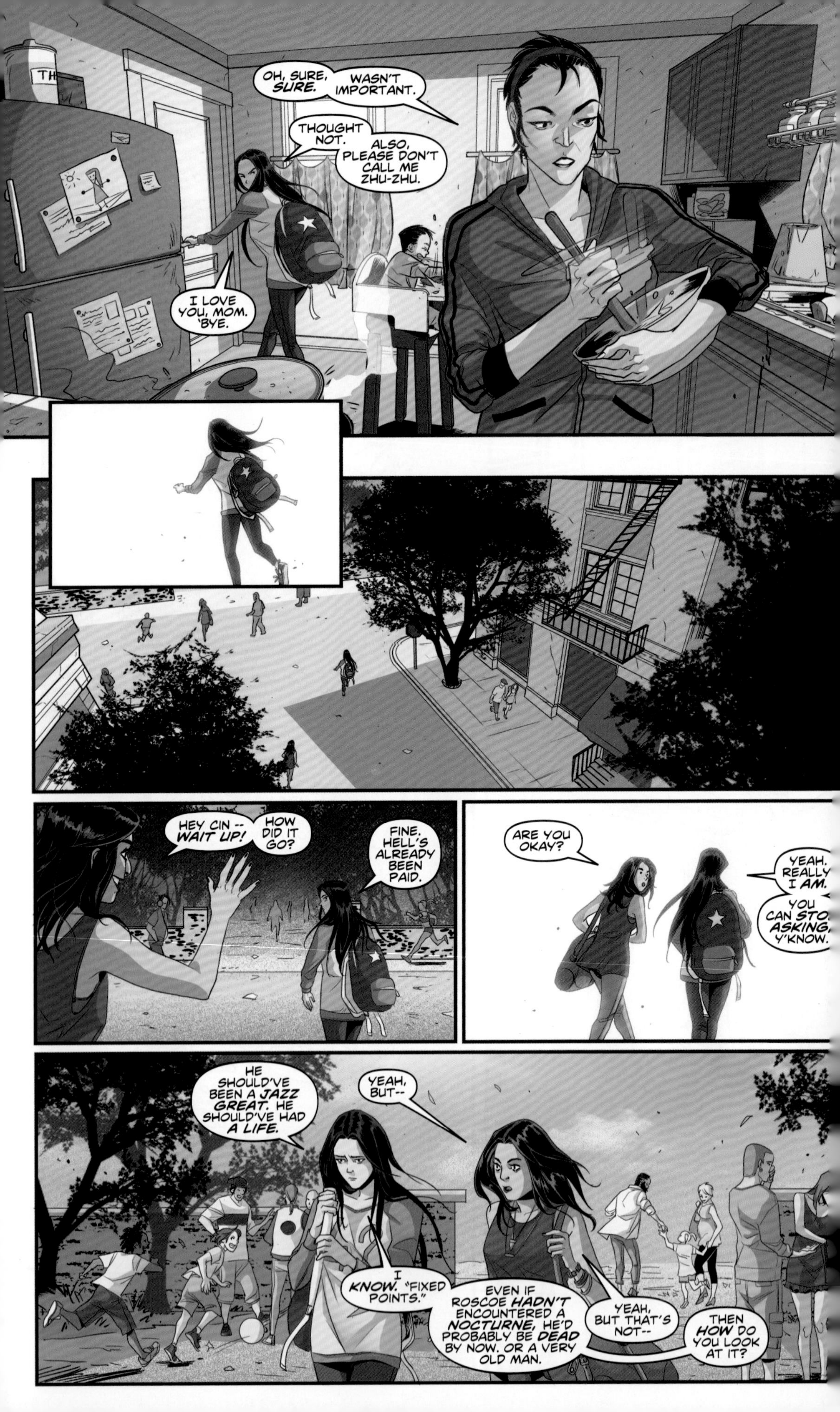

OH, SURE, SURE.
WASN'T IMPORTANT.
THOUGHT NOT.
ALSO, PLEASE DON'T CALL ME ZHU-ZHU.
I LOVE YOU, MOM. 'BYE.
HEY CIN -- WAIT UP!
HOW DID IT GO?
FINE. HELL'S ALREADY BEEN PAID.
ARE YOU OKAY?
YEAH. REALLY I AM.
YOU CAN STO ASKING, Y'KNOW.
HE SHOULD'VE BEEN A JAZZ GREAT. HE SHOULD'VE HAD A LIFE.
YEAH, BUT--
I KNOW. "FIXED POINTS."
EVEN IF ROSCOE HADN'T ENCOUNTERED A NOCTURNE, HE'D PROBABLY BE DEAD BY NOW. OR A VERY OLD MAN.
YEAH, BUT THAT'S NOT--
THEN HOW DO YOU LOOK AT IT?

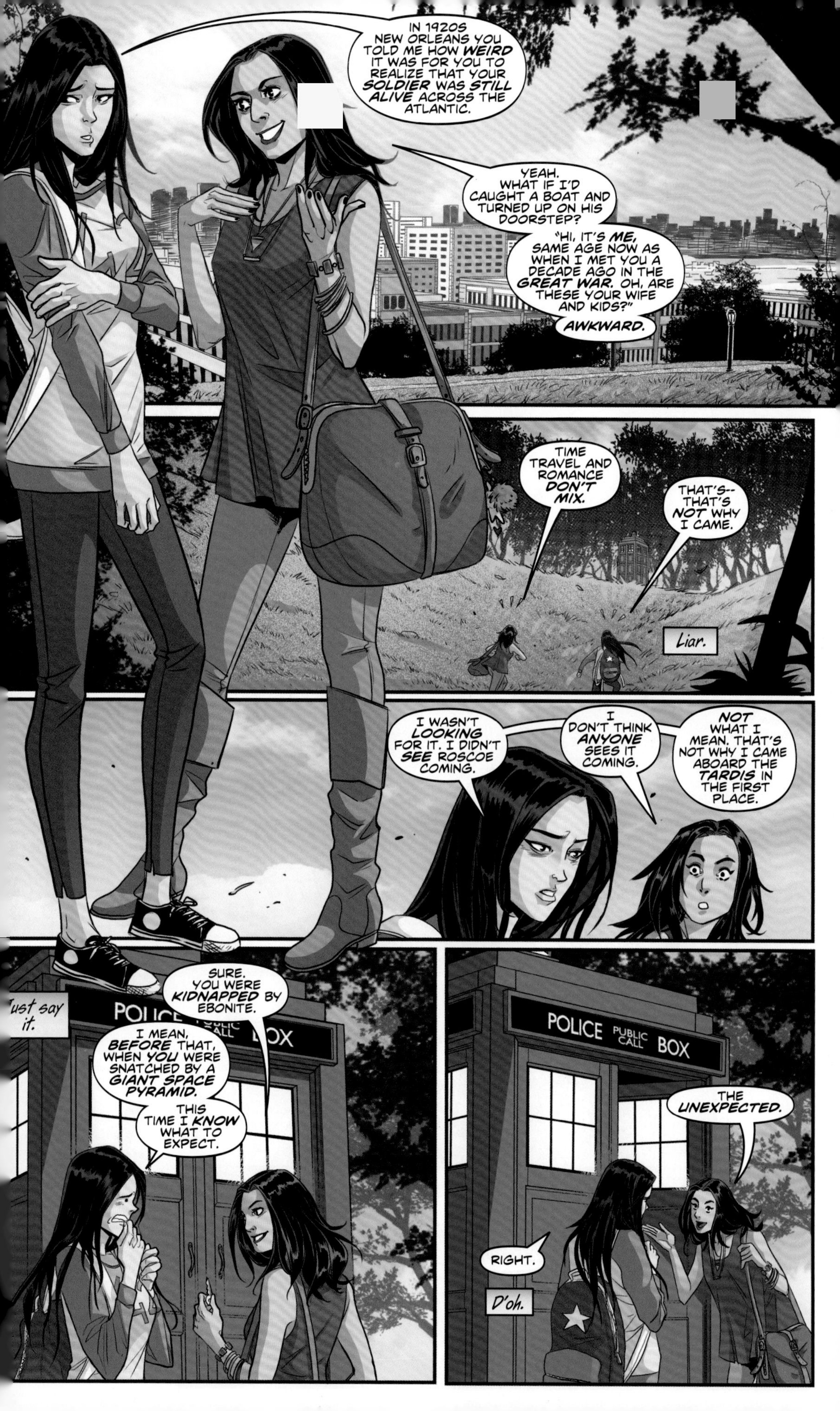
IN 1920S NEW ORLEANS YOU TOLD ME HOW WEIRD IT WAS FOR YOU TO REALIZE THAT YOUR SOLDIER WAS STILL ALIVE ACROSS THE ATLANTIC.
YEAH. WHAT IF I'D CAUGHT A BOAT AND TURNED UP ON HIS DOORSTEP?
"HI, IT'S ME, SAME AGE NOW AS WHEN I MET YOU A DECADE AGO IN THE GREAT WAR. OH, ARE THESE YOUR WIFE AND KIDS?"
AWKWARD.
TIME TRAVEL AND ROMANCE DON'T MIX.
THAT'S-- THAT'S NOT WHY I CAME.
Liar.
I WASN'T LOOKING FOR IT. I DIDN'T SEE ROSCOE COMING.
I DON'T THINK ANYONE SEES IT COMING.
NOT WHAT I MEAN. THAT'S NOT WHY I CAME ABOARD THE TARDIS IN THE FIRST PLACE.
Just say it.
SURE. YOU WERE KIDNAPPED BY EBONITE.
I MEAN, BEFORE THAT, WHEN YOU WERE SNATCHED BY A GIANT SPACE PYRAMID.
THIS TIME I KNOW WHAT TO EXPECT.
POLICE PUBLIC CALL BOX
THE UNEXPECTED.
RIGHT.
D'oh.

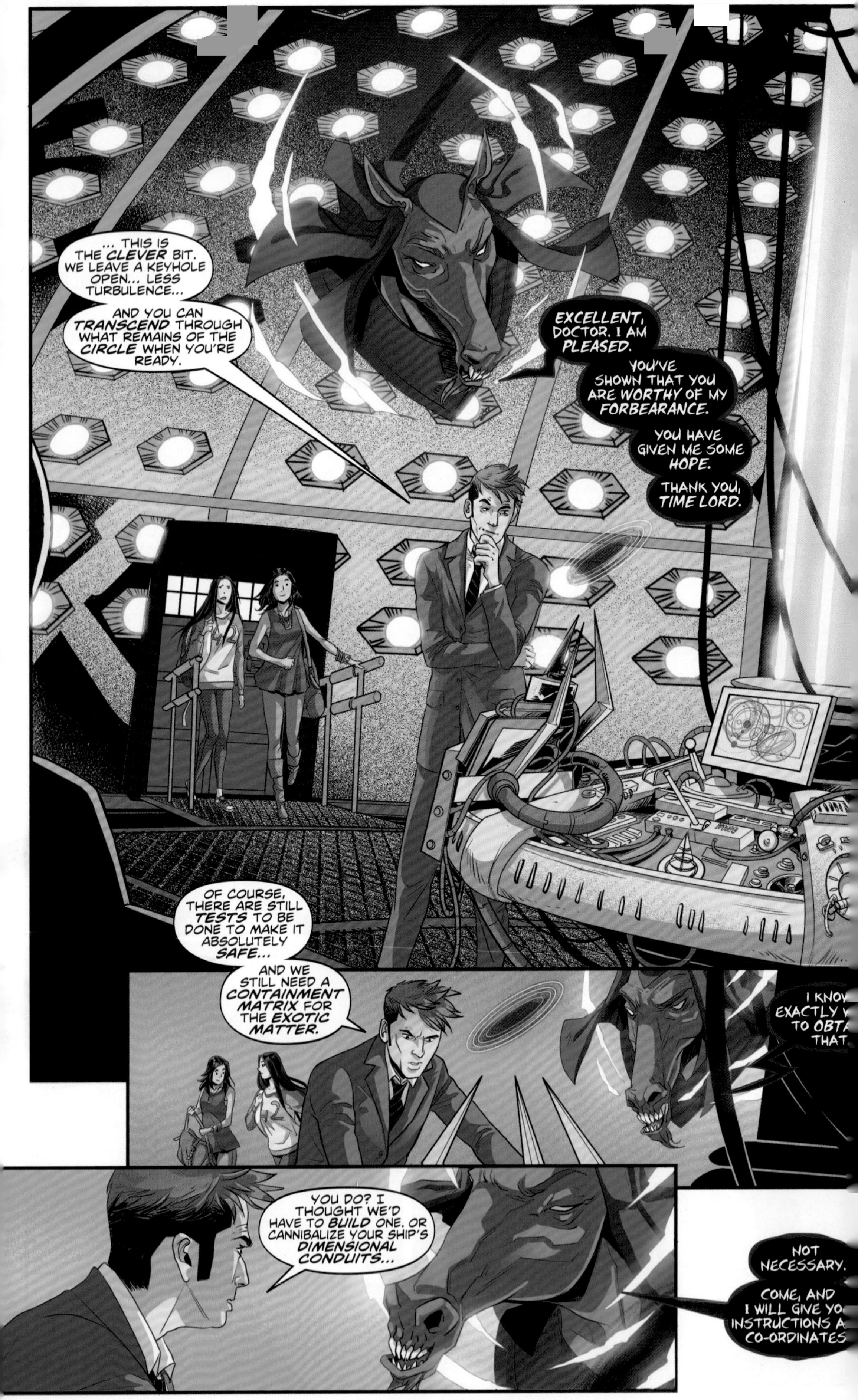
... THIS IS THE CLEVER BIT. WE LEAVE A KEYHOLE OPEN... LESS TURBULENCE...
AND YOU CAN TRANSCEND THROUGH WHAT REMAINS OF THE CIRCLE WHEN YOU'RE READY.
EXCELLENT, DOCTOR. I AM PLEASED.
YOU'VE SHOWN THAT YOU ARE WORTHY OF MY FORBEARANCE.
YOU HAVE GIVEN ME SOME HOPE.
THANK YOU, TIME LORD.
OF COURSE, THERE ARE STILL TESTS TO BE DONE TO MAKE IT ABSOLUTELY SAFE...
AND WE STILL NEED A CONTAINMENT MATRIX FOR THE EXOTIC MATTER.
YOU DO? I THOUGHT WE'D HAVE TO BUILD ONE. OR CANNIBALIZE YOUR SHIP'S DIMENSIONAL CONDUITS...
NOT NECESSARY.

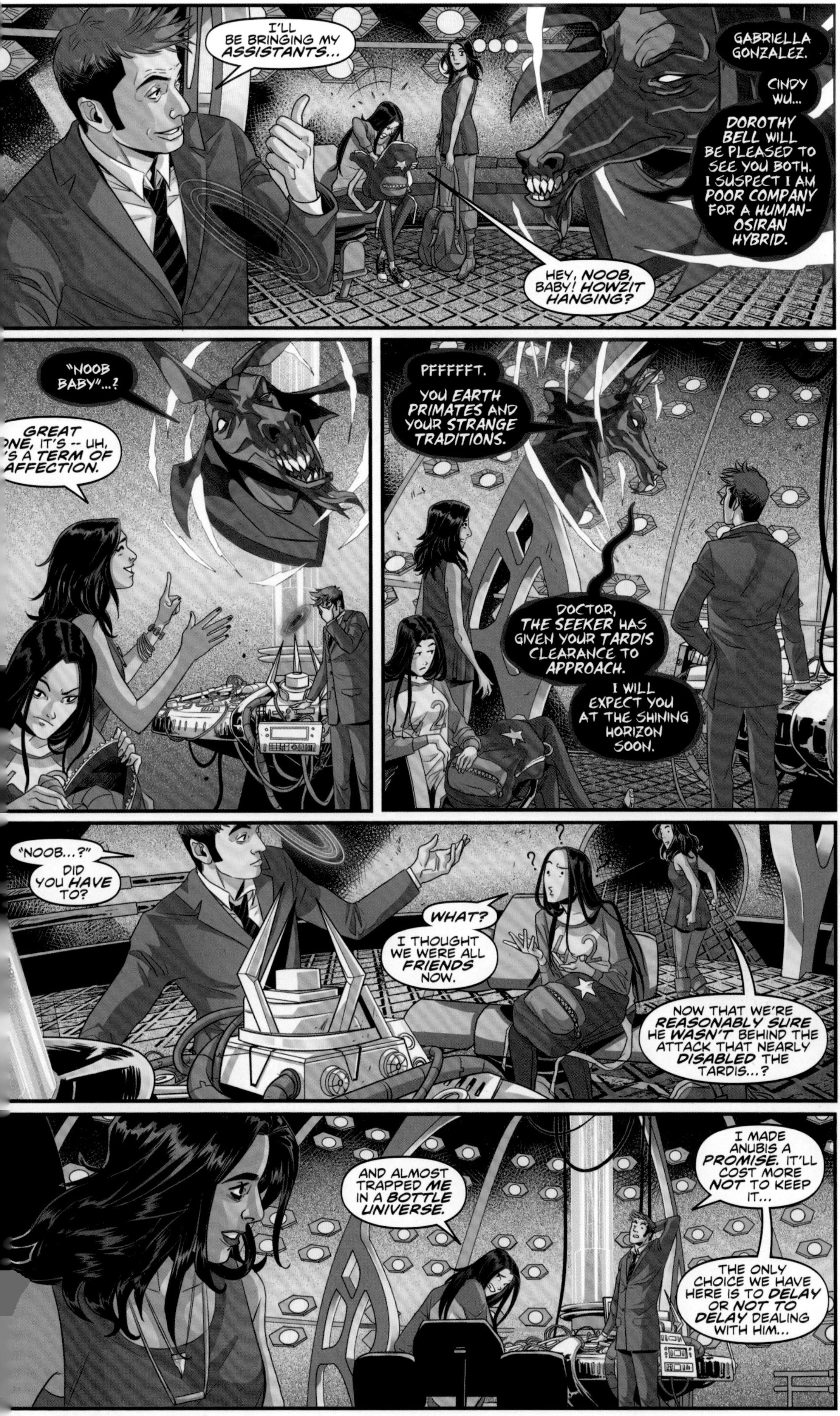

I'LL BE BRINGING MY ASSISTANTS...
GABRIELLA GONZALEZ.
CINDY WU...
DOROTHY BELL WILL BE PLEASED TO SEE YOU BOTH. I SUSPECT I AM POOR COMPANY FOR A HUMAN-OSIRAN HYBRID.
HEY, NOOB, BABY! HOWZIT HANGING?
"NOOB BABY"...?
GREAT ONE, IT'S -- UH, 'S A TERM OF AFFECTION.
PFFFFFT.
YOU EARTH PRIMATES AND YOUR STRANGE TRADITIONS.
DOCTOR, THE SEEKER HAS GIVEN YOUR TARDIS CLEARANCE TO APPROACH.
I WILL EXPECT YOU AT THE SHINING HORIZON SOON.
"NOOB...?" DID YOU HAVE TO?
WHAT?
I THOUGHT WE WERE ALL FRIENDS NOW.
NOW THAT WE'RE REASONABLY SURE HE WASN'T BEHIND THE ATTACK THAT NEARLY DISABLED THE TARDIS...?
AND ALMOST TRAPPED ME IN A BOTTLE UNIVERSE.
I MADE ANUBIS A PROMISE. IT'LL COST MORE NOT TO KEEP IT...
THE ONLY CHOICE WE HAVE HERE IS TO DELAY OR NOT TO DELAY DEALING WITH HIM...

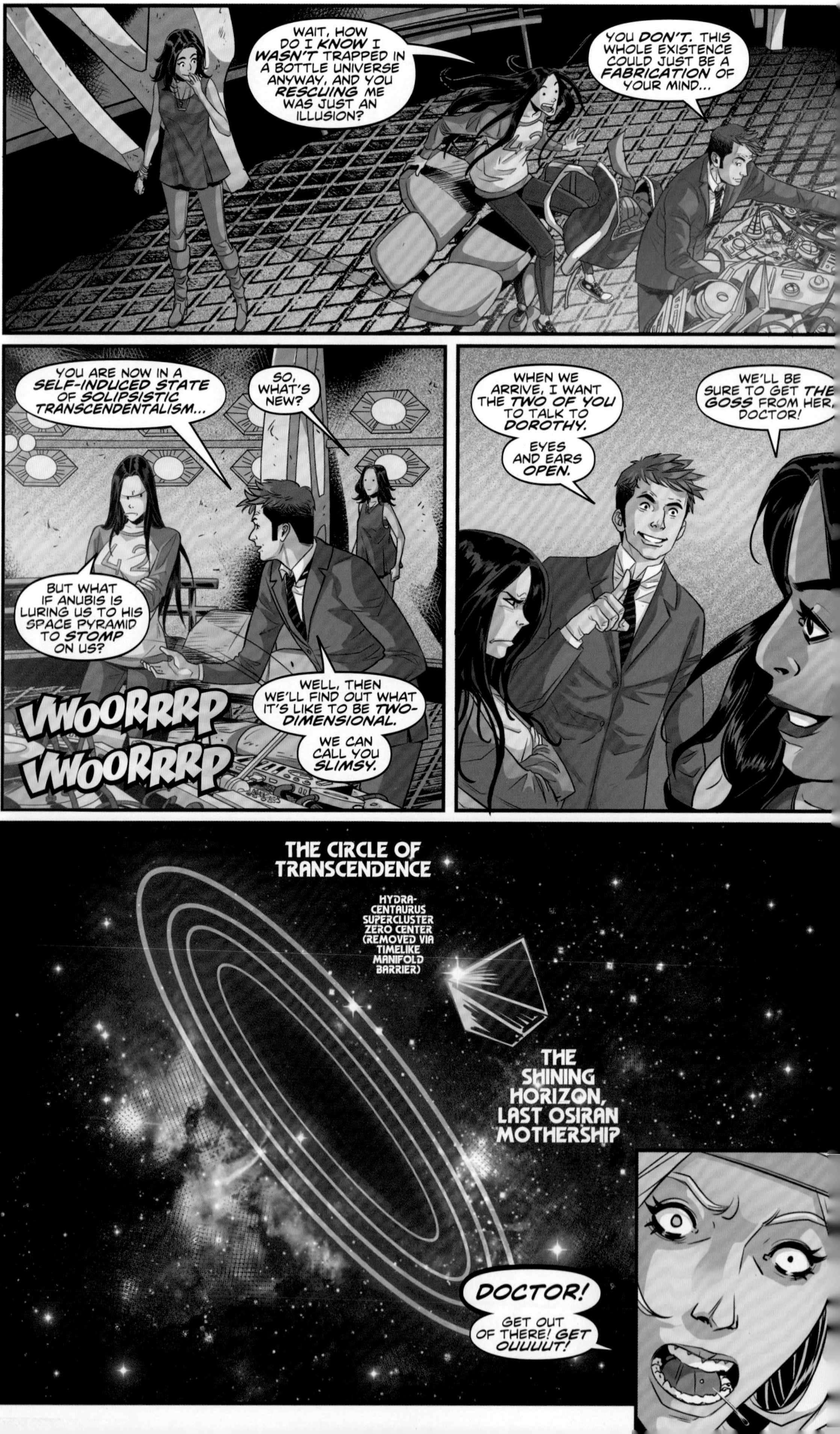
WAIT, HOW DO I KNOW I WASN'T TRAPPED IN A BOTTLE UNIVERSE ANYWAY, AND YOU RESCUING ME WAS JUST AN ILLUSION?
YOU DON'T. THIS WHOLE EXISTENCE COULD JUST BE A FABRICATION OF YOUR MIND...
YOU ARE NOW IN A SELF-INDUCED STATE OF SOLIPSISTIC TRANSCENDENTALISM...
SO, WHAT'S NEW?
BUT WHAT IF ANUBIS IS LURING US TO HIS SPACE PYRAMID TO STOMP ON US?
WELL, THEN WE'LL FIND OUT WHAT IT'S LIKE TO BE TWO-DIMENSIONAL.
WE CAN CALL YOU SLIMSY.
VWOORRRP VWOORRRP
WHEN WE ARRIVE, I WANT THE TWO OF YOU TO TALK TO DOROTHY.
EYES AND EARS OPEN.
WE'LL BE SURE TO GET THE GOSS FROM HER, DOCTOR!
THE CIRCLE OF TRANSCENDENCE
HYDRA-CENTAURUS SUPERCLUSTER ZERO CENTER (REMOVED VIA TIMELIKE MANIFOLD BARRIER)
THE SHINING HORIZON, LAST OSIRAN MOTHERSHIP
DOCTOR!
GET OUT OF THERE! GET OUUUUT!

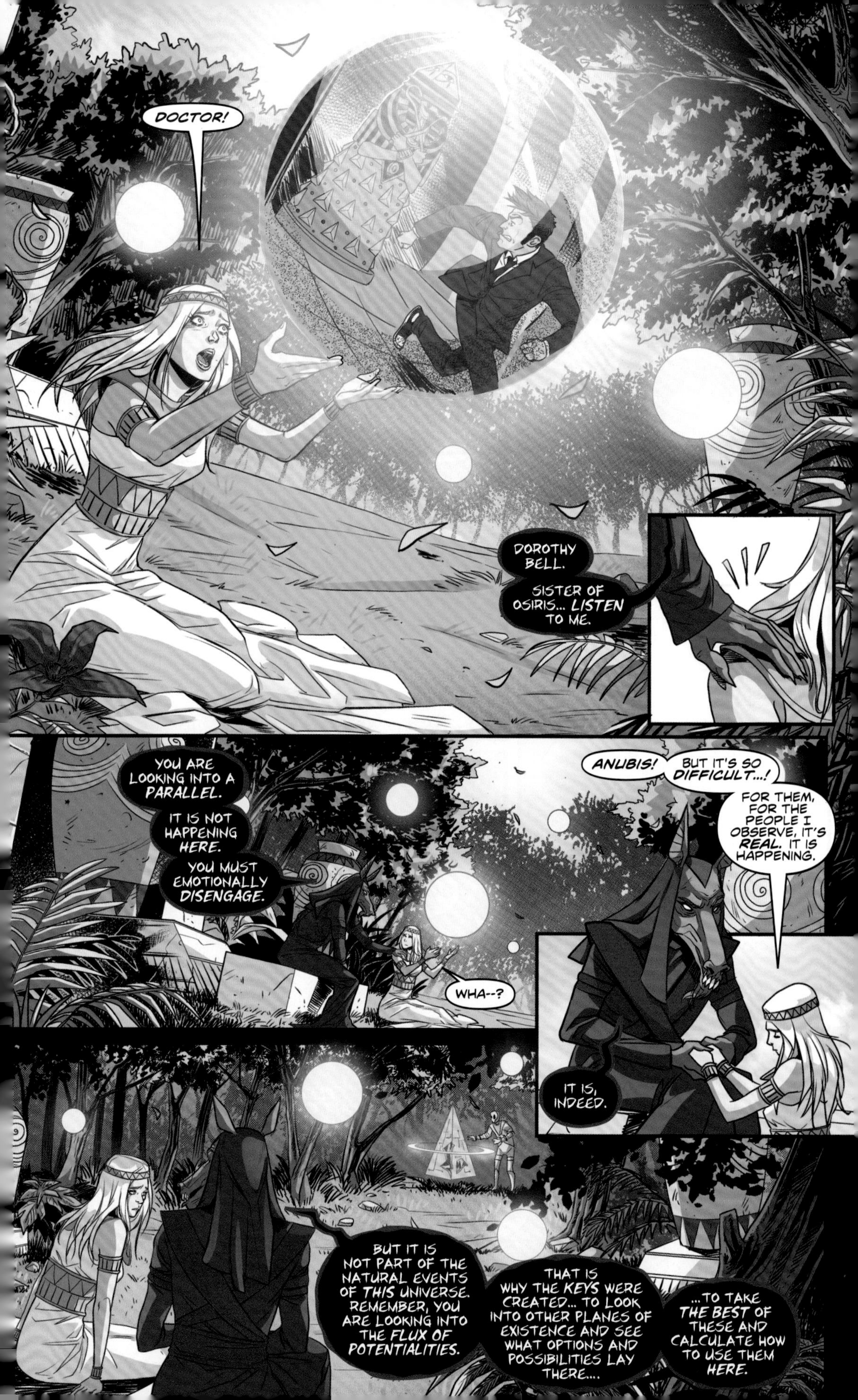
DOCTOR!
DOROTHY BELL.
SISTER OF OSIRIS... LISTEN TO ME.
YOU ARE LOOKING INTO A PARALLEL.
IT IS NOT HAPPENING HERE.
YOU MUST EMOTIONALLY DISENGAGE.
WHA--?
ANUBIS!
BUT IT'S SO DIFFICULT...!
FOR THEM, FOR THE PEOPLE I OBSERVE, IT'S REAL. IT IS HAPPENING.
IT IS, INDEED.
BUT IT IS NOT PART OF THE NATURAL EVENTS OF THIS UNIVERSE. REMEMBER, YOU ARE LOOKING INTO THE FLUX OF POTENTIALITIES.
THAT IS WHY THE KEYS WERE CREATED... TO LOOK INTO OTHER PLANES OF EXISTENCE AND SEE WHAT OPTIONS AND POSSIBILITIES LAY THERE....
...TO TAKE THE BEST OF THESE AND CALCULATE HOW TO USE THEM HERE.

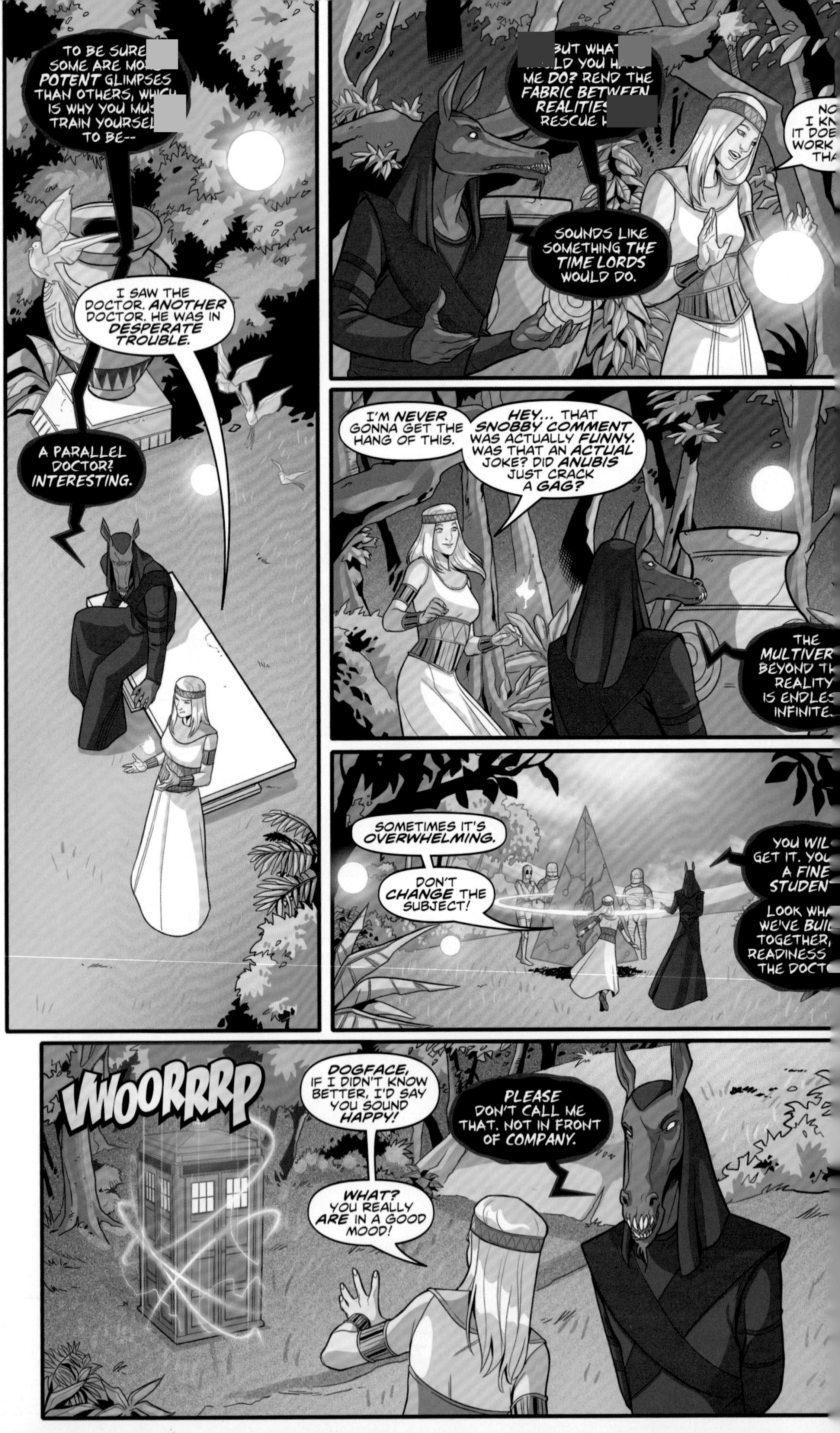

TO BE SURE SOME ARE MO POTENT GLIMPSES THAN OTHERS, WHIC IS WHY YOU MUS TRAIN YOURSEL TO BE--
I SAW THE DOCTOR. ANOTHER DOCTOR. HE WAS IN DESPERATE TROUBLE.
A PARALLEL DOCTOR? INTERESTING.
BUT WHAT LD YOU HA ME DO? REND THE FABRIC BETWEEN REALITIES RESCUE H
SOUNDS LIKE SOMETHING THE TIME LORDS WOULD DO.
NO I KN IT DOE WORK THA
I'M NEVER GONNA GET THE HANG OF THIS.
HEY... THAT SNOBBY COMMENT WAS ACTUALLY FUNNY. WAS THAT AN ACTUAL JOKE? DID ANUBIS JUST CRACK A GAG?
THE MULTIVER BEYOND TH REALITY IS ENDLES INFINITE.
SOMETIMES IT'S OVERWHELMING.
DON'T CHANGE THE SUBJECT!
YOU WIL GET IT. YOU A FINE STUDEN
LOOK WHA WE'VE BUIL TOGETHER, READINESS THE DOCT
VWOORRRP
DOGFACE, IF I DIDN'T KNOW BETTER, I'D SAY YOU SOUND HAPPY!
PLEASE DON'T CALL ME THAT. NOT IN FRONT OF COMPANY.
WHAT? YOU REALLY ARE IN A GOOD MOOD!

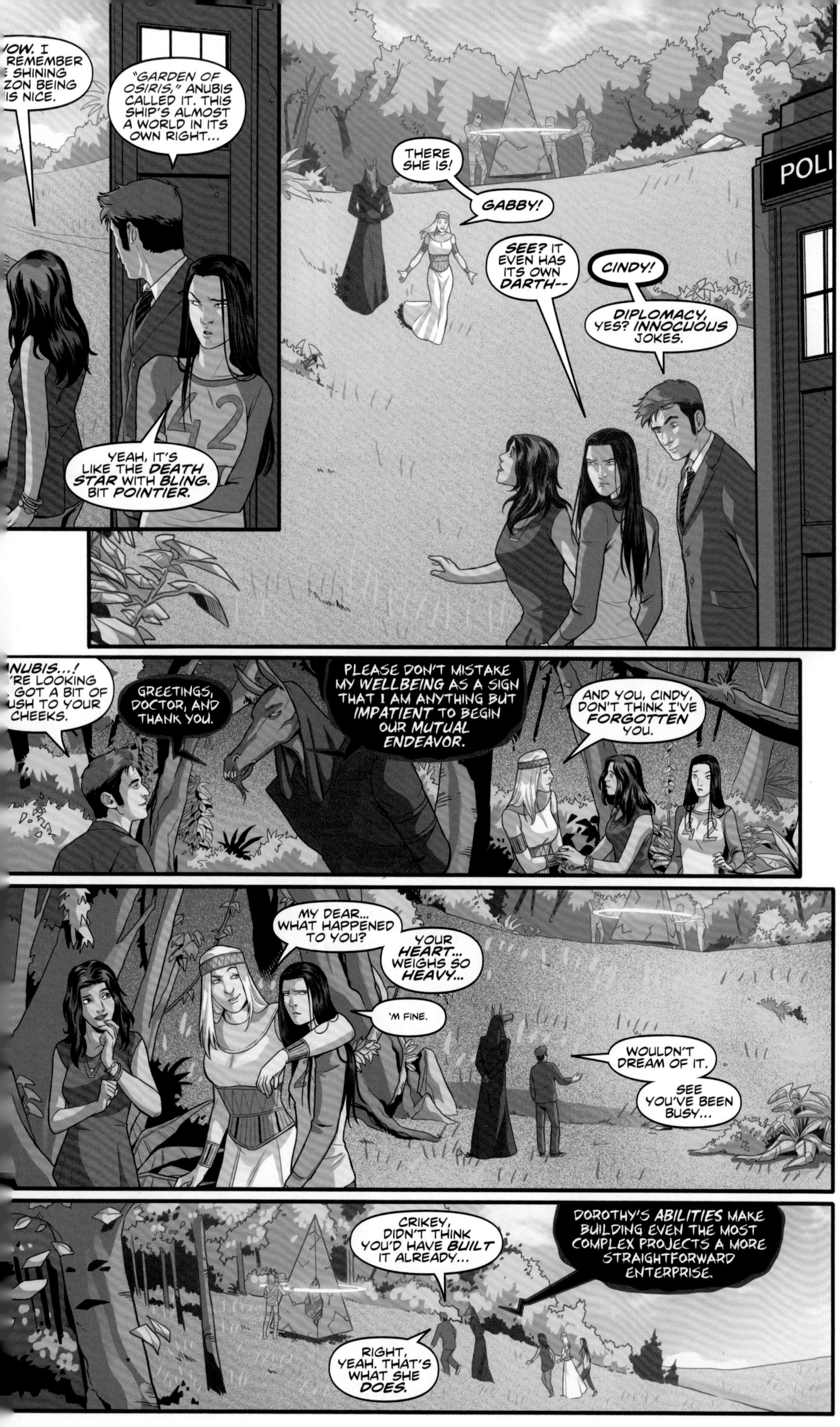

OW. I
REMEMBER
E SHINING
ZON BEING
IS NICE.
"GARDEN OF OSIRIS," ANUBIS CALLED IT. THIS SHIP'S ALMOST A WORLD IN ITS OWN RIGHT...
YEAH, IT'S LIKE THE DEATH STAR WITH BLING. BIT POINTIER.
THERE SHE IS!
GABBY!
SEE? IT EVEN HAS ITS OWN DARTH--
CINDY!
DIPLOMACY, YES? INNOCUOUS JOKES.
NUBIS...!
'RE LOOKING
. GOT A BIT OF
USH TO YOUR
CHEEKS.
GREETINGS, DOCTOR, AND THANK YOU.
PLEASE DON'T MISTAKE MY WELLBEING AS A SIGN THAT I AM ANYTHING BUT IMPATIENT TO BEGIN OUR MUTUAL ENDEAVOR.
AND YOU, CINDY, DON'T THINK I'VE FORGOTTEN YOU.
MY DEAR... WHAT HAPPENED TO YOU?
YOUR HEART... WEIGHS SO HEAVY...
'M FINE.
WOULDN'T DREAM OF IT.
SEE YOU'VE BEEN BUSY...
CRIKEY, DIDN'T THINK YOU'D HAVE BUILT IT ALREADY...
DOROTHY'S ABILITIES MAKE BUILDING EVEN THE MOST COMPLEX PROJECTS A MORE STRAIGHTFORWARD ENTERPRISE.
RIGHT, YEAH. THAT'S WHAT SHE DOES.

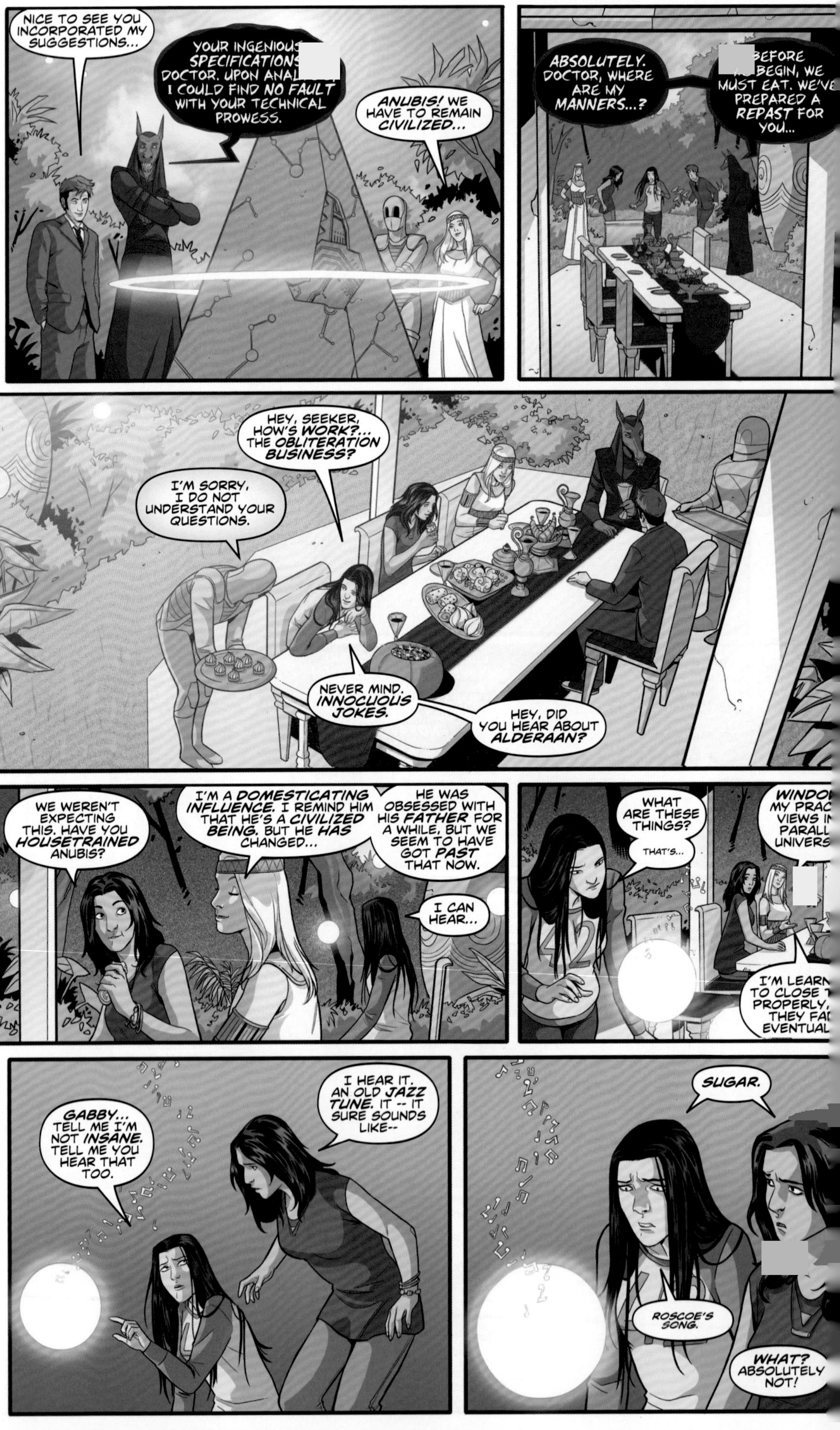
NICE TO SEE YOU INCORPORATED MY SUGGESTIONS...
YOUR INGENIOUS SPECIFICATIONS DOCTOR. UPON ANAL I COULD FIND NO FAULT WITH YOUR TECHNICAL PROWESS.
ANUBIS! WE HAVE TO REMAIN CIVILIZED...
ABSOLUTELY. DOCTOR, WHERE ARE MY MANNERS...?
BEFORE BEGIN, WE MUST EAT. WE'VE PREPARED A REPAST FOR YOU...
HEY, SEEKER, HOW'S WORK?... THE OBLITERATION BUSINESS?
I'M SORRY, I DO NOT UNDERSTAND YOUR QUESTIONS.
NEVER MIND. INNOCUOUS JOKES.
HEY, DID YOU HEAR ABOUT ALDERAAN?
WE WEREN'T EXPECTING THIS. HAVE YOU HOUSETRAINED ANUBIS?
I'M A DOMESTICATING INFLUENCE. I REMIND HIM THAT HE'S A CIVILIZED BEING. BUT HE HAS CHANGED...
HE WAS OBSESSED WITH HIS FATHER FOR A WHILE, BUT WE SEEM TO HAVE GOT PAST THAT NOW.
I CAN HEAR...
WHAT ARE THESE THINGS?
THAT'S...
WINDO MY PRAC VIEWS I PARALL UNIVERS
I'M LEARN TO CLOSE PROPERLY, THEY FA EVENTUAL
GABBY... TELL ME I'M NOT INSANE. TELL ME YOU HEAR THAT TOO.
I HEAR IT. AN OLD JAZZ TUNE. IT -- IT SURE SOUNDS LIKE--
SUGAR.
ROSCOE'S SONG.
WHAT? ABSOLUTELY NOT!

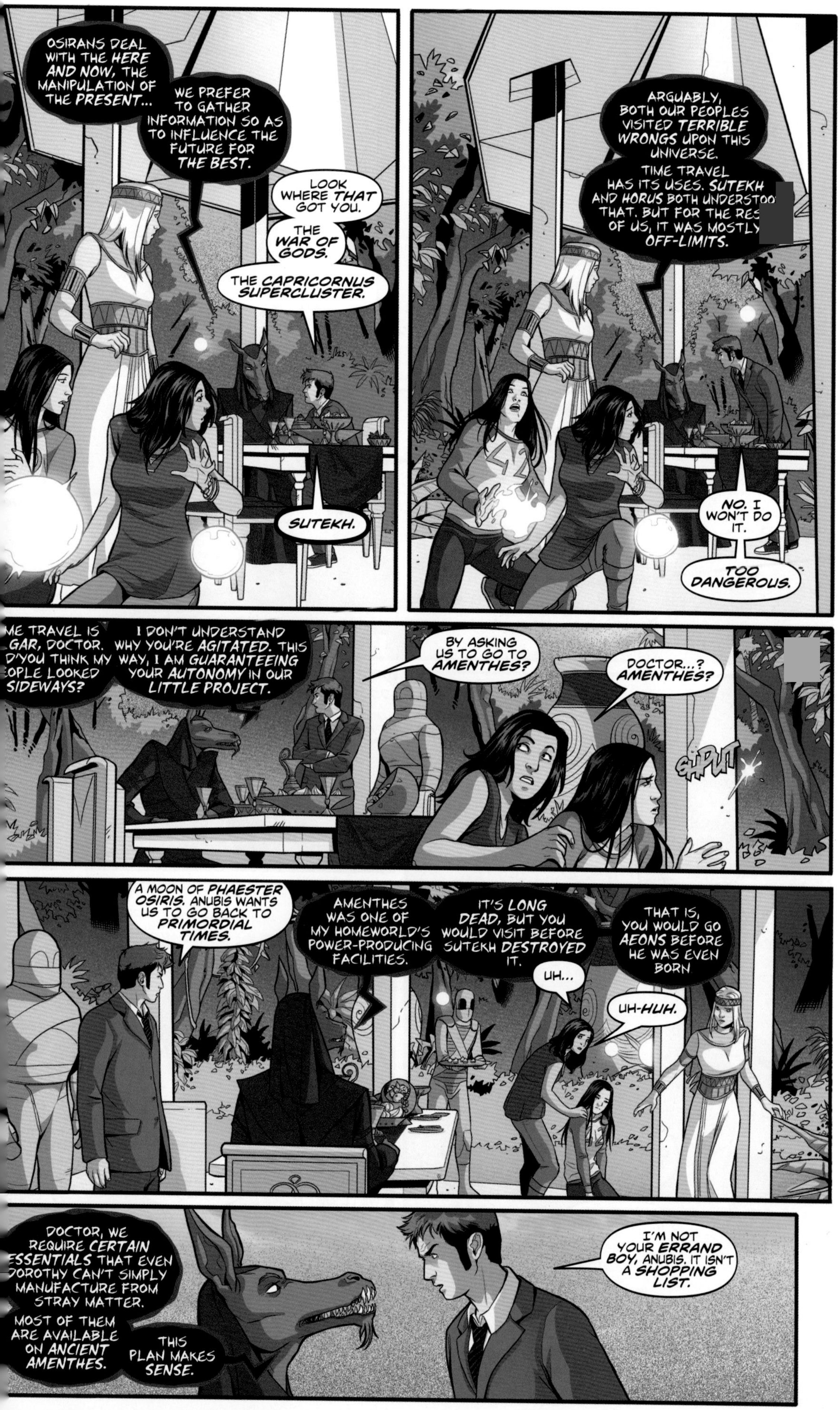
OSIRANS DEAL WITH THE HERE AND NOW, THE MANIPULATION OF THE PRESENT...
WE PREFER TO GATHER INFORMATION SO AS TO INFLUENCE THE FUTURE FOR THE BEST.
LOOK WHERE THAT GOT YOU.
THE WAR OF GODS.
THE CAPRICORNUS SUPERCLUSTER.
SUTEKH.
ARGUABLY, BOTH OUR PEOPLES VISITED TERRIBLE WRONGS UPON THIS UNIVERSE.
TIME TRAVEL HAS ITS USES. SUTEKH AND HORUS BOTH UNDERSTOO THAT. BUT FOR THE RES OF US, IT WAS MOSTLY OFF-LIMITS.
NO. I WON'T DO IT.
TOO DANGEROUS.
ME TRAVEL IS GAR, DOCTOR. D'YOU THINK MY EOPLE LOOKED SIDEWAYS?
I DON'T UNDERSTAND WHY YOU'RE AGITATED. THIS WAY, I AM GUARANTEEING YOUR AUTONOMY IN OUR LITTLE PROJECT.
BY ASKING US TO GO TO AMENTHES?
DOCTOR...? AMENTHES?
SHPUT
A MOON OF PHAESTER OSIRIS. ANUBIS WANTS US TO GO BACK TO PRIMORDIAL TIMES.
AMENTHES WAS ONE OF MY HOMEWORLD'S POWER-PRODUCING FACILITIES.
IT'S LONG DEAD, BUT YOU WOULD VISIT BEFORE SUTEKH DESTROYED IT.
UH...
THAT IS, YOU WOULD GO AEONS BEFORE HE WAS EVEN BORN
UH-HUH.
DOCTOR, WE REQUIRE CERTAIN ESSENTIALS THAT EVEN DOROTHY CAN'T SIMPLY MANUFACTURE FROM STRAY MATTER.
MOST OF THEM ARE AVAILABLE ON ANCIENT AMENTHES.
THIS PLAN MAKES SENSE.
I'M NOT YOUR ERRAND BOY, ANUBIS. IT ISN'T A SHOPPING LIST.

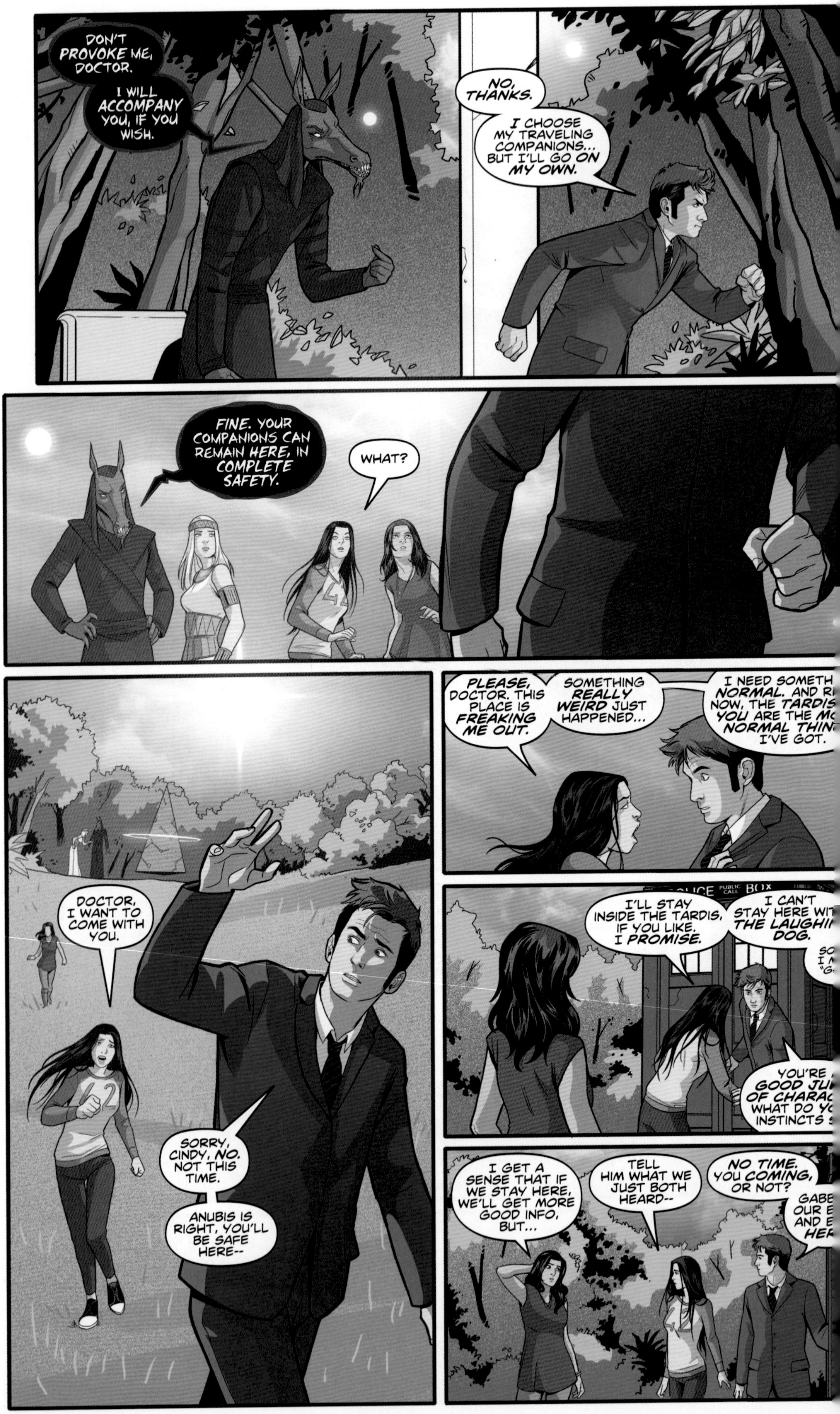
DON'T PROVOKE ME, DOCTOR.
I WILL ACCOMPANY YOU, IF YOU WISH.
NO, THANKS.
I CHOOSE MY TRAVELING COMPANIONS... BUT I'LL GO ON MY OWN.
FINE. YOUR COMPANIONS CAN REMAIN HERE, IN COMPLETE SAFETY.
WHAT?
DOCTOR, I WANT TO COME WITH YOU.
SORRY, CINDY, NO. NOT THIS TIME.
ANUBIS IS RIGHT, YOU'LL BE SAFE HERE--
PLEASE, DOCTOR. THIS PLACE IS FREAKING ME OUT.
SOMETHING REALLY WEIRD JUST HAPPENED...
I NEED SOMETH NORMAL. AND R NOW, THE TARDIS YOU ARE THE M NORMAL THIN I'VE GOT.
POLICE PUBLIC CALL BOX
I'LL STAY INSIDE THE TARDIS, IF YOU LIKE. I PROMISE.
I CAN'T STAY HERE WIT THE LAUGHI DOG.
YOU'RE GOOD JU OF CHARAC WHAT DO Y INSTINCTS
I GET A SENSE THAT IF WE STAY HERE, WE'LL GET MORE GOOD INFO, BUT...
TELL HIM WHAT WE JUST BOTH HEARD--
NO TIME. YOU COMING, OR NOT?
GABE OUR E AND E HER

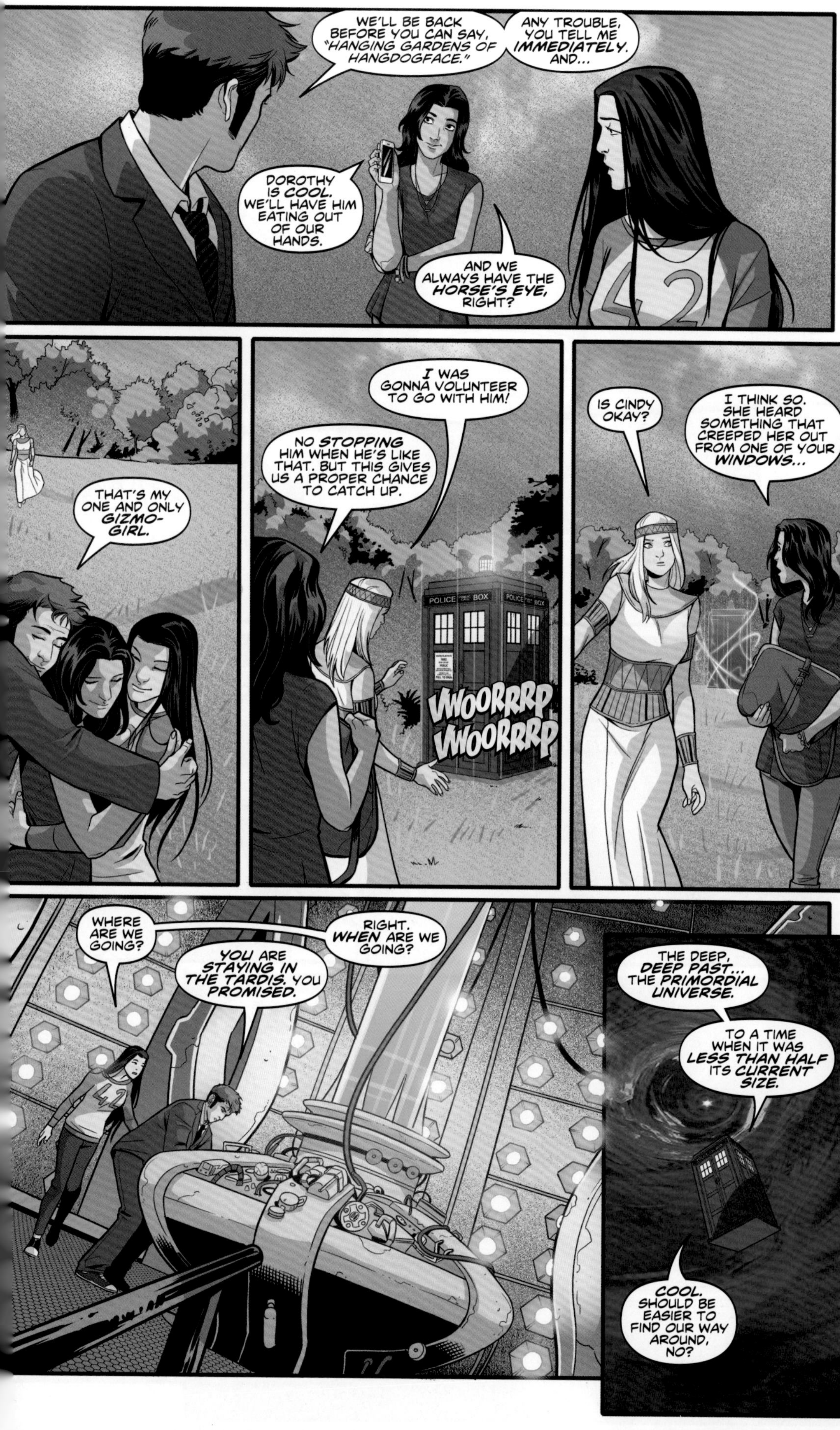
WE'LL BE BACK BEFORE YOU CAN SAY, "HANGING GARDENS OF HANGDOGFACE."
ANY TROUBLE, YOU TELL ME IMMEDIATELY. AND...
DOROTHY IS COOL. WE'LL HAVE HIM EATING OUT OF OUR HANDS.
AND WE ALWAYS HAVE THE HORSE'S EYE, RIGHT?
THAT'S MY ONE AND ONLY GIZMO-GIRL.
I WAS GONNA VOLUNTEER TO GO WITH HIM!
NO STOPPING HIM WHEN HE'S LIKE THAT. BUT THIS GIVES US A PROPER CHANCE TO CATCH UP.
POLICE BOX
VWOORRRP VWOORRRP
IS CINDY OKAY?
I THINK SO. SHE HEARD SOMETHING THAT CREEPED HER OUT FROM ONE OF YOUR WINDOWS...
WHERE ARE WE GOING?
RIGHT. WHEN ARE WE GOING?
YOU ARE STAYING IN THE TARDIS. YOU PROMISED.
THE DEEP, DEEP PAST... THE PRIMORDIAL UNIVERSE.
TO A TIME WHEN IT WAS LESS THAN HALF ITS CURRENT SIZE.
COOL. SHOULD BE EASIER TO FIND OUR WAY AROUND, NO?

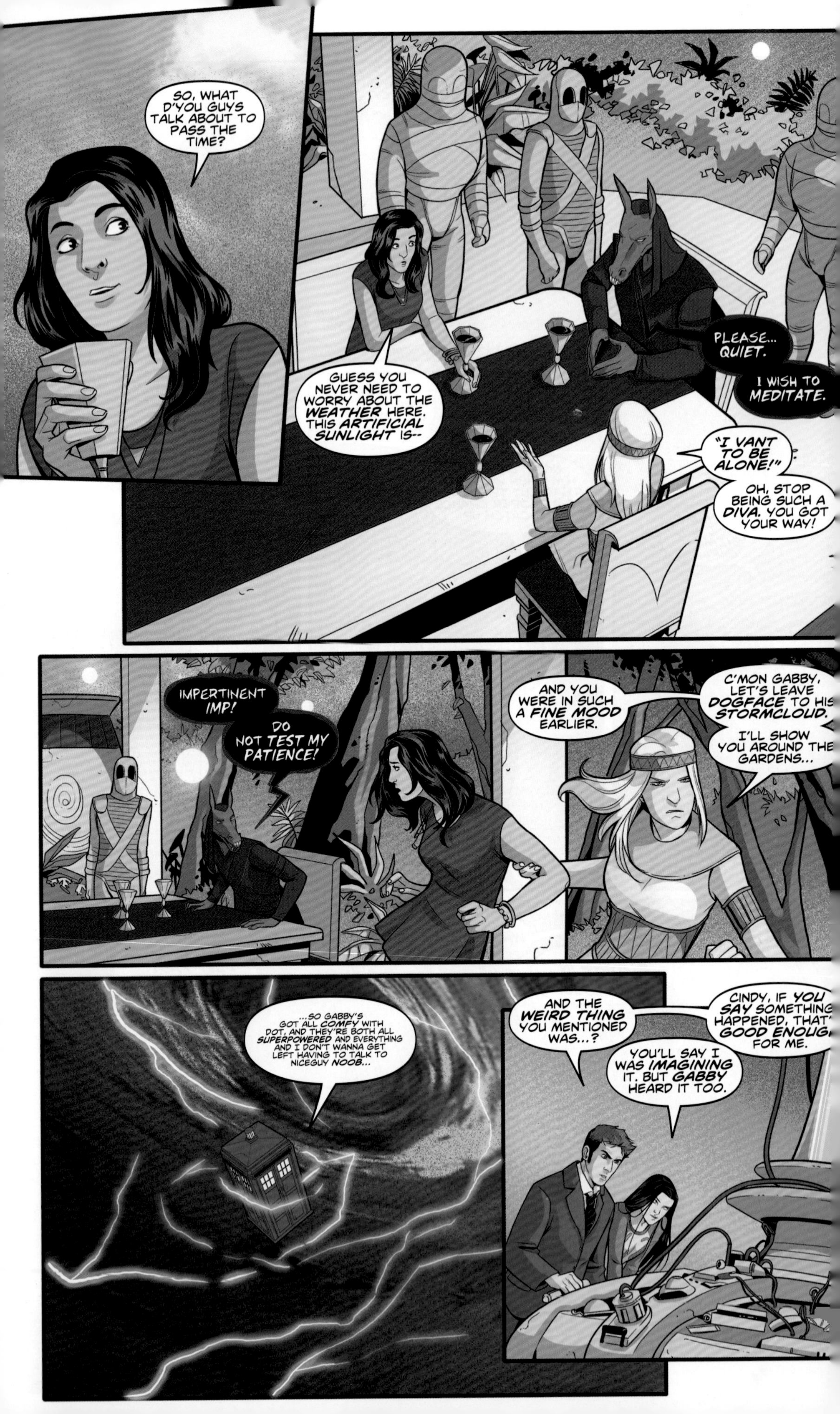
SO, WHAT D'YOU GUYS TALK ABOUT TO PASS THE TIME?
GUESS YOU NEVER NEED TO WORRY ABOUT THE WEATHER HERE. THIS ARTIFICIAL SUNLIGHT IS--
PLEASE... QUIET.
I WISH TO MEDITATE.
"I VANT TO BE ALONE!"
OH, STOP BEING SUCH A DIVA. YOU GOT YOUR WAY!
IMPERTINENT IMP!
DO NOT TEST MY PATIENCE!
AND YOU WERE IN SUCH A FINE MOOD EARLIER.
C'MON GABBY, LET'S LEAVE DOGFACE TO HIS STORMCLOUD.
I'LL SHOW YOU AROUND THE GARDENS...
...SO GABBY'S GOT ALL COMFY WITH DOT, AND THEY'RE BOTH ALL SUPERPOWERED AND EVERYTHING AND I DON'T WANNA GET LEFT HAVING TO TALK TO NICEGUY NOOB...
AND THE WEIRD THING YOU MENTIONED WAS...?
YOU'LL SAY I WAS IMAGINING IT. BUT GABBY HEARD IT TOO.
CINDY, IF YOU SAY SOMETHING HAPPENED, THAT' GOOD ENOUG FOR ME.

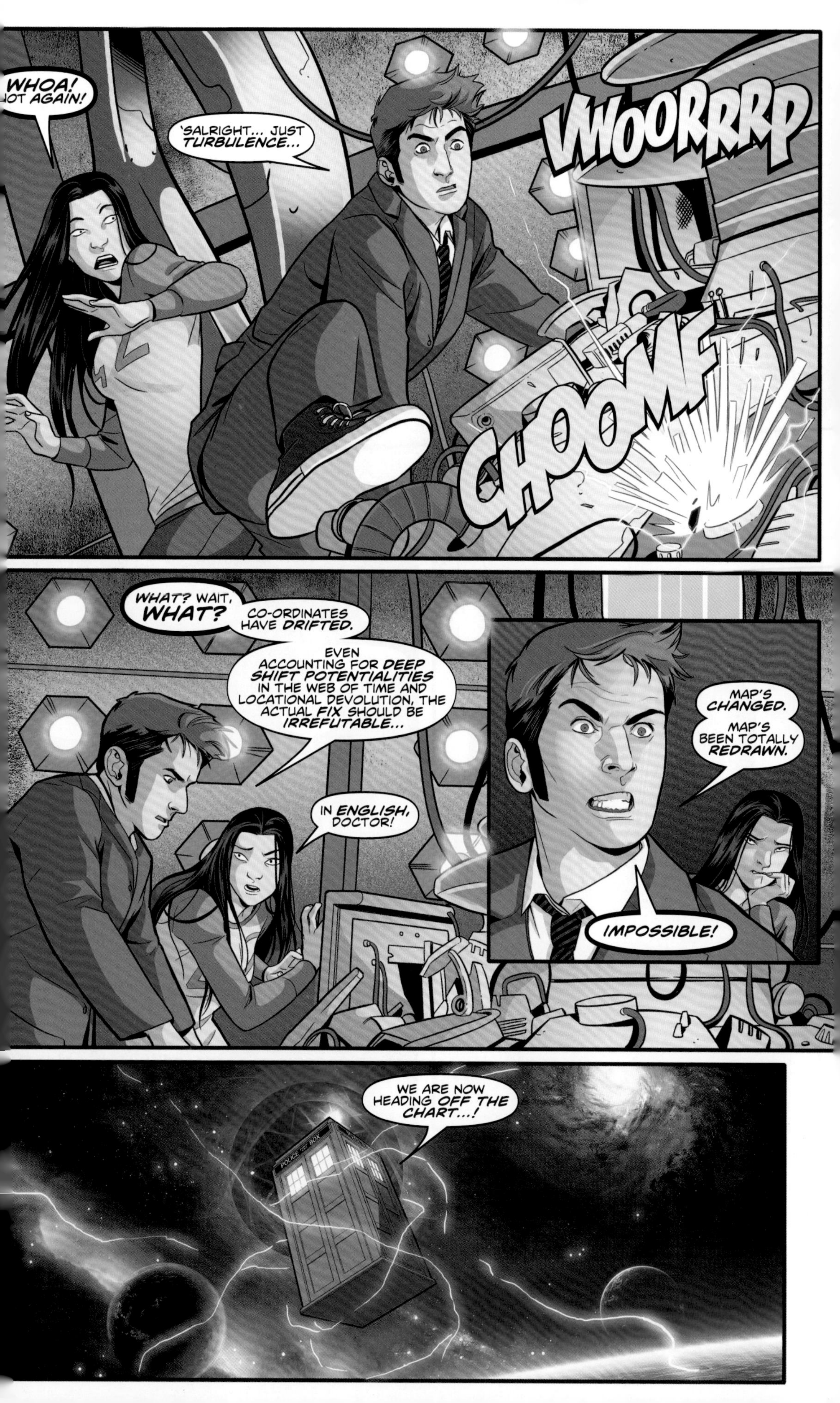
WHOA! NOT AGAIN!
'SALRIGHT... JUST TURBULENCE...
VWOORRRP
CHOOMF
WHAT? WAIT, WHAT?
CO-ORDINATES HAVE DRIFTED.
EVEN ACCOUNTING FOR DEEP SHIFT POTENTIALITIES IN THE WEB OF TIME AND LOCATIONAL DEVOLUTION, THE ACTUAL FIX SHOULD BE IRREFUTABLE...
IN ENGLISH, DOCTOR!
MAP'S CHANGED.
MAP'S BEEN TOTALLY REDRAWN.
IMPOSSIBLE!
WE ARE NOW HEADING OFF THE CHART...!
POLICE BOX

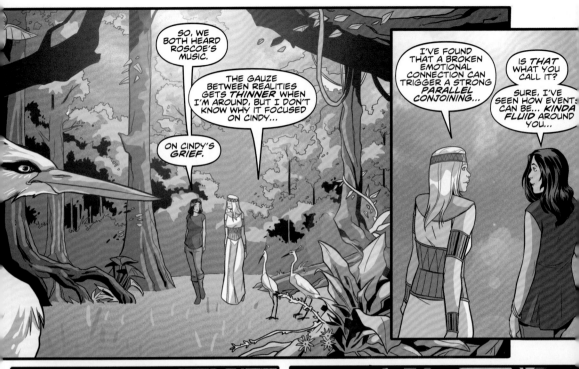

SO, WE BOTH HEARD ROSCOE'S MUSIC.

THE GAUZE BETWEEN REALITIES GETS *THINNER* WHEN I'M AROUND, BUT I DON'T KNOW WHY IT FOCUSED ON CINDY...

ON CINDY'S *GRIEF*.

I'VE FOUND THAT A BROKEN EMOTIONAL CONNECTION CAN TRIGGER A STRONG *PARALLEL CONJOINING*...

IS *THAT* WHAT YOU CALL IT?

SURE, I'VE SEEN HOW EVENTS CAN BE... *KINDA FLUID* AROUND YOU...

WHAT IS THIS PLACE?

I CALL IT THE *GLADE OF THE GODS*. BASICALLY, IT'S LOTS OF *STATUES* OF DEAD OSIRANS...

HEY, WANT TO SEE ANUBIS' *DAD*?

SUTEKH?

UH... SURE.

HE'S GOT HIS *OWN* GLOOMY SPOT. THIS WAY...

IT CAN'T HAVE BEEN FUN TO KNOW YOU WERE ONCE USED BY *SUTEKH*...

EARLIER INCARNATION THAN THE *CONSCIOUSNESS* IN THIS SKULL, M'DEAR. ALL *UNDER* CONTROL.

I'M STILL *DOROTHY BELL*. I'M NOT RESPONSIBLE FOR SUTEKH'S *WAR CRIMES*.

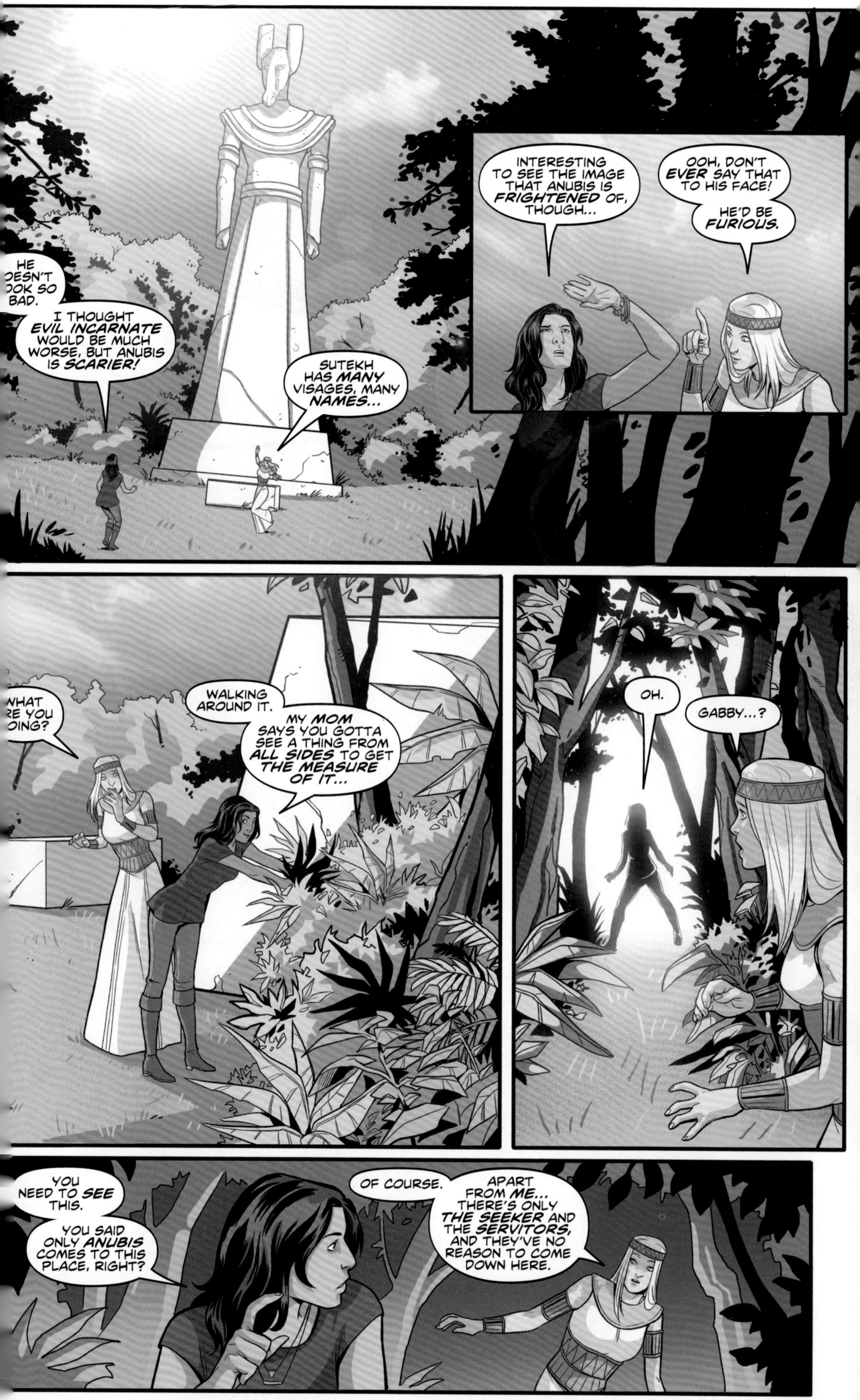
HE OESN'T OOK SO BAD.
I THOUGHT EVIL INCARNATE WOULD BE MUCH WORSE, BUT ANUBIS IS SCARIER!
SUTEKH HAS MANY VISAGES, MANY NAMES...
INTERESTING TO SEE THE IMAGE THAT ANUBIS IS FRIGHTENED OF, THOUGH...
OOH, DON'T EVER SAY THAT TO HIS FACE!
HE'D BE FURIOUS.
WHAT RE YOU OING?
WALKING AROUND IT.
MY MOM SAYS YOU GOTTA SEE A THING FROM ALL SIDES TO GET THE MEASURE OF IT...
OH.
GABBY...?
YOU NEED TO SEE THIS.
YOU SAID ONLY ANUBIS COMES TO THIS PLACE, RIGHT?
OF COURSE.
APART FROM ME... THERE'S ONLY THE SEEKER AND THE SERVITORS, AND THEY'VE NO REASON TO COME DOWN HERE.

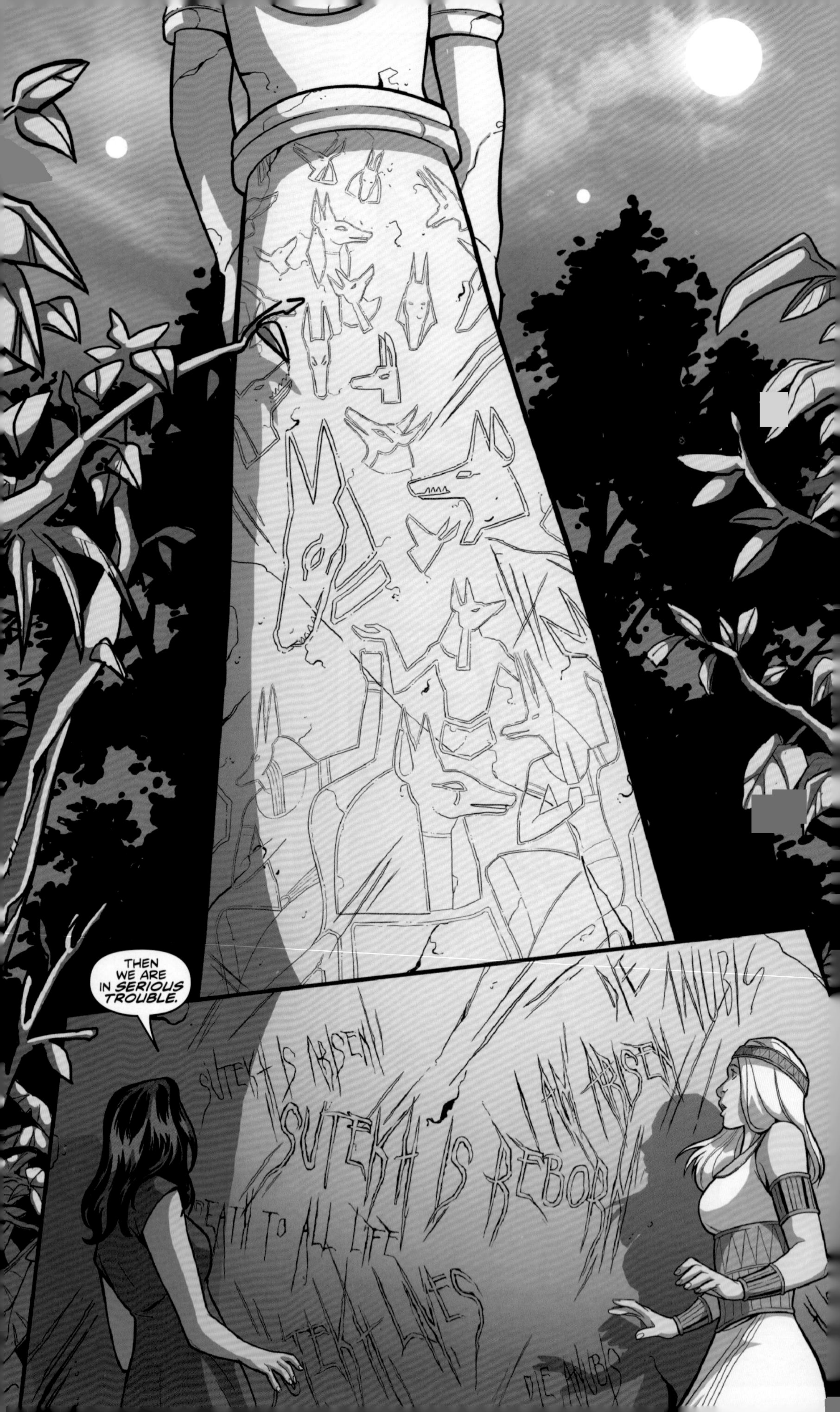
THEN WE ARE IN *SERIOUS* TROUBLE.
DIE ANUBIS
SUTEKH IS ARISEN
I AM ARISEN
SUTEKH IS REBORN
DEATH TO ALL LIFE
DIE ANUBIS

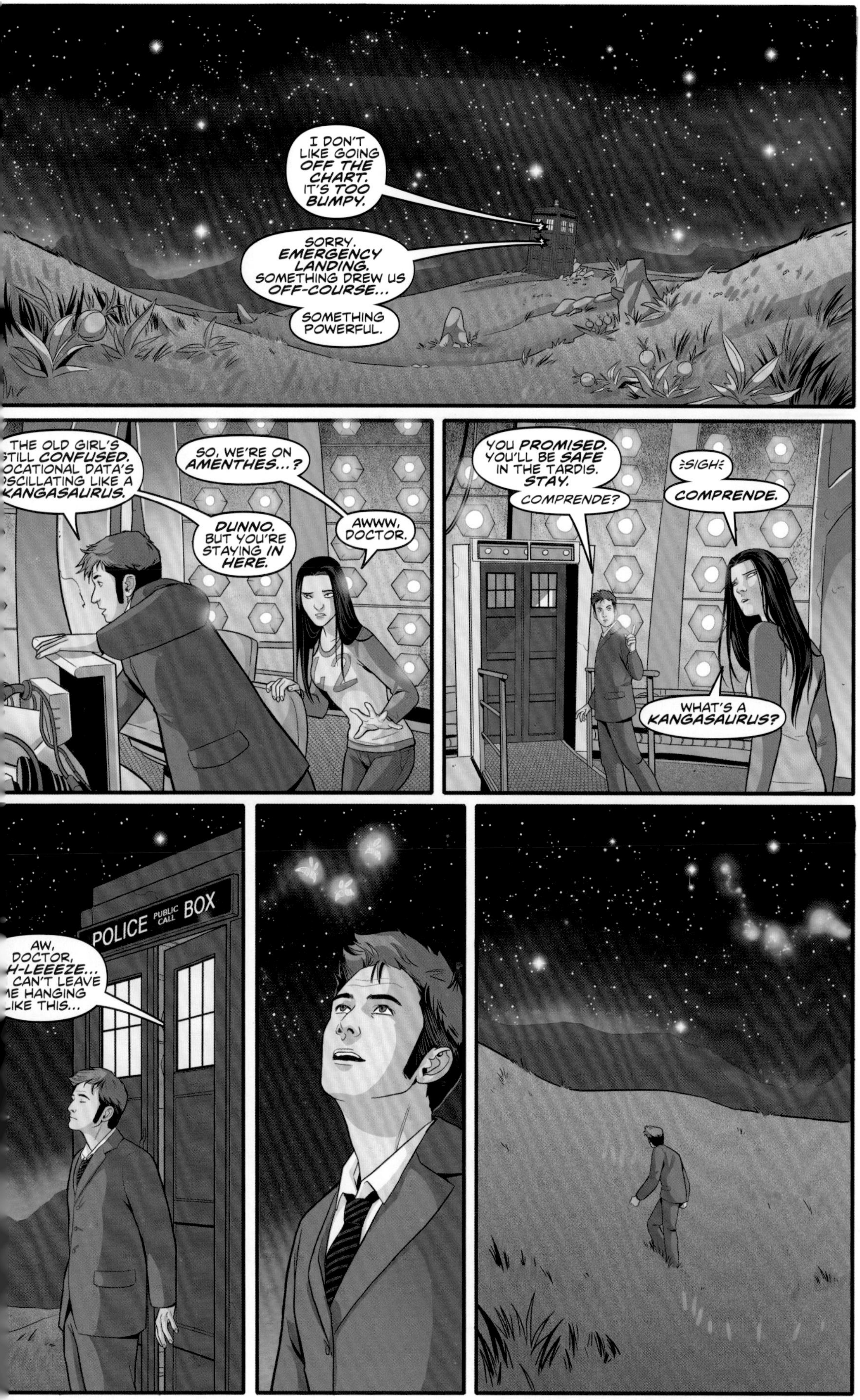
I DON'T LIKE GOING OFF THE CHART. IT'S TOO BUMPY.
SORRY. EMERGENCY LANDING. SOMETHING DREW US OFF-COURSE...
SOMETHING POWERFUL.
THE OLD GIRL'S STILL CONFUSED. OCATIONAL DATA'S OSCILLATING LIKE A KANGASAURUS.
SO, WE'RE ON AMENTHES...?
DUNNO. BUT YOU'RE STAYING IN HERE.
AWWW, DOCTOR.
YOU PROMISED. YOU'LL BE SAFE IN THE TARDIS. STAY.
COMPRENDE?
SIGH
COMPRENDE.
WHAT'S A KANGASAURUS?
POLICE PUBLIC CALL BOX
AW, DOCTOR, H-LEEEZE... CAN'T LEAVE ME HANGING LIKE THIS...

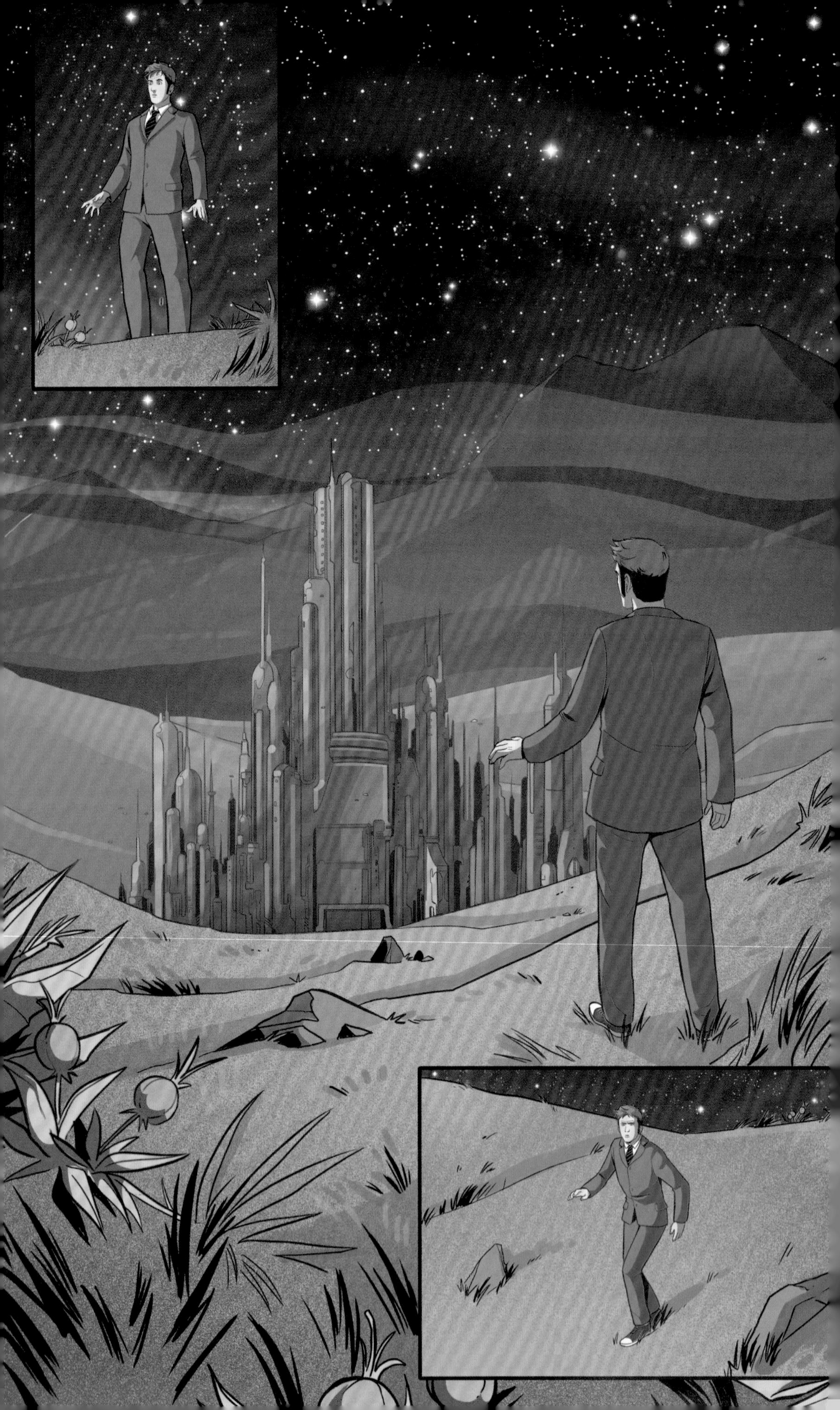

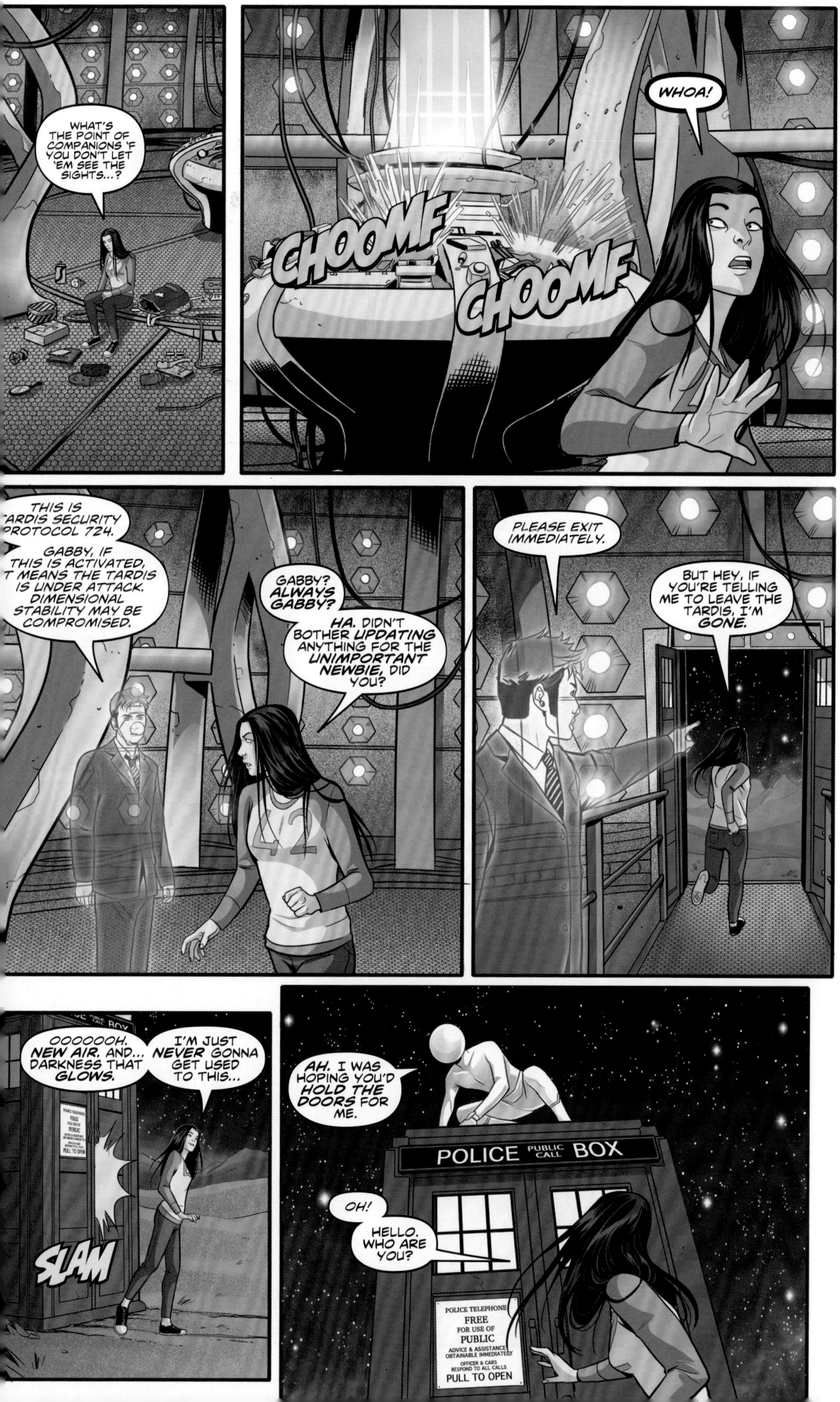

WHAT'S THE POINT OF COMPANIONS 'F YOU DON'T LET 'EM SEE THE SIGHTS...?
WHOA!
CHOOMF
CHOOMF
THIS IS TARDIS SECURITY PROTOCOL 724.
GABBY, IF THIS IS ACTIVATED, IT MEANS THE TARDIS IS UNDER ATTACK. DIMENSIONAL STABILITY MAY BE COMPROMISED.
GABBY? ALWAYS GABBY?
HA. DIDN'T BOTHER UPDATING ANYTHING FOR THE UNIMPORTANT NEWBIE, DID YOU?
PLEASE EXIT IMMEDIATELY.
BUT HEY, IF YOU'RE TELLING ME TO LEAVE THE TARDIS, I'M GONE.
OOOOOOH. NEW AIR. AND... DARKNESS THAT GLOWS.
I'M JUST NEVER GONNA GET USED TO THIS...
SLAM
AH. I WAS HOPING YOU'D HOLD THE DOORS FOR ME.
POLICE PUBLIC CALL BOX
OH!
HELLO. WHO ARE YOU?
POLICE TELEPHONE
FREE
FOR USE OF
PUBLIC
ADVICE & ASSISTANCE OBTAINABLE IMMEDIATELY
OFFICER & CARS RESPOND TO ALL CALLS
PULL TO OPEN

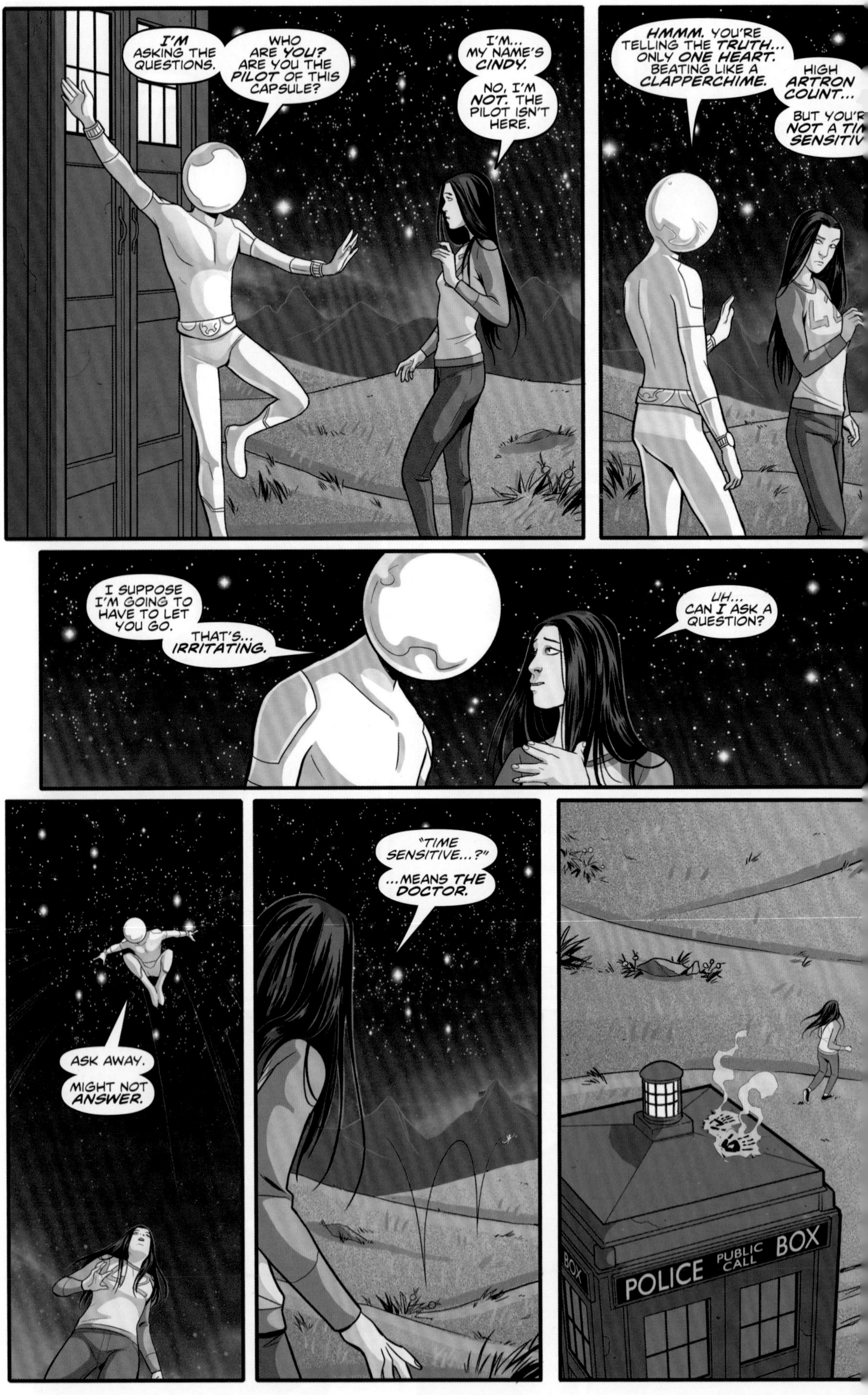
I'M ASKING THE QUESTIONS.
WHO ARE YOU? ARE YOU THE PILOT OF THIS CAPSULE?
I'M... MY NAME'S CINDY.
NO, I'M NOT. THE PILOT ISN'T HERE.
HMMM. YOU'RE TELLING THE TRUTH... ONLY ONE HEART. BEATING LIKE A CLAPPERCHIME.
HIGH ARTRON COUNT...
BUT YOU'R NOT A TIM SENSITIV
I SUPPOSE I'M GOING TO HAVE TO LET YOU GO.
THAT'S... IRRITATING.
UH... CAN I ASK A QUESTION?
ASK AWAY.
MIGHT NOT ANSWER.
"TIME SENSITIVE...?"
...MEANS THE DOCTOR.
POLICE PUBLIC CALL BOX
BOX

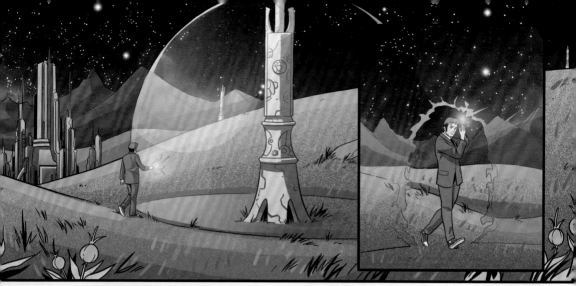

HELLO! ANYONE OUT HERE? HELLO...?

CINDY...?

CINDY!

HELLO!

GET INSIDE THE FORCE SCREEN... QUICKLY!

DOCTOR! NO!

DOCTOR, THAT'S NOT ME!

≥HUNH... HUNH≤

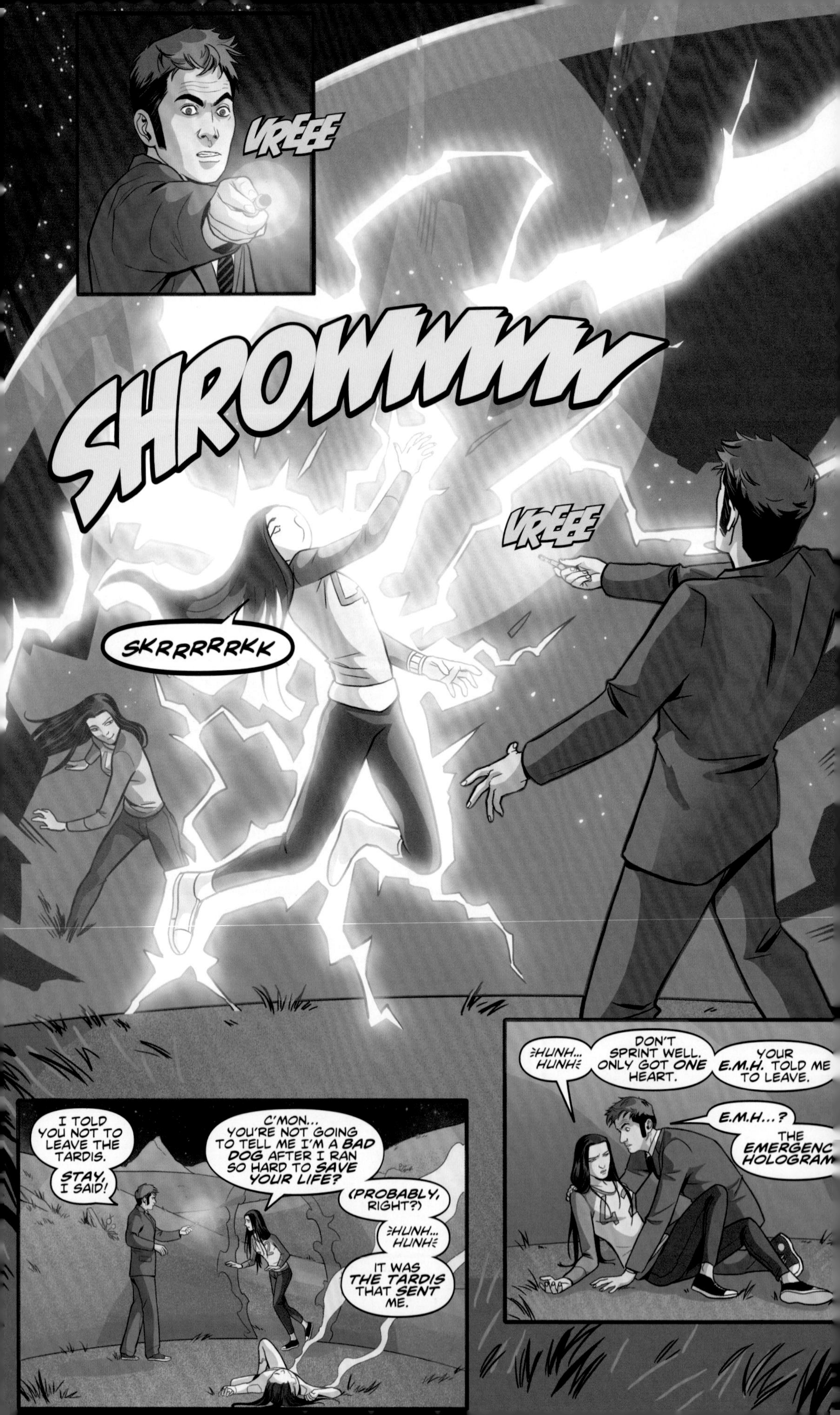

VREEE
SHROWWWW
VREEE
SKRRRRRKK
I TOLD YOU NOT TO LEAVE THE TARDIS.
STAY, I SAID!
C'MON... YOU'RE NOT GOING TO TELL ME I'M A BAD DOG AFTER I RAN SO HARD TO SAVE YOUR LIFE?
(PROBABLY, RIGHT?)
HUNH... HUNH
IT WAS THE TARDIS THAT SENT ME.
HUNH... HUNH
DON'T SPRINT WELL. ONLY GOT ONE HEART.
YOUR E.M.H. TOLD ME TO LEAVE.
E.M.H...?
THE EMERGENC HOLOGRAM

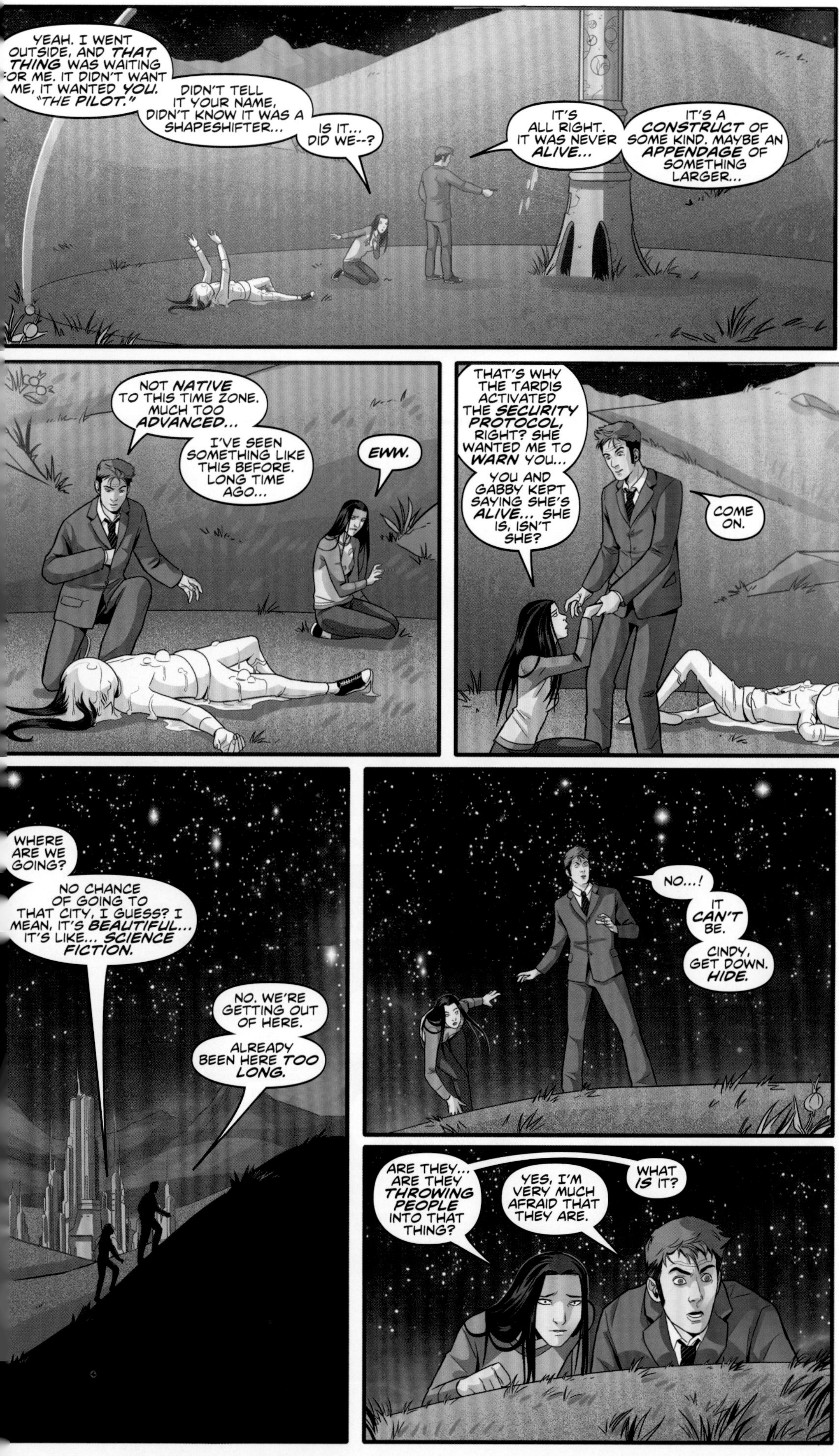
YEAH. I WENT OUTSIDE, AND THAT THING WAS WAITING FOR ME. IT DIDN'T WANT ME, IT WANTED YOU. "THE PILOT."
DIDN'T TELL IT YOUR NAME, DIDN'T KNOW IT WAS A SHAPESHIFTER...
IS IT... DID WE--?
IT'S ALL RIGHT. IT WAS NEVER ALIVE...
IT'S A CONSTRUCT OF SOME KIND. MAYBE AN APPENDAGE OF SOMETHING LARGER...
NOT NATIVE TO THIS TIME ZONE. MUCH TOO ADVANCED...
I'VE SEEN SOMETHING LIKE THIS BEFORE. LONG TIME AGO...
EWW.
THAT'S WHY THE TARDIS ACTIVATED THE SECURITY PROTOCOL, RIGHT? SHE WANTED ME TO WARN YOU...
YOU AND GABBY KEPT SAYING SHE'S ALIVE... SHE IS, ISN'T SHE?
COME ON.
WHERE ARE WE GOING?
NO CHANCE OF GOING TO THAT CITY, I GUESS? I MEAN, IT'S BEAUTIFUL... IT'S LIKE... SCIENCE FICTION.
NO. WE'RE GETTING OUT OF HERE.
ALREADY BEEN HERE TOO LONG.
NO...!
IT CAN'T BE.
CINDY, GET DOWN. HIDE.
ARE THEY... ARE THEY THROWING PEOPLE INTO THAT THING?
YES, I'M VERY MUCH AFRAID THAT THEY ARE.
WHAT IS IT?

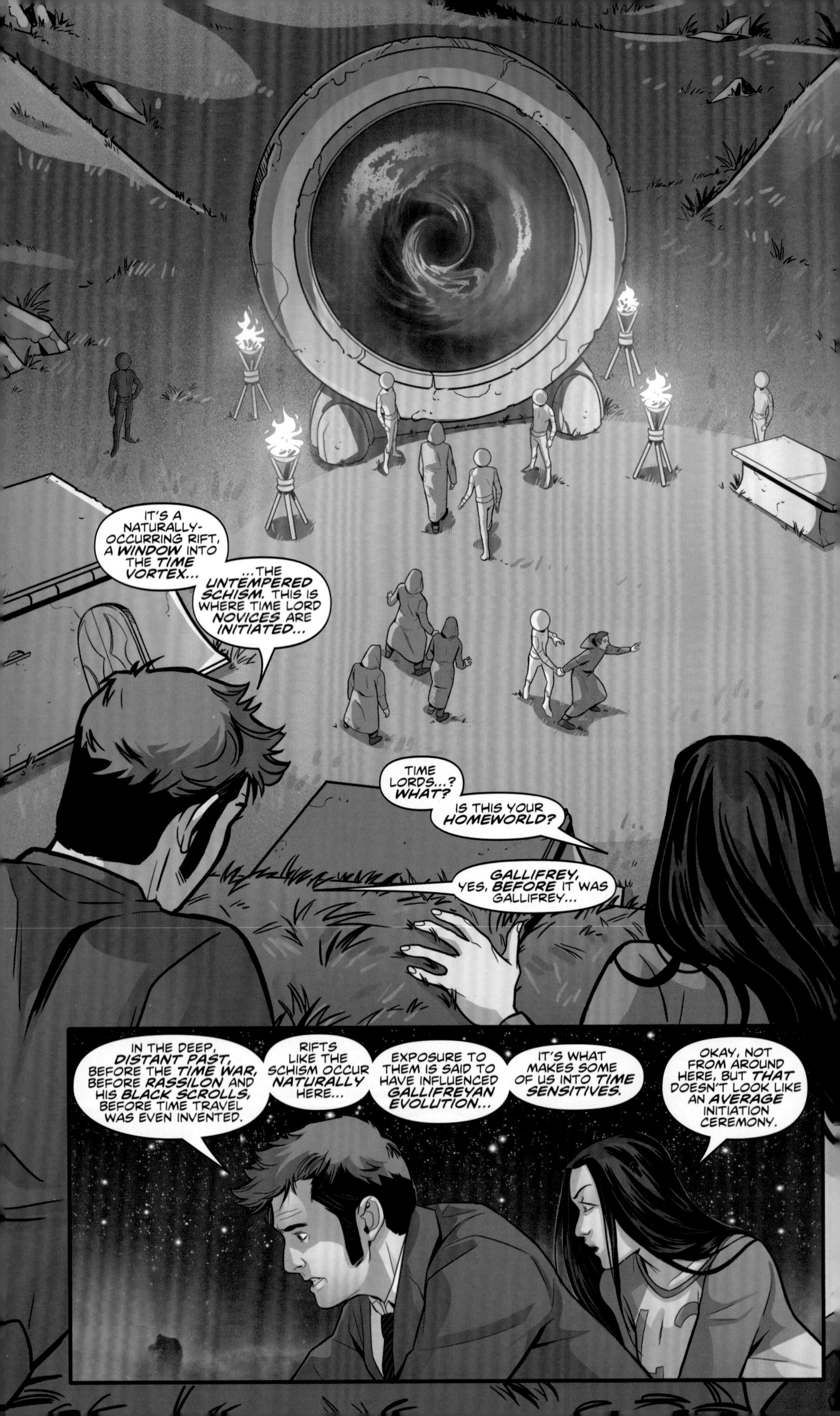
IT'S A NATURALLY-OCCURRING RIFT, A *WINDOW* INTO THE *TIME VORTEX...*
...THE *UNTEMPERED SCHISM.* THIS IS WHERE TIME LORD *NOVICES* ARE *INITIATED...*
TIME LORDS...? *WHAT?*
IS THIS YOUR *HOMEWORLD?*
GALLIFREY, YES, *BEFORE* IT WAS GALLIFREY...
IN THE DEEP, *DISTANT PAST,* BEFORE THE *TIME WAR,* BEFORE *RASSILON* AND HIS *BLACK SCROLLS,* BEFORE TIME TRAVEL WAS EVEN INVENTED.
RIFTS LIKE THE SCHISM OCCUR *NATURALLY* HERE...
EXPOSURE TO THEM IS SAID TO HAVE INFLUENCED *GALLIFREYAN EVOLUTION...*
IT'S WHAT MAKES SOME OF US INTO *TIME SENSITIVES.*
OKAY, NOT FROM AROUND HERE, BUT *THAT* DOESN'T LOOK LIKE AN *AVERAGE* INITIATION CEREMONY.

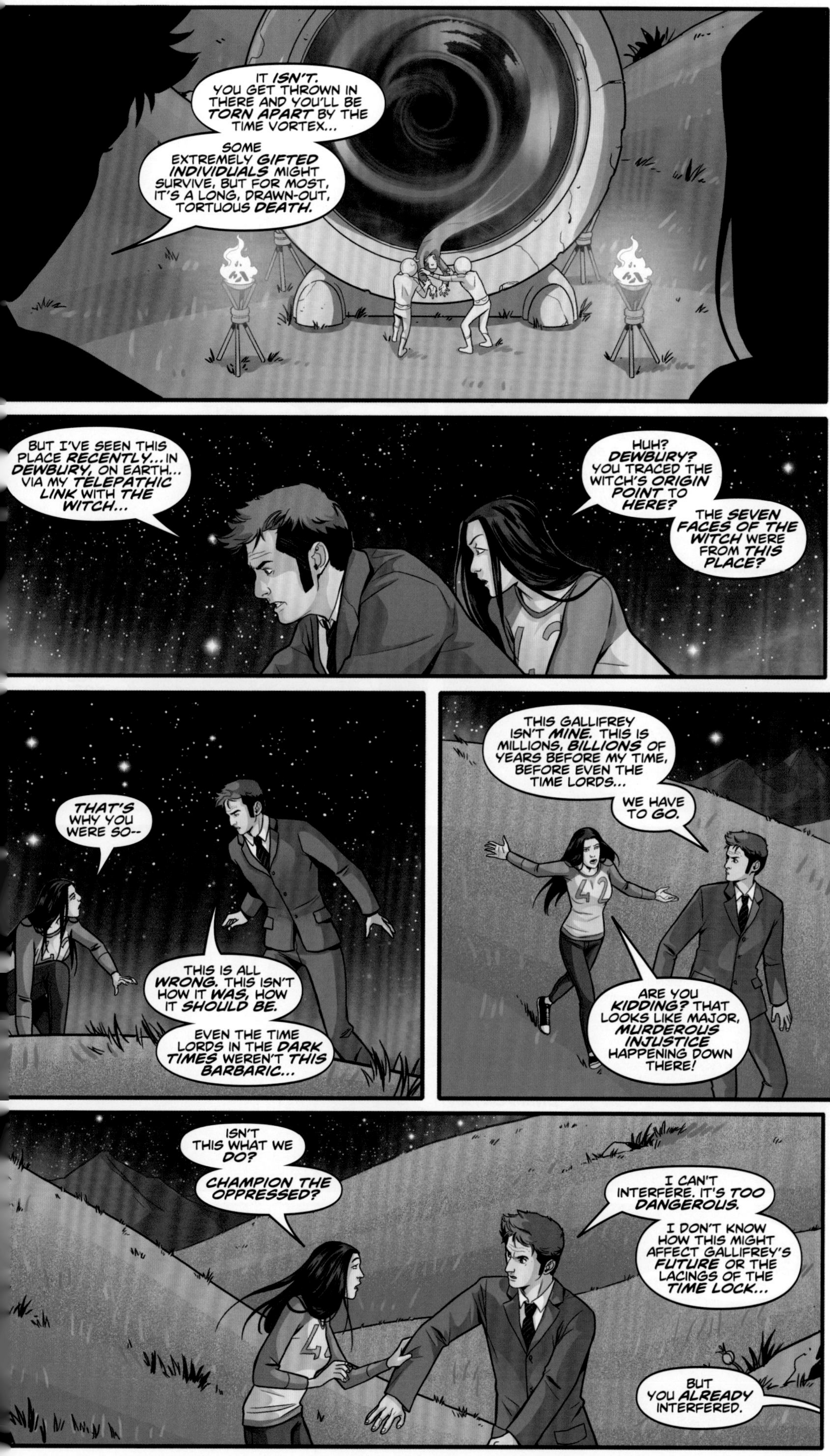
IT ISN'T. YOU GET THROWN IN THERE AND YOU'LL BE TORN APART BY THE TIME VORTEX...
SOME EXTREMELY GIFTED INDIVIDUALS MIGHT SURVIVE, BUT FOR MOST, IT'S A LONG, DRAWN-OUT, TORTUOUS DEATH.
BUT I'VE SEEN THIS PLACE RECENTLY... IN DEWBURY, ON EARTH... VIA MY TELEPATHIC LINK WITH THE WITCH...
HUH? DEWBURY? YOU TRACED THE WITCH'S ORIGIN POINT TO HERE?
THE SEVEN FACES OF THE WITCH WERE FROM THIS PLACE?
THAT'S WHY YOU WERE SO--
THIS IS ALL WRONG. THIS ISN'T HOW IT WAS, HOW IT SHOULD BE.
EVEN THE TIME LORDS IN THE DARK TIMES WEREN'T THIS BARBARIC...
THIS GALLIFREY ISN'T MINE. THIS IS MILLIONS, BILLIONS OF YEARS BEFORE MY TIME, BEFORE EVEN THE TIME LORDS...
WE HAVE TO GO.
ARE YOU KIDDING? THAT LOOKS LIKE MAJOR, MURDEROUS INJUSTICE HAPPENING DOWN THERE!
ISN'T THIS WHAT WE DO?
CHAMPION THE OPPRESSED?
I CAN'T INTERFERE. IT'S TOO DANGEROUS.
I DON'T KNOW HOW THIS MIGHT AFFECT GALLIFREY'S FUTURE OR THE LACINGS OF THE TIME LOCK...
BUT YOU ALREADY INTERFERED.

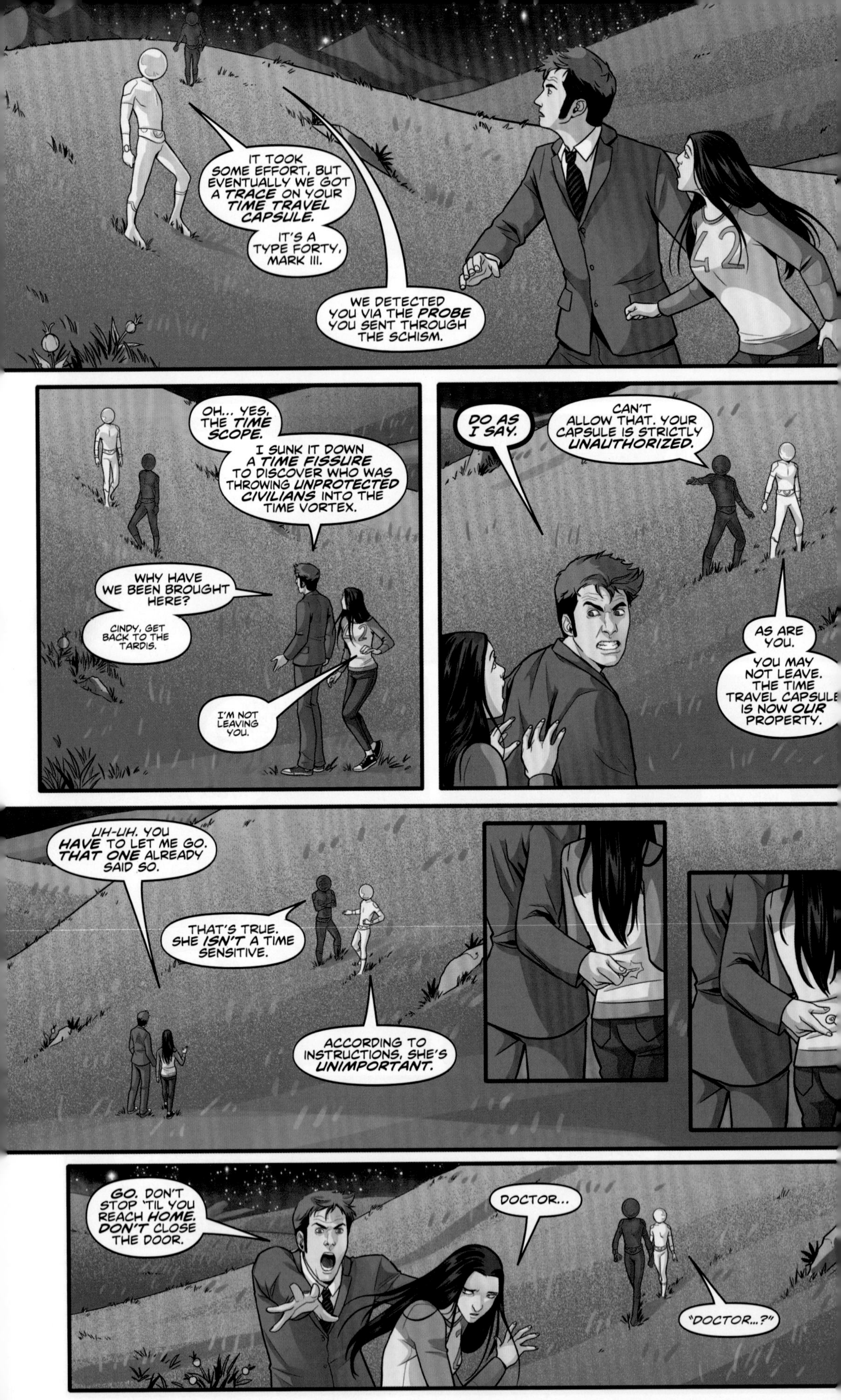
IT TOOK SOME EFFORT, BUT EVENTUALLY WE GOT A TRACE ON YOUR TIME TRAVEL CAPSULE.
IT'S A TYPE FORTY, MARK III.
WE DETECTED YOU VIA THE PROBE YOU SENT THROUGH THE SCHISM.
OH... YES, THE TIME SCOPE.
I SUNK IT DOWN A TIME FISSURE TO DISCOVER WHO WAS THROWING UNPROTECTED CIVILIANS INTO THE TIME VORTEX.
WHY HAVE WE BEEN BROUGHT HERE?
CINDY, GET BACK TO THE TARDIS.
I'M NOT LEAVING YOU.
CAN'T ALLOW THAT. YOUR CAPSULE IS STRICTLY UNAUTHORIZED.
DO AS I SAY.
AS ARE YOU.
YOU MAY NOT LEAVE. THE TIME TRAVEL CAPSULE IS NOW OUR PROPERTY.
UH-UH. YOU HAVE TO LET ME GO. THAT ONE ALREADY SAID SO.
THAT'S TRUE. SHE ISN'T A TIME SENSITIVE.
ACCORDING TO INSTRUCTIONS, SHE'S UNIMPORTANT.
GO. DON'T STOP 'TIL YOU REACH HOME. DON'T CLOSE THE DOOR.
DOCTOR...
"DOCTOR...?"

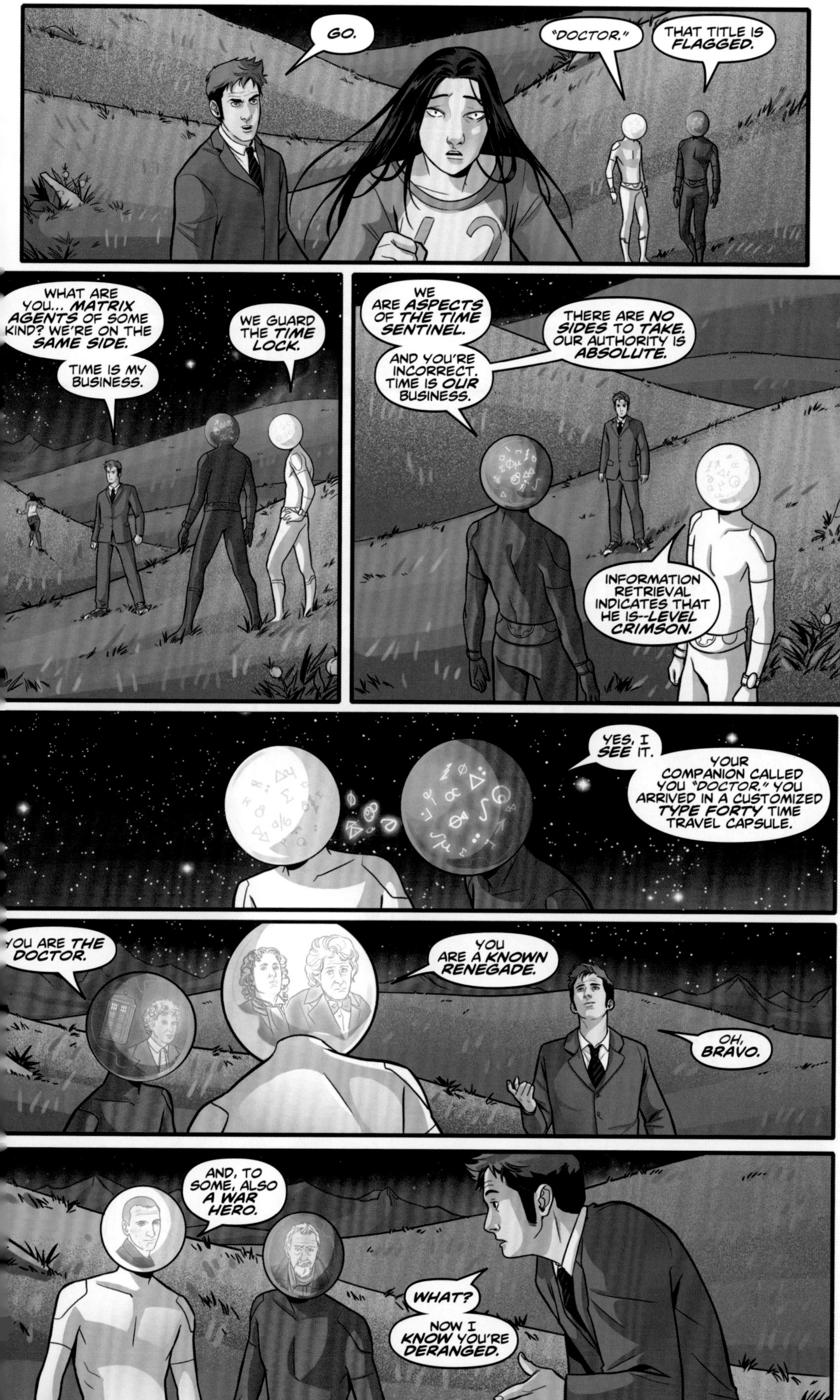
GO.
"DOCTOR."
THAT TITLE IS FLAGGED.
WHAT ARE YOU... MATRIX AGENTS OF SOME KIND? WE'RE ON THE SAME SIDE.
TIME IS MY BUSINESS.
WE GUARD THE TIME LOCK.
WE ARE ASPECTS OF THE TIME SENTINEL.
AND YOU'RE INCORRECT. TIME IS OUR BUSINESS.
THERE ARE NO SIDES TO TAKE. OUR AUTHORITY IS ABSOLUTE.
INFORMATION RETRIEVAL INDICATES THAT HE IS--LEVEL CRIMSON.
YES, I SEE IT.
YOUR COMPANION CALLED YOU "DOCTOR." YOU ARRIVED IN A CUSTOMIZED TYPE FORTY TIME TRAVEL CAPSULE.
YOU ARE THE DOCTOR.
YOU ARE A KNOWN RENEGADE.
OH, BRAVO.
AND, TO SOME, ALSO A WAR HERO.
WHAT?
NOW I KNOW YOU'RE DERANGED.

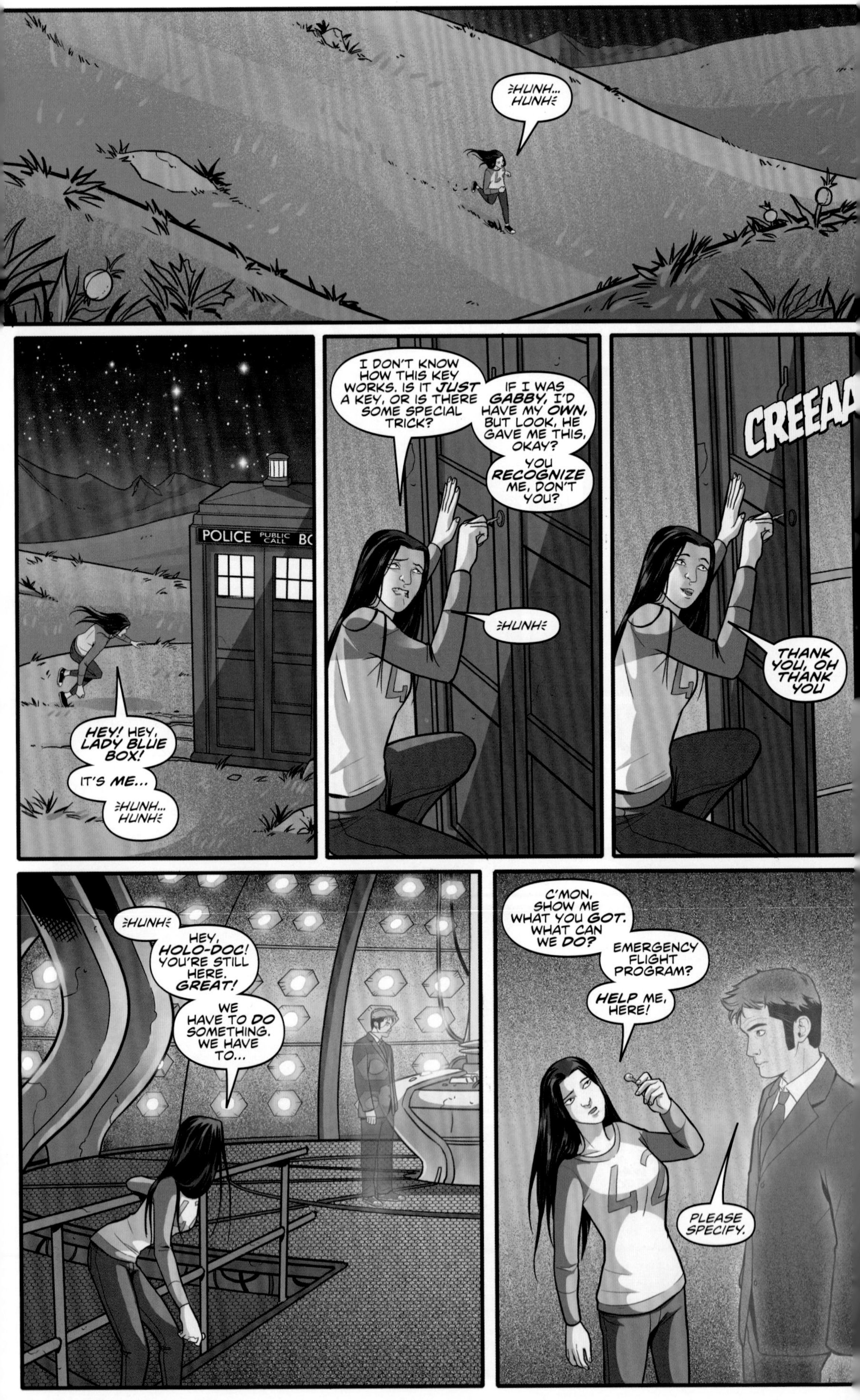

HUNH... HUNH
HEY! HEY, LADY BLUE BOX!
IT'S ME...
HUNH... HUNH
POLICE PUBLIC CALL BO
I DON'T KNOW HOW THIS KEY WORKS. IS IT JUST A KEY, OR IS THERE SOME SPECIAL TRICK?
IF I WAS GABBY, I'D HAVE MY OWN, BUT LOOK, HE GAVE ME THIS, OKAY?
YOU RECOGNIZE ME, DON'T YOU?
HUNH
CREEAA
THANK YOU, OH THANK YOU
HUNH
HEY, HOLO-DOC! YOU'RE STILL HERE. GREAT!
WE HAVE TO DO SOMETHING. WE HAVE TO...
C'MON, SHOW ME WHAT YOU GOT. WHAT CAN WE DO?
EMERGENCY FLIGHT PROGRAM?
HELP ME, HERE!
PLEASE SPECIFY.

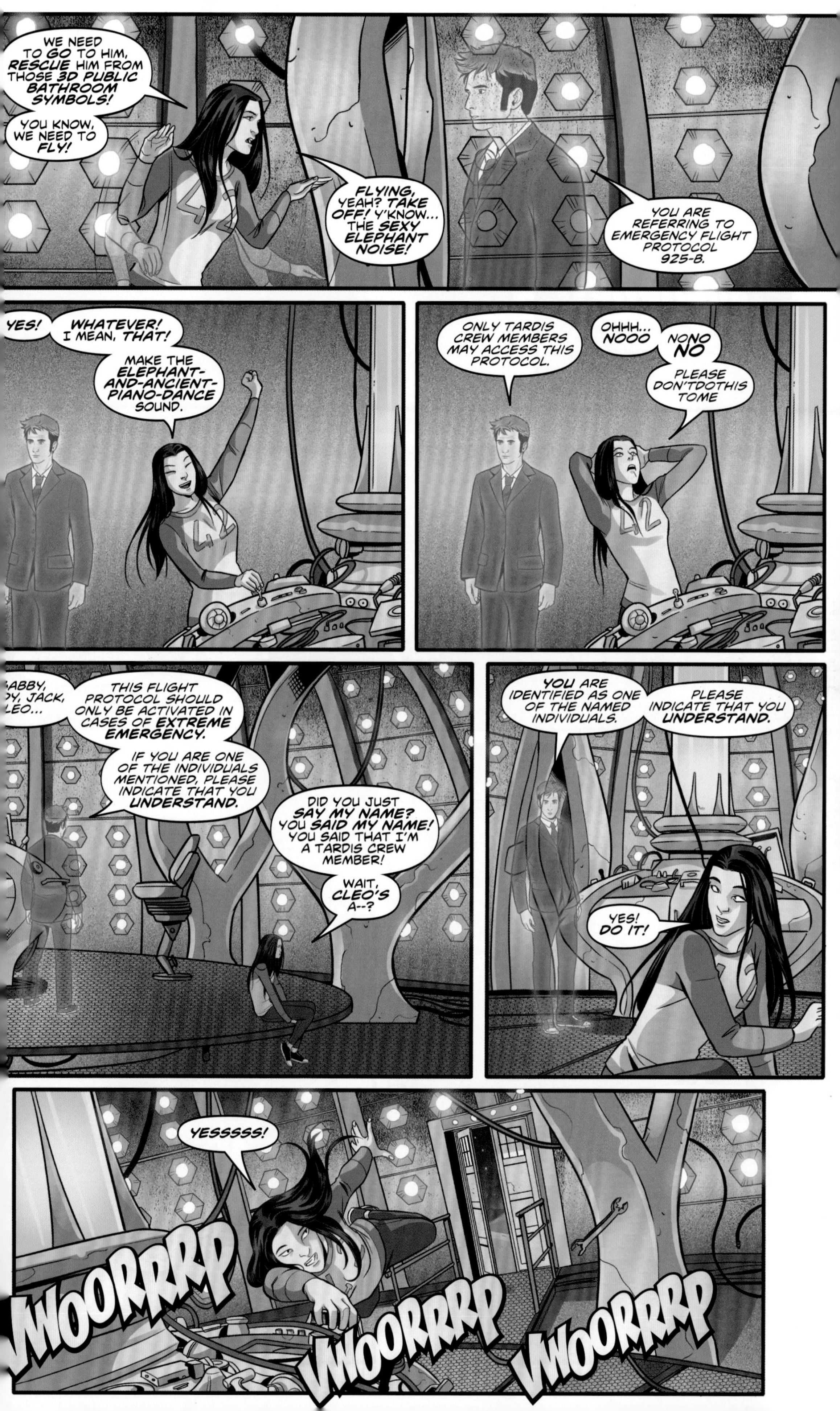
WE NEED TO GO TO HIM, RESCUE HIM FROM THOSE 3D PUBLIC BATHROOM SYMBOLS!
YOU KNOW, WE NEED TO FLY!
FLYING, YEAH? TAKE OFF! Y'KNOW... THE SEXY ELEPHANT NOISE!
YOU ARE REFERRING TO EMERGENCY FLIGHT PROTOCOL 925-B.
YES!
WHATEVER! I MEAN, THAT!
MAKE THE ELEPHANT-AND-ANCIENT-PIANO-DANCE SOUND.
ONLY TARDIS CREW MEMBERS MAY ACCESS THIS PROTOCOL.
OHHH... NOOO
NONO NO
PLEASE DON'TDOTHIS TOME
ABBY, DY, JACK, LEO...
THIS FLIGHT PROTOCOL SHOULD ONLY BE ACTIVATED IN CASES OF EXTREME EMERGENCY.
IF YOU ARE ONE OF THE INDIVIDUALS MENTIONED, PLEASE INDICATE THAT YOU UNDERSTAND.
DID YOU JUST SAY MY NAME? YOU SAID MY NAME! YOU SAID THAT I'M A TARDIS CREW MEMBER!
WAIT, CLEO'S A--?
YOU ARE IDENTIFIED AS ONE OF THE NAMED INDIVIDUALS.
PLEASE INDICATE THAT YOU UNDERSTAND.
YES! DO IT!
YESSSSS!
WOORRRP
WOORRRP
WOORRRP

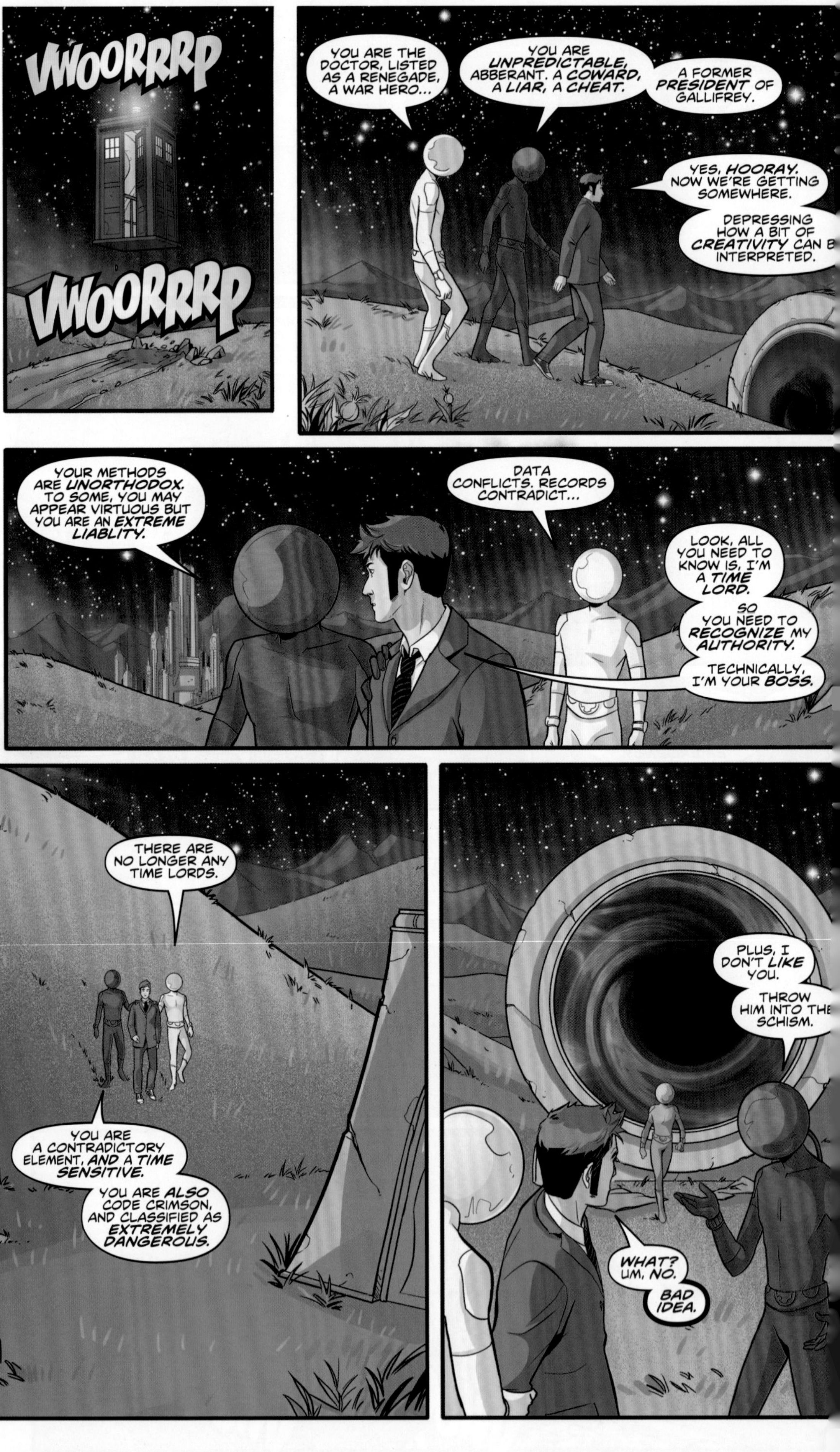
VWOORRRP
VWOORRRP
YOU ARE THE DOCTOR, LISTED AS A RENEGADE, A WAR HERO...
YOU ARE UNPREDICTABLE, ABBERANT. A COWARD, A LIAR, A CHEAT.
A FORMER PRESIDENT OF GALLIFREY.
YES, HOORAY. NOW WE'RE GETTING SOMEWHERE.
DEPRESSING HOW A BIT OF CREATIVITY CAN B INTERPRETED.
YOUR METHODS ARE UNORTHODOX. TO SOME, YOU MAY APPEAR VIRTUOUS BUT YOU ARE AN EXTREME LIABLITY.
DATA CONFLICTS. RECORDS CONTRADICT...
LOOK, ALL YOU NEED TO KNOW IS, I'M A TIME LORD.
SO YOU NEED TO RECOGNIZE MY AUTHORITY.
TECHNICALLY, I'M YOUR BOSS.
THERE ARE NO LONGER ANY TIME LORDS.
YOU ARE A CONTRADICTORY ELEMENT, AND A TIME SENSITIVE.
YOU ARE ALSO CODE CRIMSON, AND CLASSIFIED AS EXTREMELY DANGEROUS.
PLUS, I DON'T LIKE YOU.
THROW HIM INTO THE SCHISM.
WHAT? UM, NO.
BAD IDEA.

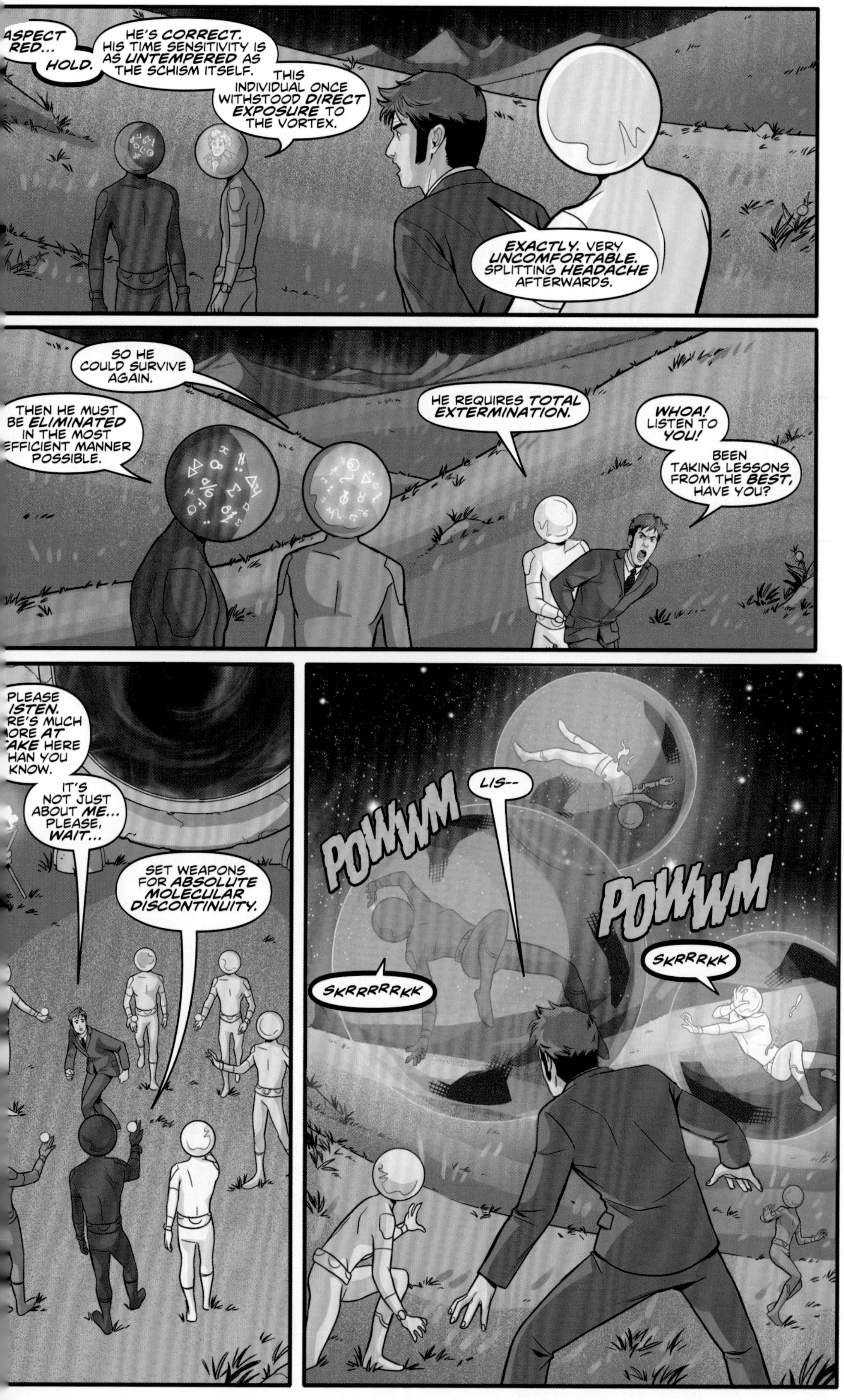
ASPECT RED... HOLD.
HE'S CORRECT. HIS TIME SENSITIVITY IS AS UNTEMPERED AS THE SCHISM ITSELF.
THIS INDIVIDUAL ONCE WITHSTOOD DIRECT EXPOSURE TO THE VORTEX.
EXACTLY. VERY UNCOMFORTABLE. SPLITTING HEADACHE AFTERWARDS.
SO HE COULD SURVIVE AGAIN.
THEN HE MUST BE ELIMINATED IN THE MOST EFFICIENT MANNER POSSIBLE.
HE REQUIRES TOTAL EXTERMINATION.
WHOA! LISTEN TO YOU!
BEEN TAKING LESSONS FROM THE BEST, HAVE YOU?
PLEASE LISTEN. RE'S MUCH ORE AT AKE HERE HAN YOU KNOW.
IT'S NOT JUST ABOUT ME... PLEASE, WAIT...
SET WEAPONS FOR ABSOLUTE MOLECULAR DISCONTINUITY.
POWWM
LIS--
POWWM
SKRRRRRKK
SKRRRKK

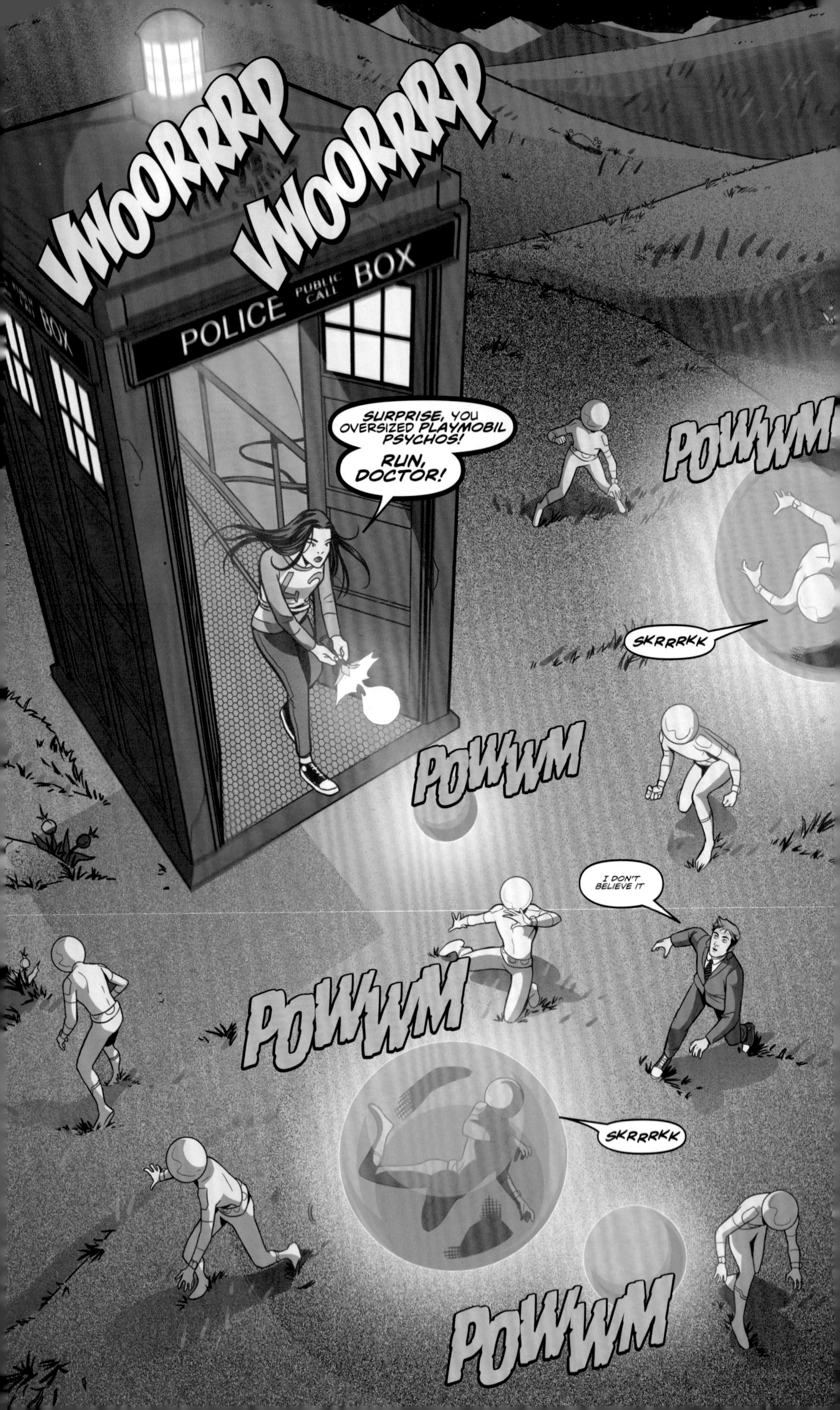
WOORRRP WOORRRP
POLICE PUBLIC CALL BOX
SURPRISE, YOU OVERSIZED PLAYMOBIL PSYCHOS!
RUN, DOCTOR!
POWWM
SKRRRKK
POWWM
I DON'T BELIEVE IT
POWWM
SKRRRKK
POWWM

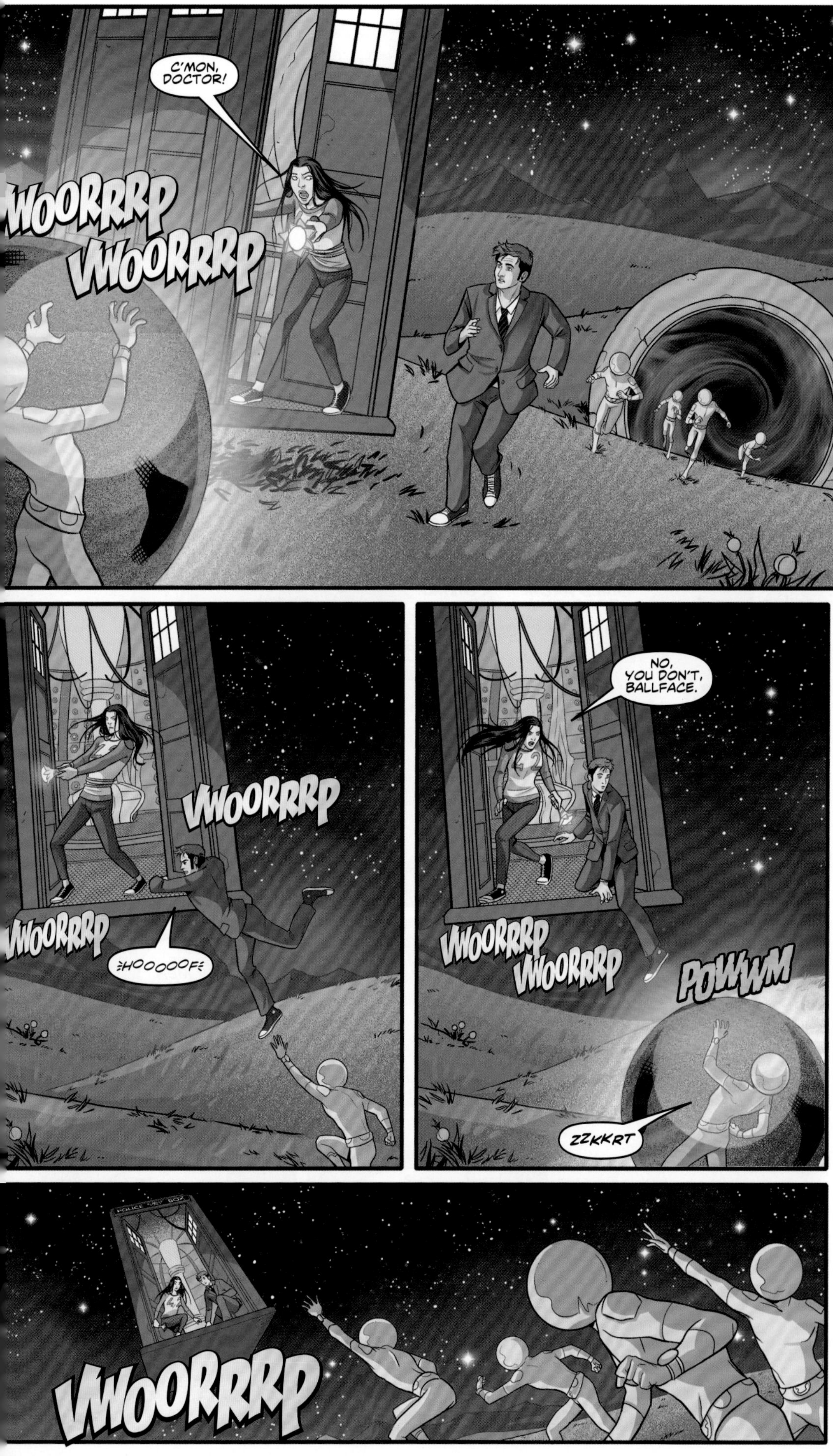
C'MON, DOCTOR!
WOORRRP
VWOORRRP
VWOORRRP
VWOORRRP
HOOOOOF
NO, YOU DON'T, BALLFACE.
VWOORRRP
VWOORRRP
POWWM
ZZKKRT
VWOORRRP

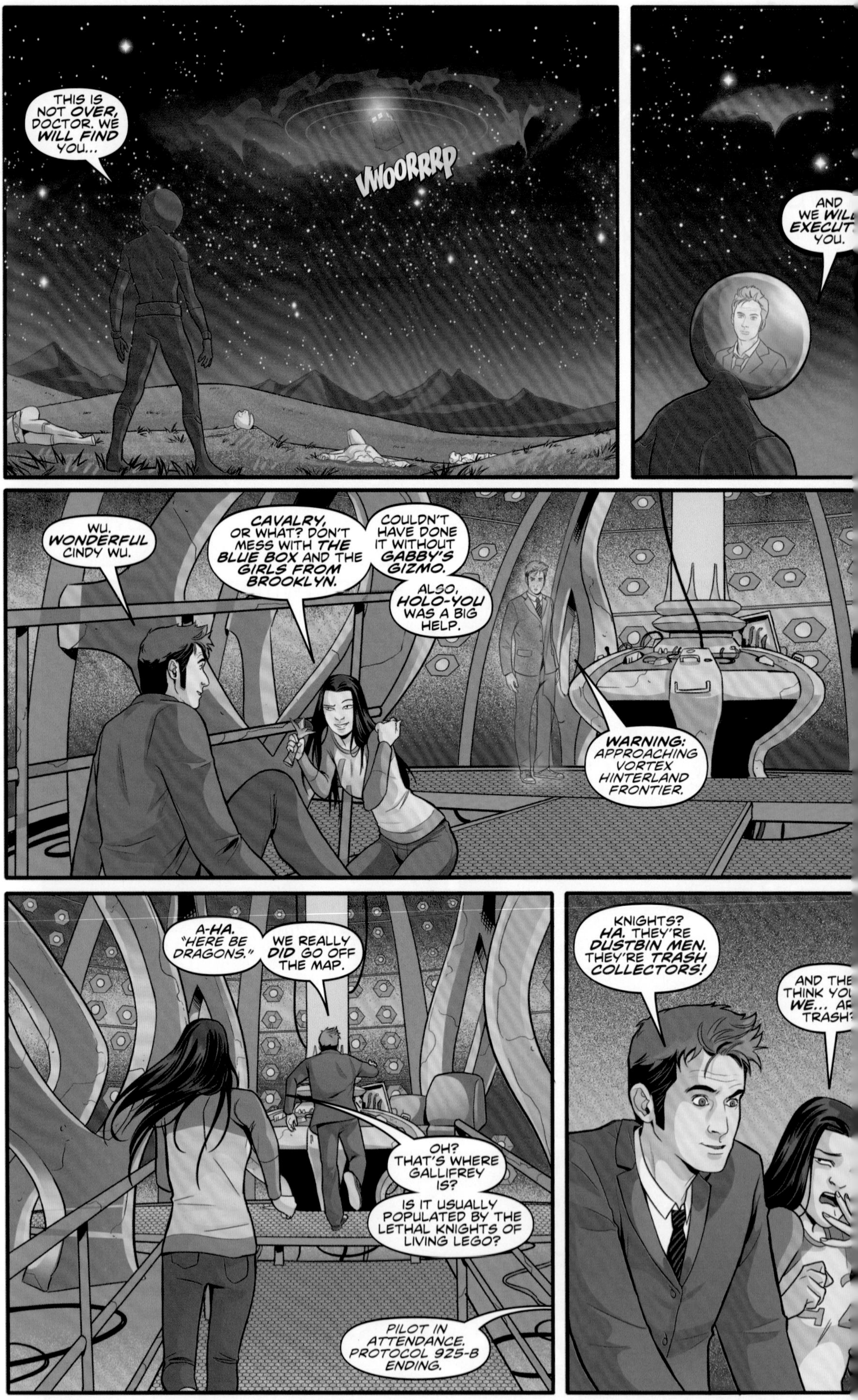

THIS IS NOT OVER, DOCTOR. WE WILL FIND YOU...
VWOORRRP
AND WE WILL EXECUT YOU.
WU. WONDERFUL CINDY WU.
CAVALRY, OR WHAT? DON'T MESS WITH THE BLUE BOX AND THE GIRLS FROM BROOKLYN.
COULDN'T HAVE DONE IT WITHOUT GABBY'S GIZMO.
ALSO, HOLO-YOU WAS A BIG HELP.
WARNING: APPROACHING VORTEX HINTERLAND FRONTIER.
A-HA. "HERE BE DRAGONS."
WE REALLY DID GO OFF THE MAP.
OH? THAT'S WHERE GALLIFREY IS?
IS IT USUALLY POPULATED BY THE LETHAL KNIGHTS OF LIVING LEGO?
PILOT IN ATTENDANCE. PROTOCOL 925-B ENDING.
KNIGHTS? HA. THEY'RE DUSTBIN MEN. THEY'RE TRASH COLLECTORS!
AND THE THINK YOU WE... AR TRASH?

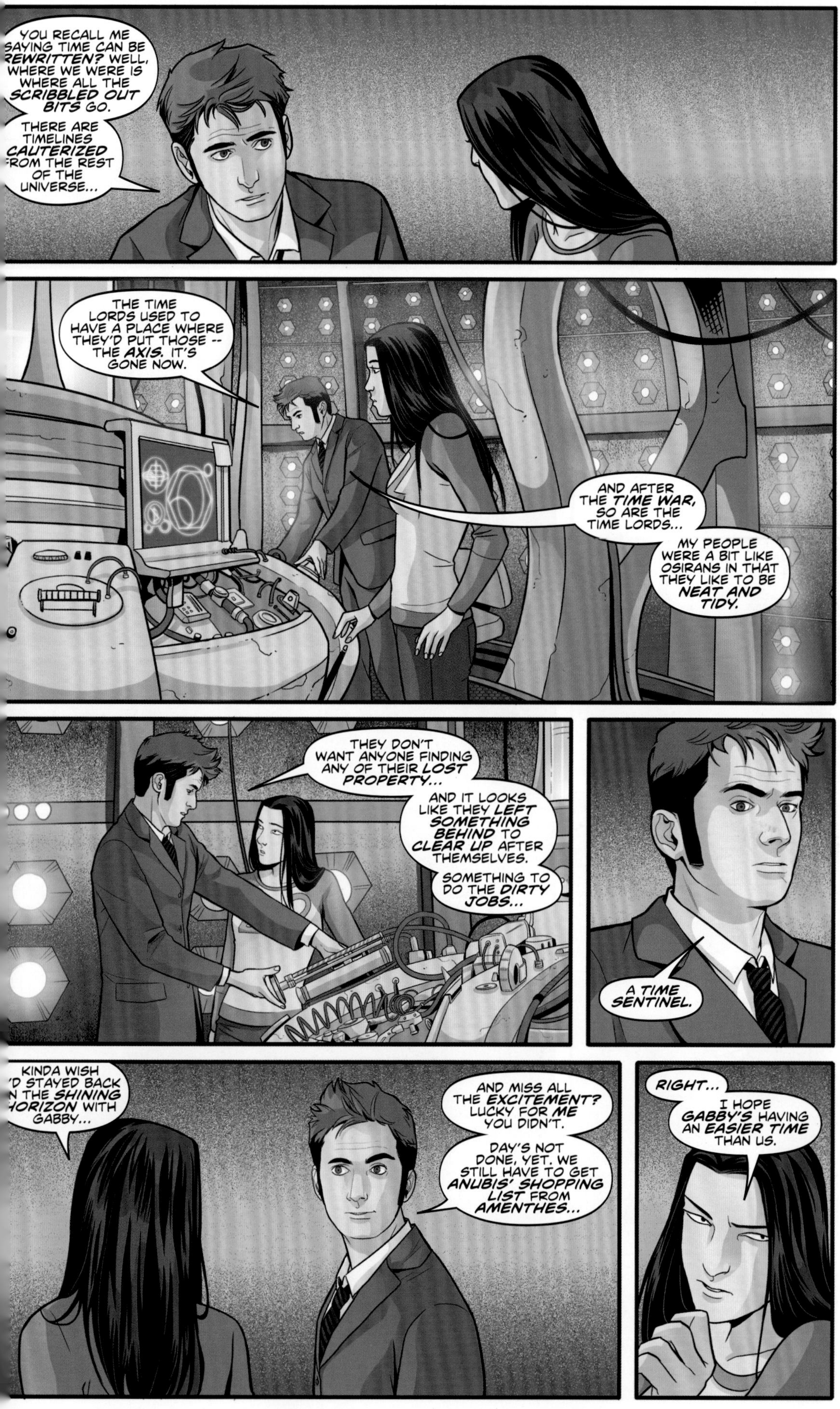
YOU RECALL ME SAYING TIME CAN BE REWRITTEN? WELL, WHERE WE WERE IS WHERE ALL THE SCRIBBLED OUT BITS GO.
THERE ARE TIMELINES CAUTERIZED FROM THE REST OF THE UNIVERSE...
THE TIME LORDS USED TO HAVE A PLACE WHERE THEY'D PUT THOSE -- THE AXIS. IT'S GONE NOW.
AND AFTER THE TIME WAR, SO ARE THE TIME LORDS...
MY PEOPLE WERE A BIT LIKE OSIRANS IN THAT THEY LIKE TO BE NEAT AND TIDY.
THEY DON'T WANT ANYONE FINDING ANY OF THEIR LOST PROPERTY...
AND IT LOOKS LIKE THEY LEFT SOMETHING BEHIND TO CLEAR UP AFTER THEMSELVES.
SOMETHING TO DO THE DIRTY JOBS...
A TIME SENTINEL.
KINDA WISH I'D STAYED BACK IN THE SHINING HORIZON WITH GABBY...
AND MISS ALL THE EXCITEMENT? LUCKY FOR ME YOU DIDN'T.
DAY'S NOT DONE, YET. WE STILL HAVE TO GET ANUBIS' SHOPPING LIST FROM AMENTHES...
RIGHT...
I HOPE GABBY'S HAVING AN EASIER TIME THAN US.

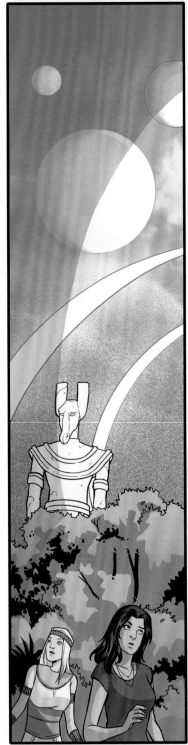

THE SUNLIGHT HERE IS *ARTIFICIAL,* SO HOW IS IT WE'RE EXPERIENCING AN *ECLIPSE?*

DON'T *KNOW.* SOME KIND OF *POWER DRAIN...?*

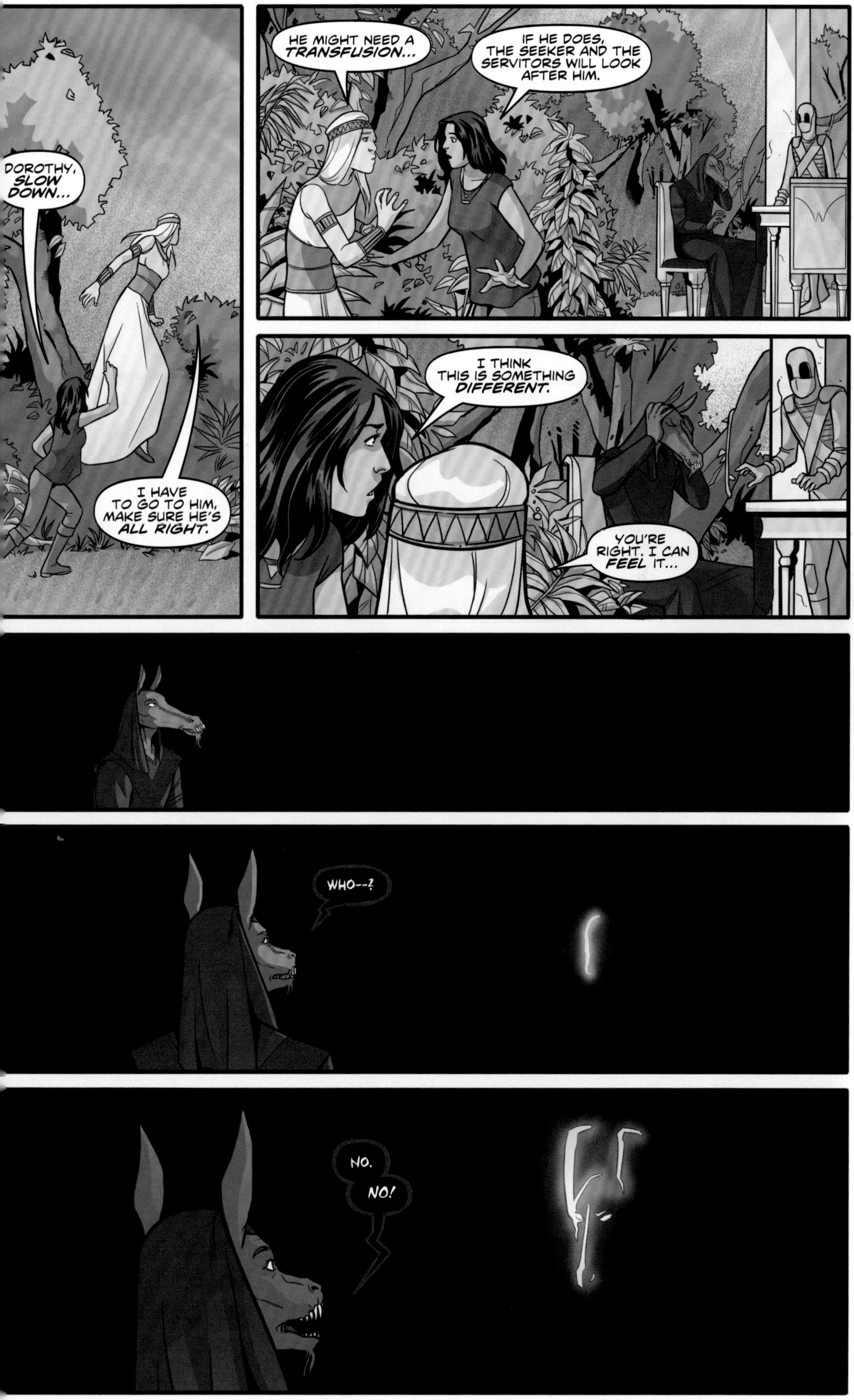
DOROTHY, SLOW DOWN...
I HAVE TO GO TO HIM, MAKE SURE HE'S ALL RIGHT.
HE MIGHT NEED A TRANSFUSION...
IF HE DOES, THE SEEKER AND THE SERVITORS WILL LOOK AFTER HIM.
I THINK THIS IS SOMETHING DIFFERENT.
YOU'RE RIGHT. I CAN FEEL IT...
WHO--?
NO.
NO!

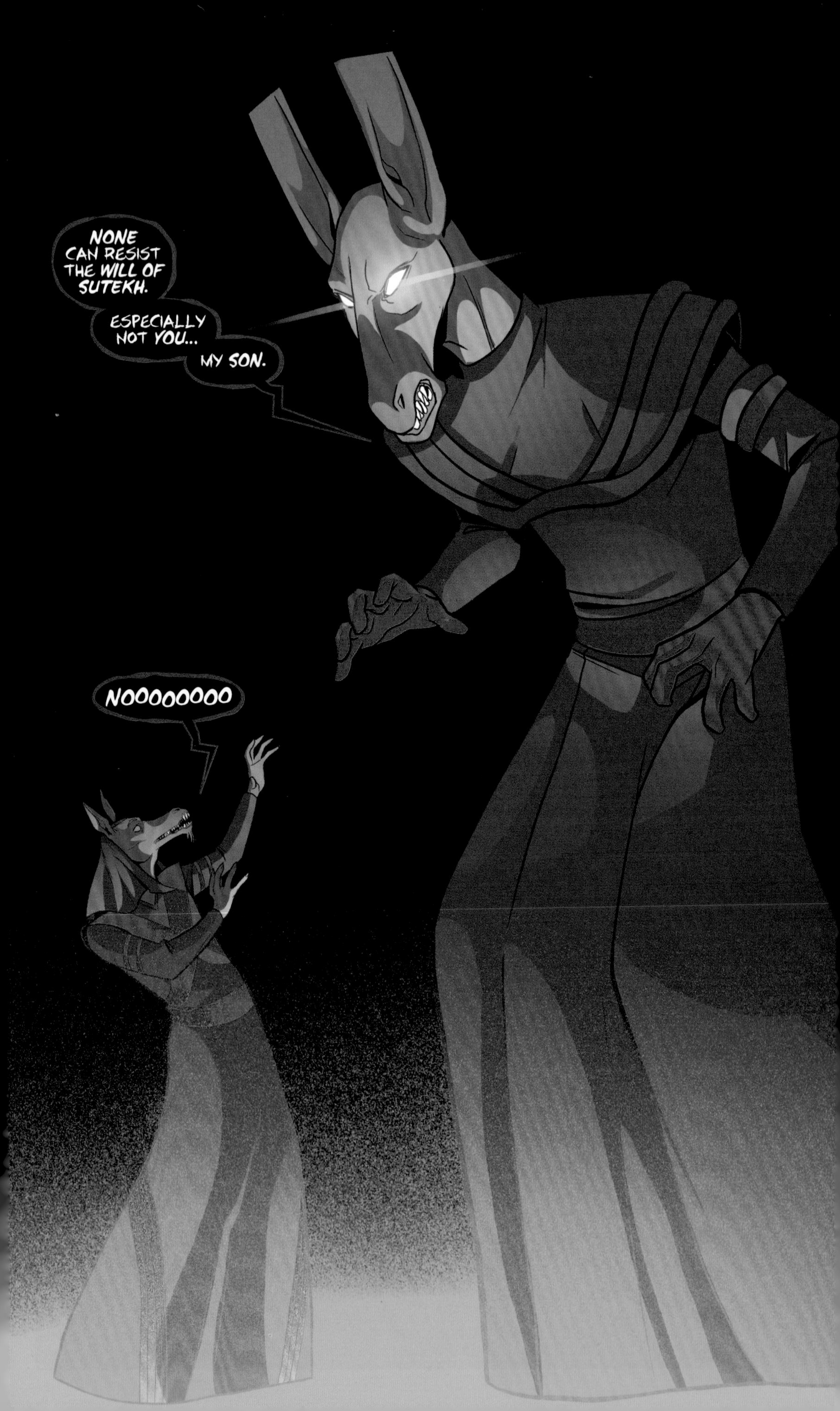
NONE CAN RESIST THE WILL OF SUTEKH.
ESPECIALLY NOT YOU...
MY SON.
NOOOOOOOO

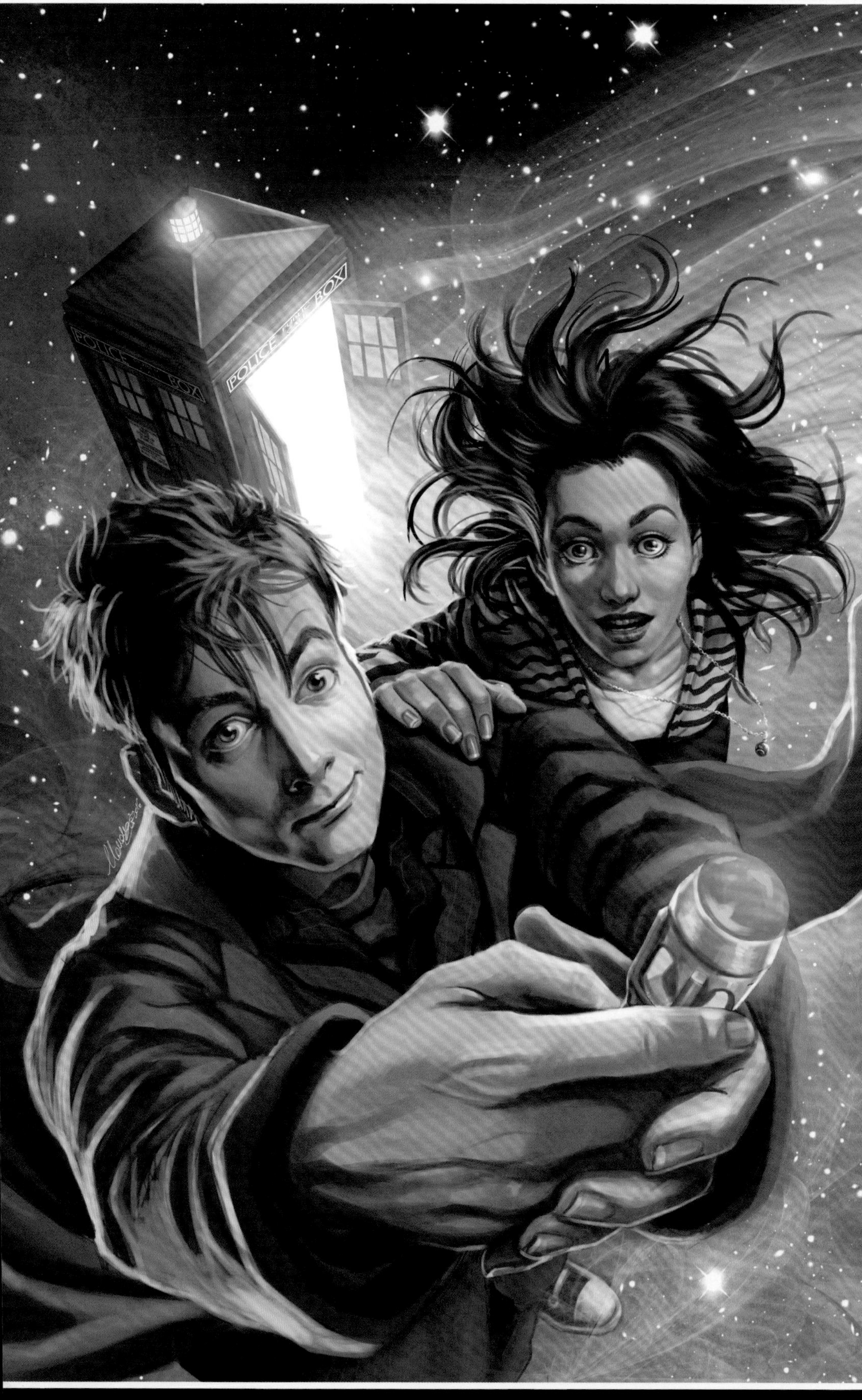
POLICE BOX
POLICE BOX

10D #2.11 Cover A: CLAUDIA IANNICIELO

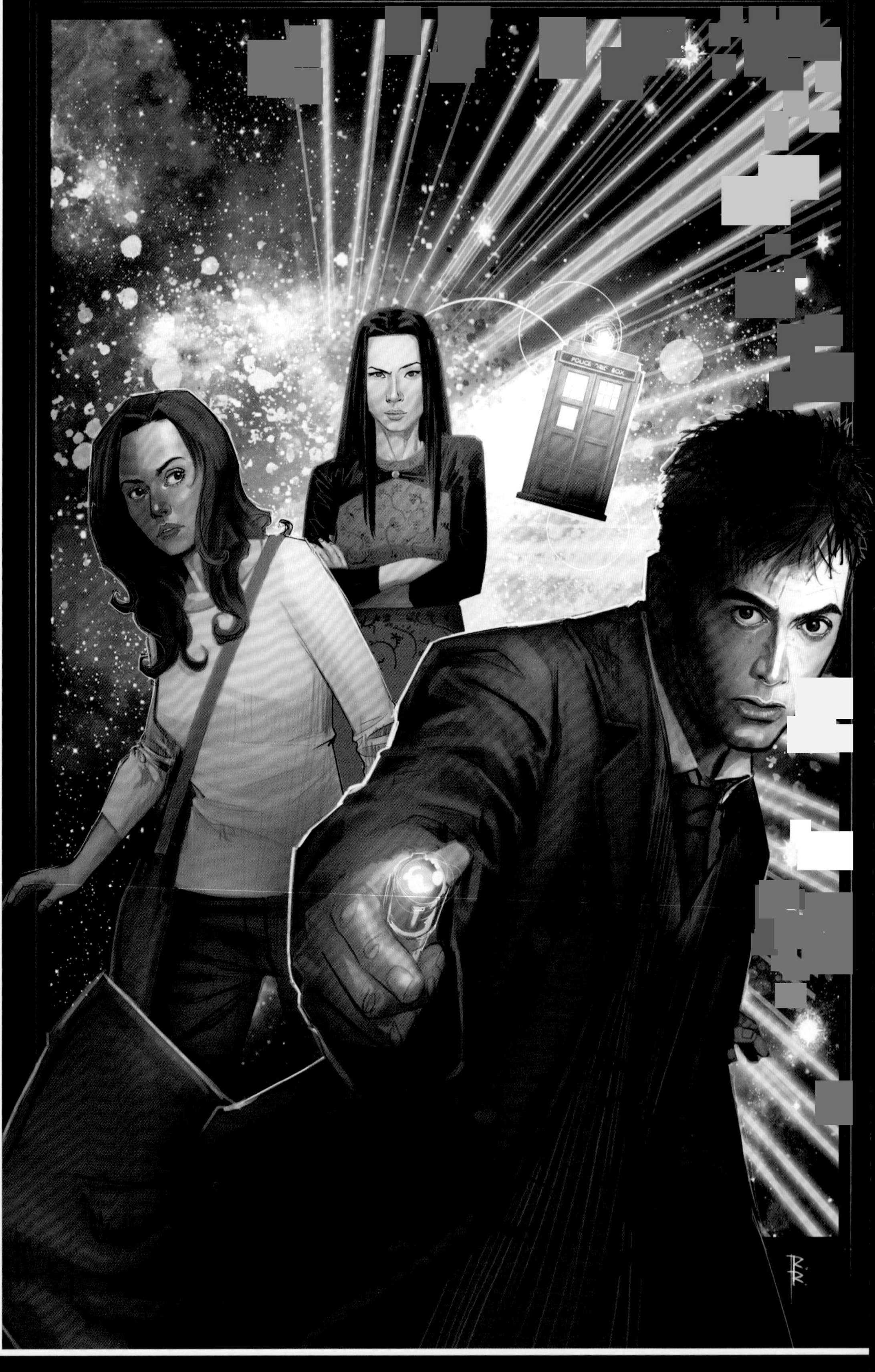

10D #2.13 Cover A: ROD REIS

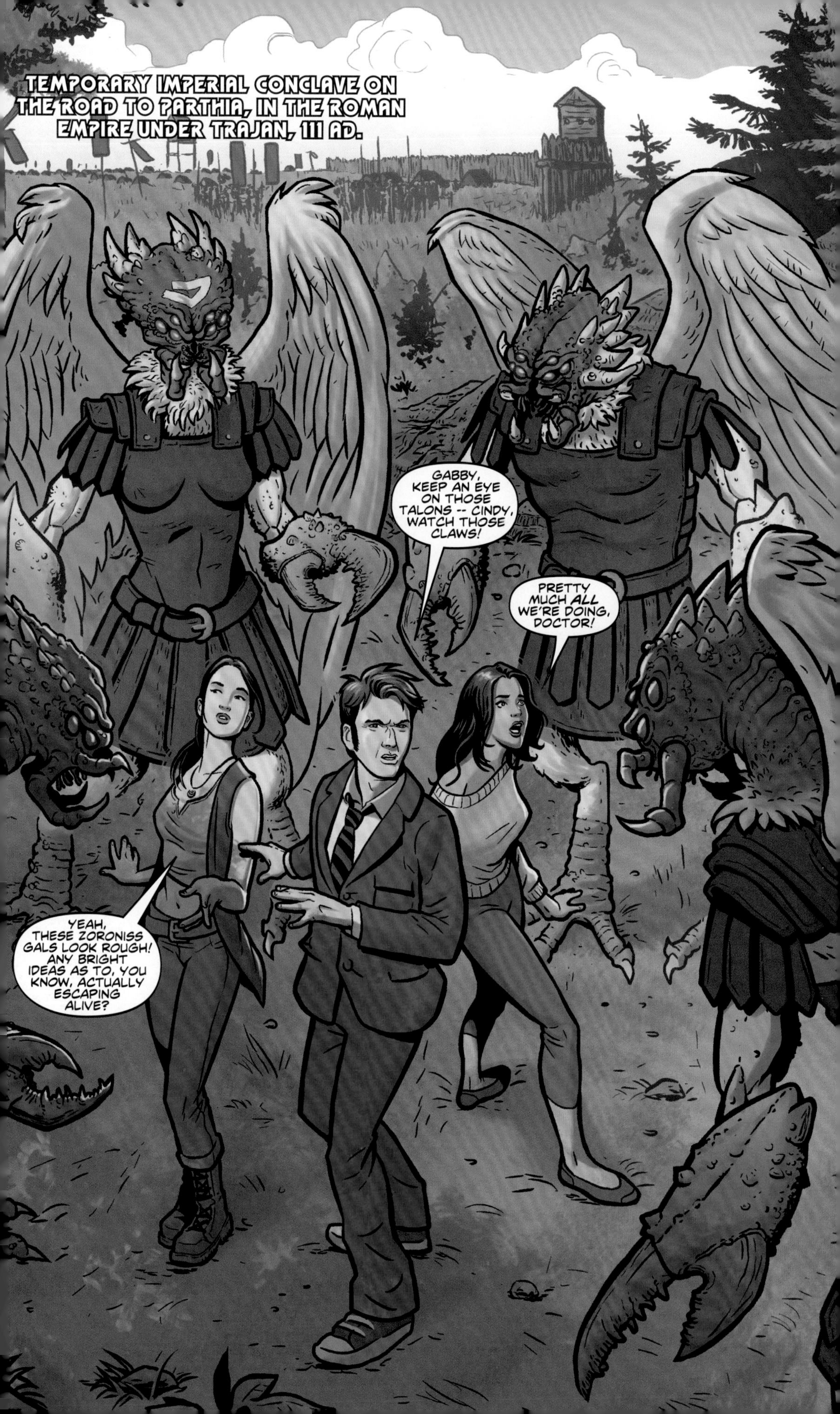
TEMPORARY IMPERIAL CONCLAVE ON THE ROAD TO PARTHIA, IN THE ROMAN EMPIRE UNDER TRAJAN, 111 AD.
GABBY, KEEP AN EYE ON THOSE TALONS -- CINDY, WATCH THOSE CLAWS!
PRETTY MUCH ALL WE'RE DOING, DOCTOR!
YEAH, THESE ZORONISS GALS LOOK ROUGH! ANY BRIGHT IDEAS AS TO, YOU KNOW, ACTUALLY ESCAPING ALIVE?

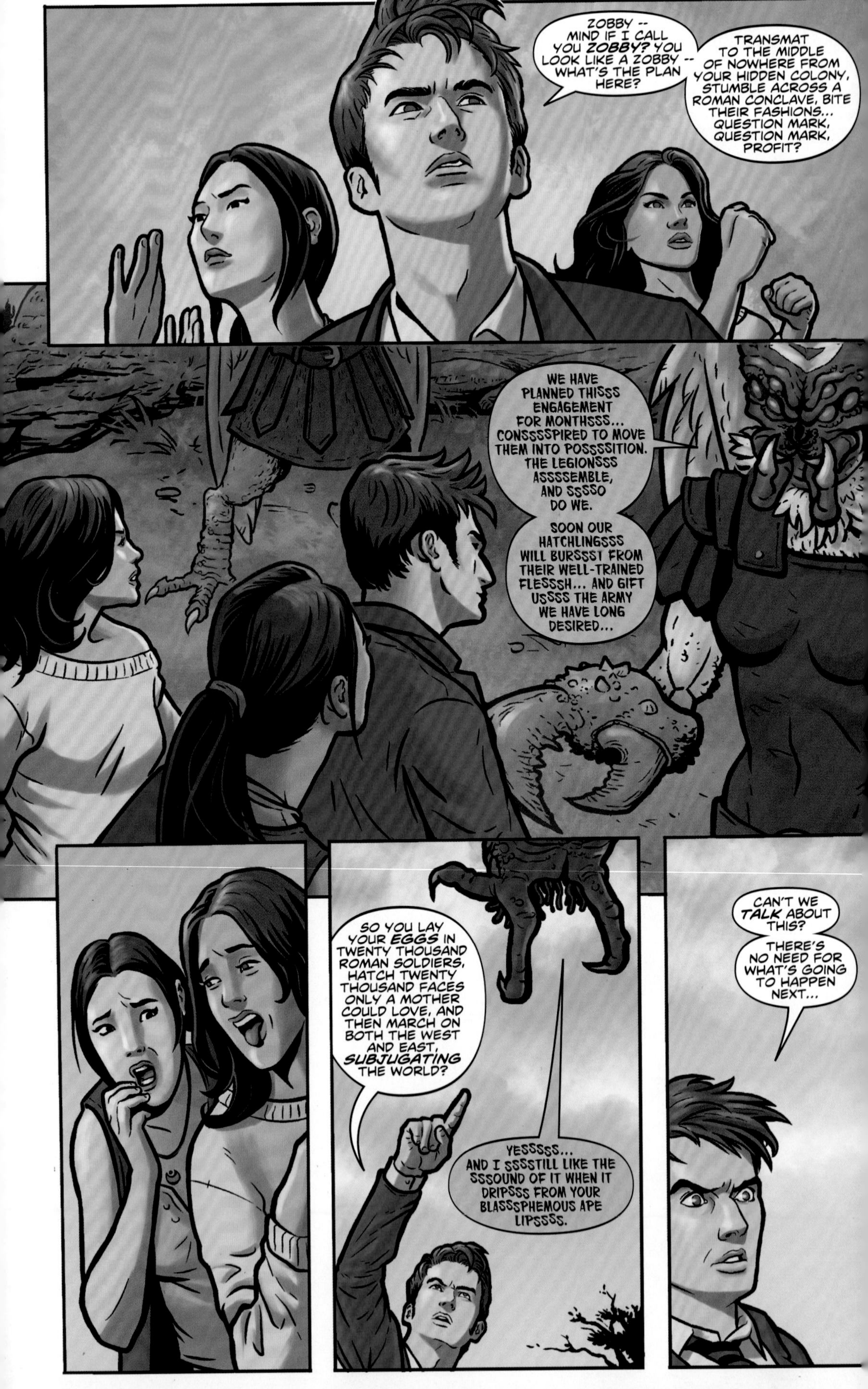
ZOBBY -- MIND IF I CALL YOU ZOBBY? YOU LOOK LIKE A ZOBBY -- WHAT'S THE PLAN HERE?
TRANSMAT TO THE MIDDLE OF NOWHERE FROM YOUR HIDDEN COLONY, STUMBLE ACROSS A ROMAN CONCLAVE, BITE THEIR FASHIONS... QUESTION MARK, QUESTION MARK, PROFIT?
WE HAVE PLANNED THISSS ENGAGEMENT FOR MONTHSSS... CONSSSSPIRED TO MOVE THEM INTO POSSSSITION. THE LEGIONSSS ASSSSEMBLE, AND SSSSO DO WE.
SOON OUR HATCHLINGSSS WILL BURSSST FROM THEIR WELL-TRAINED FLESSSH... AND GIFT USSSS THE ARMY WE HAVE LONG DESIRED...
SO YOU LAY YOUR EGGS IN TWENTY THOUSAND ROMAN SOLDIERS, HATCH TWENTY THOUSAND FACES ONLY A MOTHER COULD LOVE, AND THEN MARCH ON BOTH THE WEST AND EAST, SUBJUGATING THE WORLD?
YESSSSS... AND I SSSSTILL LIKE THE SSSOUND OF IT WHEN IT DRIPSSS FROM YOUR BLASSSPHEMOUS APE LIPSSSS.
CAN'T WE TALK ABOUT THIS?
THERE'S NO NEED FOR WHAT'S GOING TO HAPPEN NEXT...

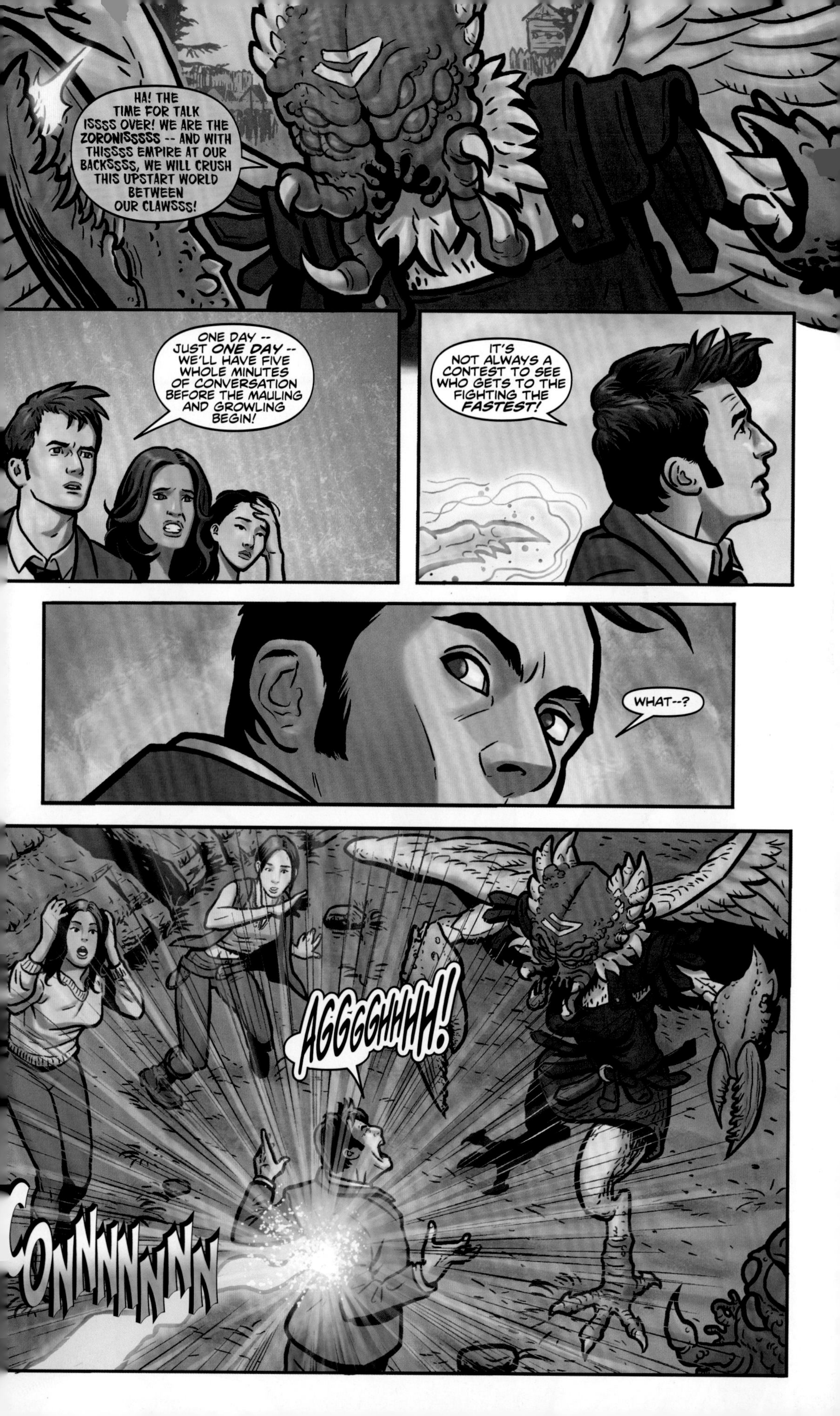
HA! THE TIME FOR TALK ISSSS OVER! WE ARE THE ZORONISSSSS -- AND WITH THISSSS EMPIRE AT OUR BACKSSSS, WE WILL CRUSH THIS UPSTART WORLD BETWEEN OUR CLAWSSS!
ONE DAY -- JUST ONE DAY -- WE'LL HAVE FIVE WHOLE MINUTES OF CONVERSATION BEFORE THE MAULING AND GROWLING BEGIN!
IT'S NOT ALWAYS A CONTEST TO SEE WHO GETS TO THE FIGHTING THE FASTEST!
WHAT--?
AGGGGHHHH!
CONNNNNNN

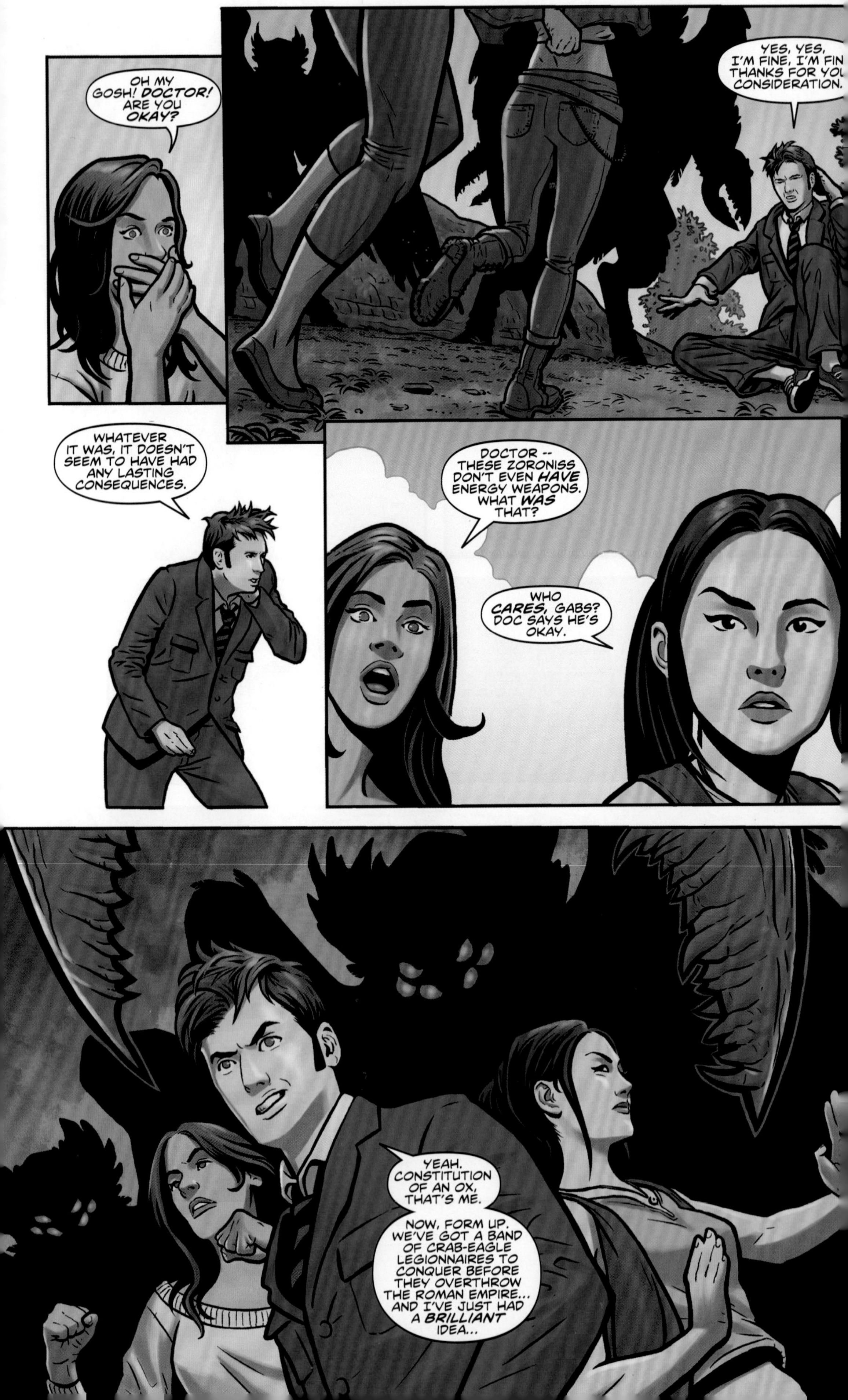
OH MY GOSH! DOCTOR! ARE YOU OKAY?
YES, YES, I'M FINE, I'M FIN THANKS FOR YOU CONSIDERATION.
WHATEVER IT WAS, IT DOESN'T SEEM TO HAVE HAD ANY LASTING CONSEQUENCES.
DOCTOR -- THESE ZORONISS DON'T EVEN HAVE ENERGY WEAPONS. WHAT WAS THAT?
WHO CARES, GABS? DOC SAYS HE'S OKAY.
YEAH. CONSTITUTION OF AN OX, THAT'S ME.
NOW, FORM UP. WE'VE GOT A BAND OF CRAB-EAGLE LEGIONNAIRES TO CONQUER BEFORE THEY OVERTHROW THE ROMAN EMPIRE... AND I'VE JUST HAD A BRILLIANT IDEA...

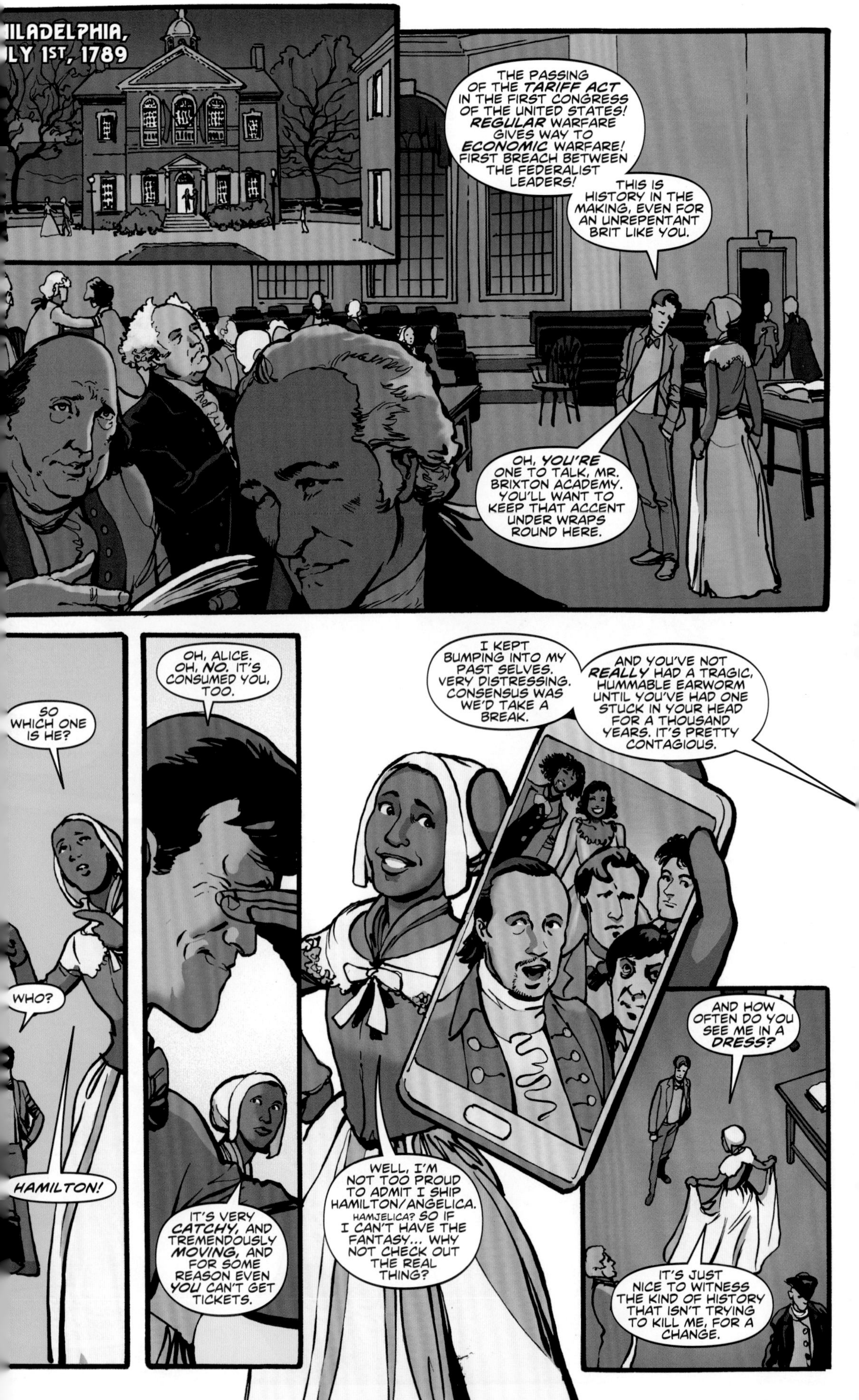

ILADELPHIA,
LY 1ST, 1789
THE PASSING OF THE TARIFF ACT IN THE FIRST CONGRESS OF THE UNITED STATES! REGULAR WARFARE GIVES WAY TO ECONOMIC WARFARE! FIRST BREACH BETWEEN THE FEDERALIST LEADERS!
THIS IS HISTORY IN THE MAKING, EVEN FOR AN UNREPENTANT BRIT LIKE YOU.
OH, YOU'RE ONE TO TALK, MR. BRIXTON ACADEMY. YOU'LL WANT TO KEEP THAT ACCENT UNDER WRAPS ROUND HERE.
SO WHICH ONE IS HE?
WHO?
HAMILTON!
OH, ALICE. OH, NO. IT'S CONSUMED YOU, TOO.
IT'S VERY CATCHY, AND TREMENDOUSLY MOVING, AND FOR SOME REASON EVEN YOU CAN'T GET TICKETS.
WELL, I'M NOT TOO PROUD TO ADMIT I SHIP HAMILTON/ANGELICA. HAMJELICA? SO IF I CAN'T HAVE THE FANTASY... WHY NOT CHECK OUT THE REAL THING?
I KEPT BUMPING INTO MY PAST SELVES. VERY DISTRESSING. CONSENSUS WAS WE'D TAKE A BREAK.
AND YOU'VE NOT REALLY HAD A TRAGIC, HUMMABLE EARWORM UNTIL YOU'VE HAD ONE STUCK IN YOUR HEAD FOR A THOUSAND YEARS. IT'S PRETTY CONTAGIOUS.
AND HOW OFTEN DO YOU SEE ME IN A DRESS?
IT'S JUST NICE TO WITNESS THE KIND OF HISTORY THAT ISN'T TRYING TO KILL ME, FOR A CHANGE.

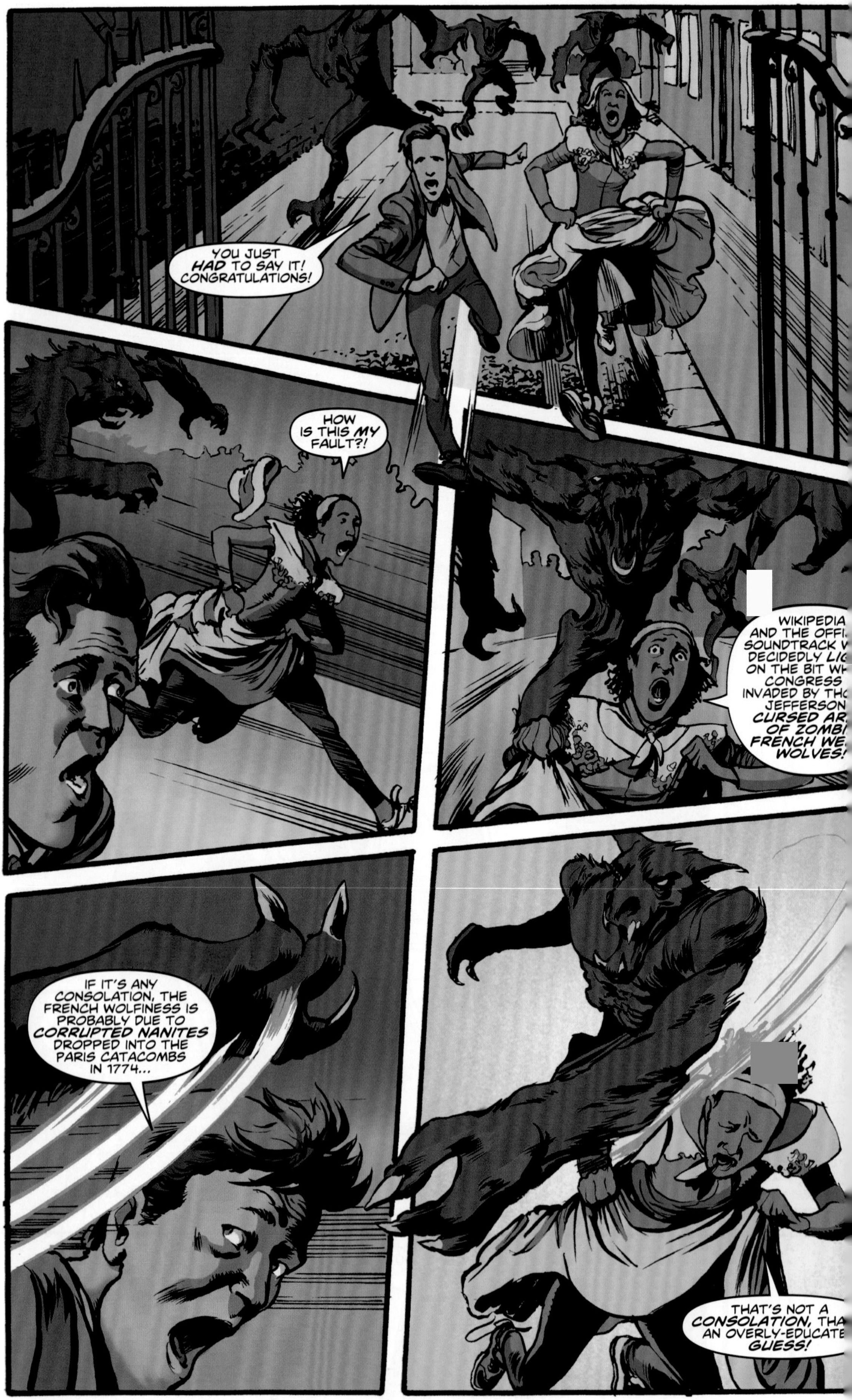
YOU JUST HAD TO SAY IT! CONGRATULATIONS!
HOW IS THIS MY FAULT?!
WIKIPEDIA AND THE OFFI SOUNDTRACK W DECIDEDLY LIG ON THE BIT WH CONGRESS INVADED BY THO JEFFERSON CURSED AR OF ZOMBI FRENCH WE WOLVES!
IF IT'S ANY CONSOLATION, THE FRENCH WOLFINESS IS PROBABLY DUE TO CORRUPTED NANITES DROPPED INTO THE PARIS CATACOMBS IN 1774...
THAT'S NOT A CONSOLATION, THA AN OVERLY-EDUCATE GUESS!

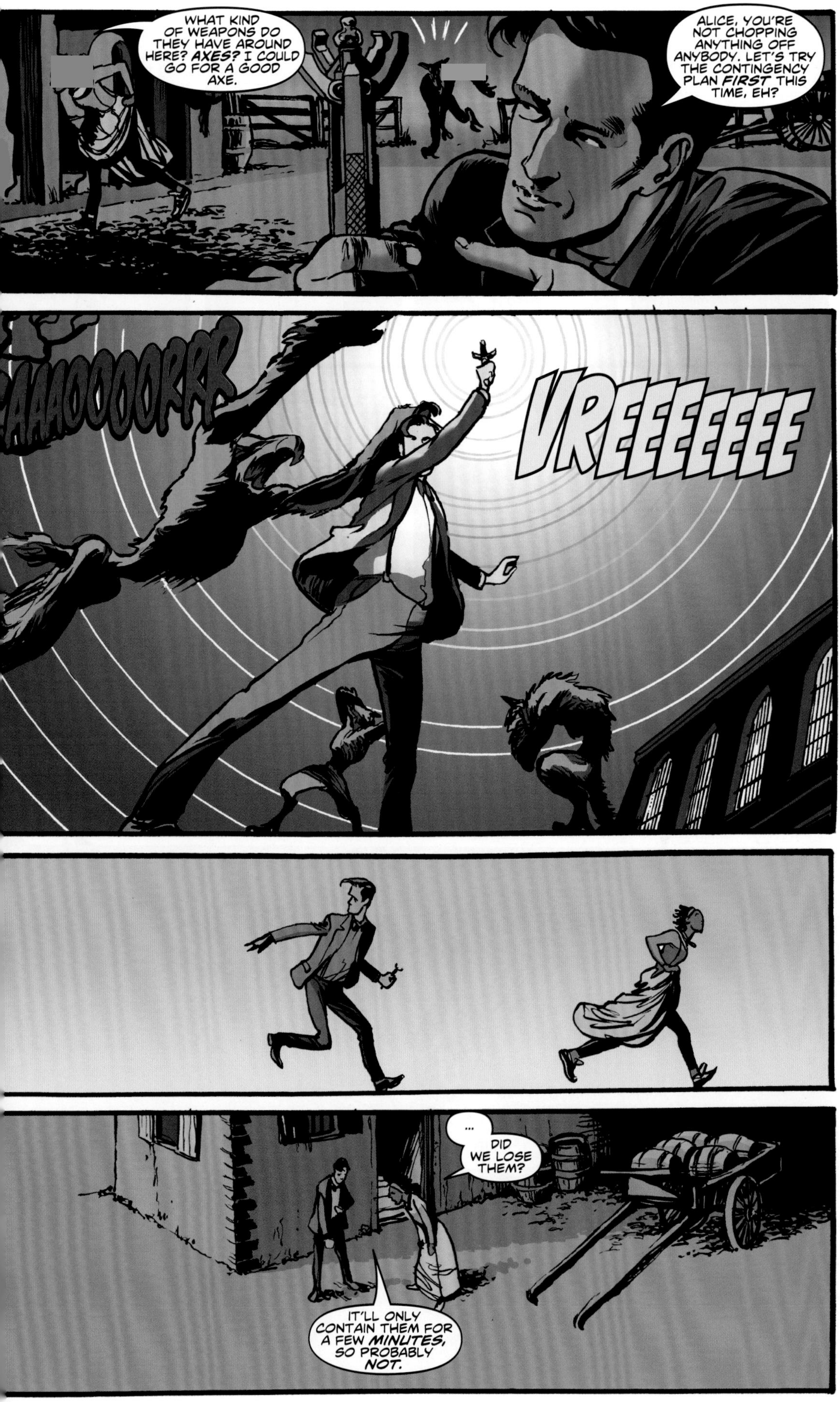
WHAT KIND OF WEAPONS DO THEY HAVE AROUND HERE? AXES? I COULD GO FOR A GOOD AXE.
ALICE, YOU'RE NOT CHOPPING ANYBODY OFF. LET'S TRY THE CONTINGENCY PLAN FIRST THIS TIME, EH?
AAAOOOORRR
VREEEEEEEE
... DID WE LOSE THEM?
IT'LL ONLY CONTAIN THEM FOR A FEW MINUTES, SO PROBABLY NOT.

I CAN'T PUT MY FINGER ON IT, DOCTOR, BUT EVER SINCE WE GOT HERE, THERE'S BEEN SOMETHING... OFF... ABOUT YOU.

IS THIS ABOUT THE AXES? YOU CAN'T GO AROUND BEHEADING FUTURE PRESIDENTS, ALICE. YOU *KNOW* I DON'T CONDONE BEHEADINGS.

NO, NOT *THAT.* THOUGH HE PROBABLY DESERVED IT.

HISTORY WOULD VINDICATE ME. OR AT LEAST TUMBLR WOULD.

SO CONSIDERATE.

IT'S SOMETHING ABOUT... YOUR VOCABULARY.

VAST, EXPANSIVE, *LABYRINTHINE...* WORDS AND PUNCTUATION WORKING IN PERFECT CONCERT...?

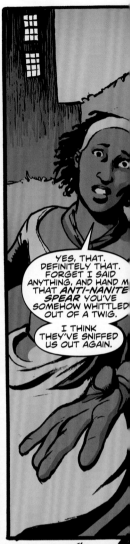

YES, THAT. DEFINITELY THAT. FORGET I SAID ANYTHING, AND HAND M THAT *ANTI-NANITE SPEAR* YOU'VE SOMEHOW WHITTLED OUT OF A TWIG.

I THINK THEY'VE SNIFFED US OUT AGAIN.

NO NEED FOR CONCERN -- I'M SIXTY-FIVE PERCENT *DEFINITELY CERTAIN* MY PLAN WILL WORK...!

ARROOOO-GRAR!

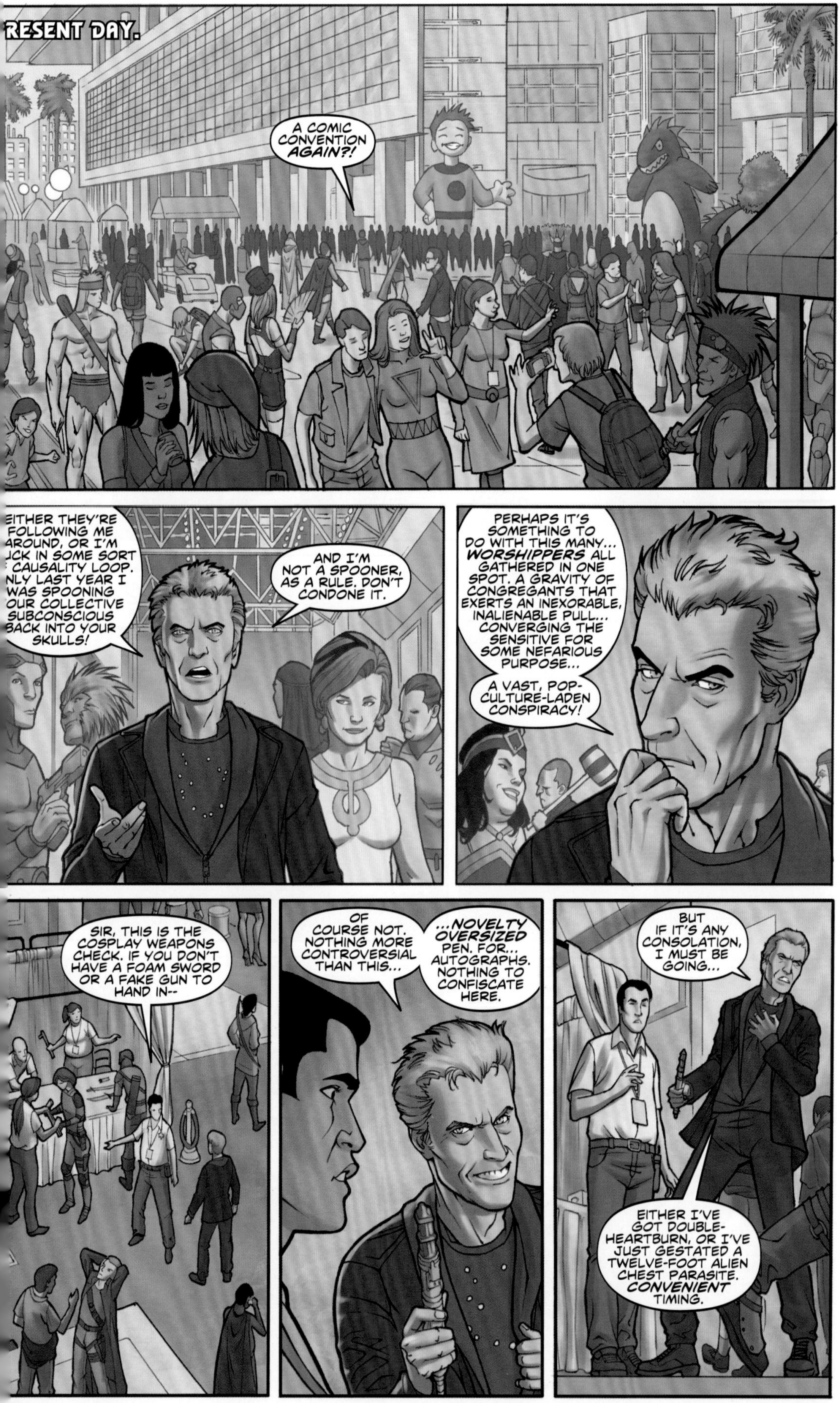
RESENT DAY.
A COMIC CONVENTION AGAIN?!
EITHER THEY'RE FOLLOWING ME AROUND, OR I'M UCK IN SOME SORT CAUSALITY LOOP. NLY LAST YEAR I WAS SPOONING OUR COLLECTIVE SUBCONSCIOUS BACK INTO YOUR SKULLS!
AND I'M NOT A SPOONER, AS A RULE. DON'T CONDONE IT.
PERHAPS IT'S SOMETHING TO DO WITH THIS MANY... WORSHIPPERS ALL GATHERED IN ONE SPOT. A GRAVITY OF CONGREGANTS THAT EXERTS AN INEXORABLE, INALIENABLE PULL... CONVERGING THE SENSITIVE FOR SOME NEFARIOUS PURPOSE...
A VAST, POP-CULTURE-LADEN CONSPIRACY!
SIR, THIS IS THE COSPLAY WEAPONS CHECK. IF YOU DON'T HAVE A FOAM SWORD OR A FAKE GUN TO HAND IN--
OF COURSE NOT. NOTHING MORE CONTROVERSIAL THAN THIS...
...NOVELTY OVERSIZED PEN. FOR... AUTOGRAPHS. NOTHING TO CONFISCATE HERE.
BUT IF IT'S ANY CONSOLATION, I MUST BE GOING...
EITHER I'VE GOT DOUBLE-HEARTBURN, OR I'VE JUST GESTATED A TWELVE-FOOT ALIEN CHEST PARASITE. CONVENIENT TIMING.

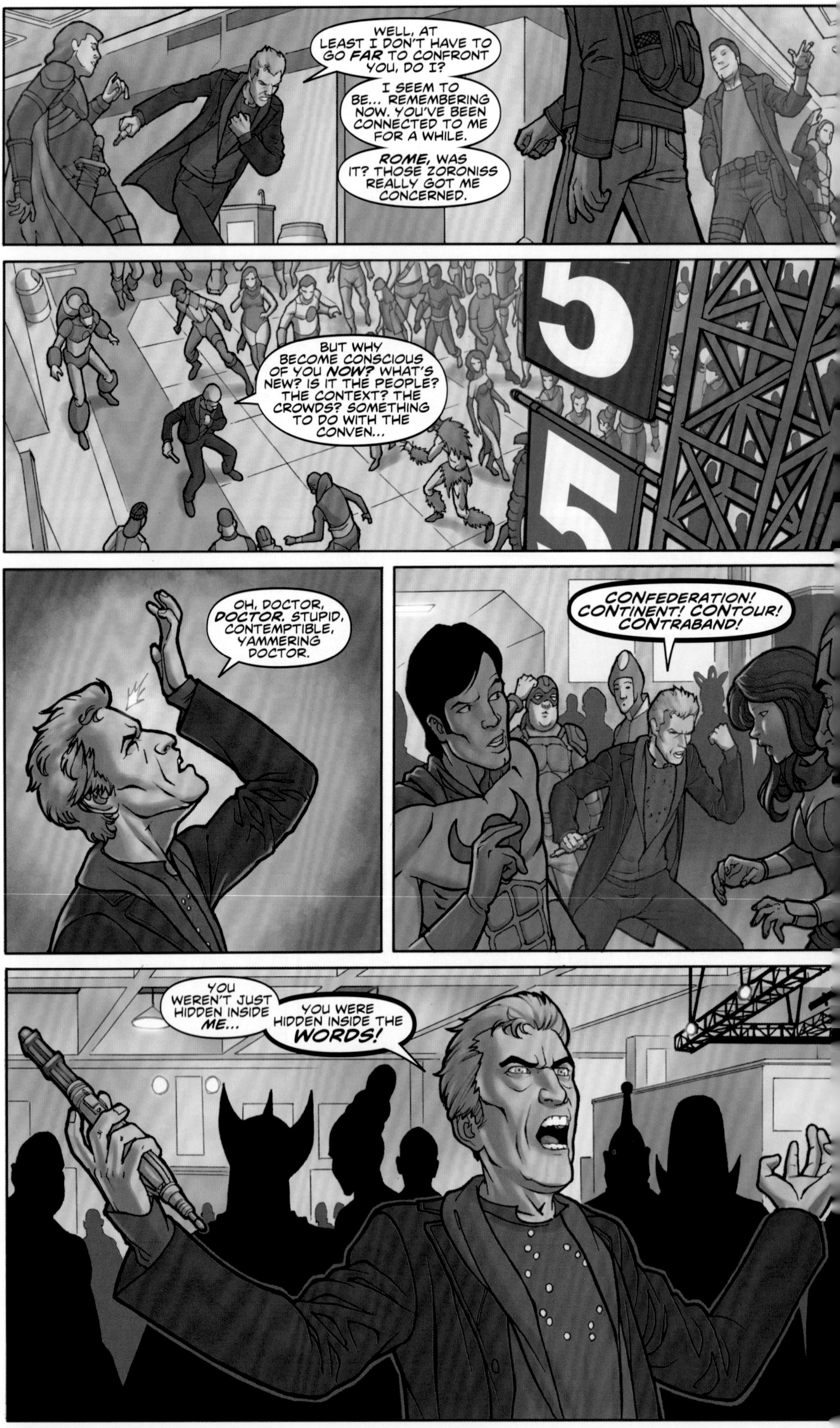
WELL, AT LEAST I DON'T HAVE TO GO FAR TO CONFRONT YOU, DO I?
I SEEM TO BE... REMEMBERING NOW. YOU'VE BEEN CONNECTED TO ME FOR A WHILE.
ROME, WAS IT? THOSE ZORONISS REALLY GOT ME CONCERNED.
BUT WHY BECOME CONSCIOUS OF YOU NOW? WHAT'S NEW? IS IT THE PEOPLE? THE CONTEXT? THE CROWDS? SOMETHING TO DO WITH THE CONVEN...
OH, DOCTOR, DOCTOR. STUPID, CONTEMPTIBLE, YAMMERING DOCTOR.
CONFEDERATION! CONTINENT! CONTOUR! CONTRABAND!
YOU WEREN'T JUST HIDDEN INSIDE ME...
YOU WERE HIDDEN INSIDE THE WORDS!

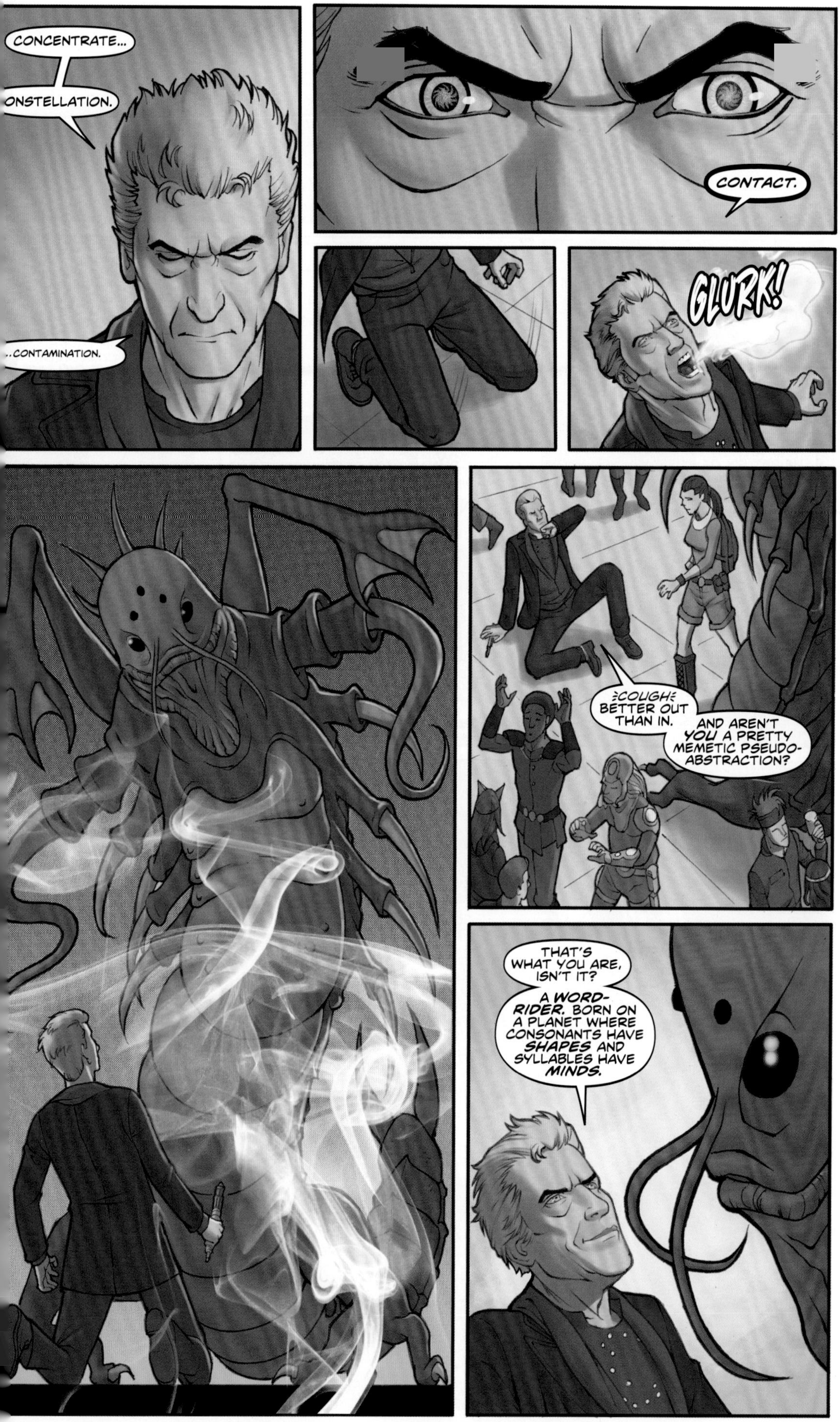
CONCENTRATE...
ONSTELLATION.
...CONTAMINATION.
CONTACT.
GLURK!
COUGH BETTER OUT THAN IN.
AND AREN'T *YOU* A PRETTY MEMETIC PSEUDO-ABSTRACTION?
THAT'S WHAT YOU ARE, ISN'T IT?
A *WORD-RIDER.* BORN ON A PLANET WHERE CONSONANTS HAVE *SHAPES* AND SYLLABLES HAVE *MINDS.*

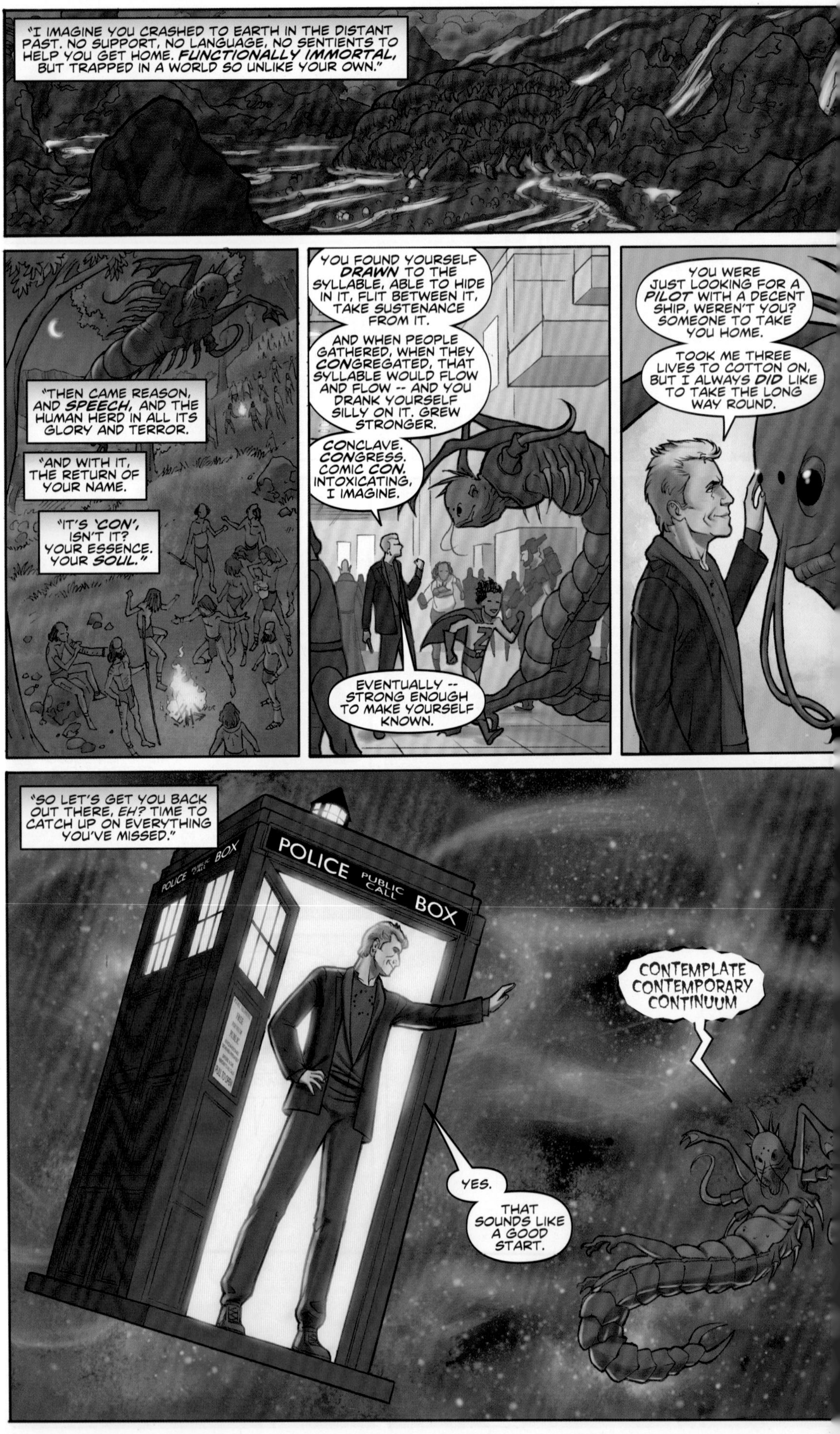
"I IMAGINE YOU CRASHED TO EARTH IN THE DISTANT PAST. NO SUPPORT, NO LANGUAGE, NO SENTIENTS TO HELP YOU GET HOME. FUNCTIONALLY IMMORTAL, BUT TRAPPED IN A WORLD SO UNLIKE YOUR OWN."
"THEN CAME REASON, AND SPEECH, AND THE HUMAN HERD IN ALL ITS GLORY AND TERROR.
"AND WITH IT, THE RETURN OF YOUR NAME.
"IT'S 'CON', ISN'T IT? YOUR ESSENCE. YOUR SOUL."
YOU FOUND YOURSELF DRAWN TO THE SYLLABLE, ABLE TO HIDE IN IT, FLIT BETWEEN IT, TAKE SUSTENANCE FROM IT.
AND WHEN PEOPLE GATHERED, WHEN THEY CONGREGATED, THAT SYLLABLE WOULD FLOW AND FLOW -- AND YOU DRANK YOURSELF SILLY ON IT. GREW STRONGER.
CONCLAVE. CONGRESS. COMIC CON. INTOXICATING, I IMAGINE.
EVENTUALLY -- STRONG ENOUGH TO MAKE YOURSELF KNOWN.
YOU WERE JUST LOOKING FOR A PILOT WITH A DECENT SHIP, WEREN'T YOU? SOMEONE TO TAKE YOU HOME.
TOOK ME THREE LIVES TO COTTON ON, BUT I ALWAYS DID LIKE TO TAKE THE LONG WAY ROUND.
"SO LET'S GET YOU BACK OUT THERE, EH? TIME TO CATCH UP ON EVERYTHING YOU'VE MISSED."
POLICE PUBLIC CALL BOX
CONTEMPLATE CONTEMPORARY CONTINUUM
YES.
THAT SOUNDS LIKE A GOOD START.

DOCTOR WHO
THE TENTH DOCTOR

COVER GALLERY

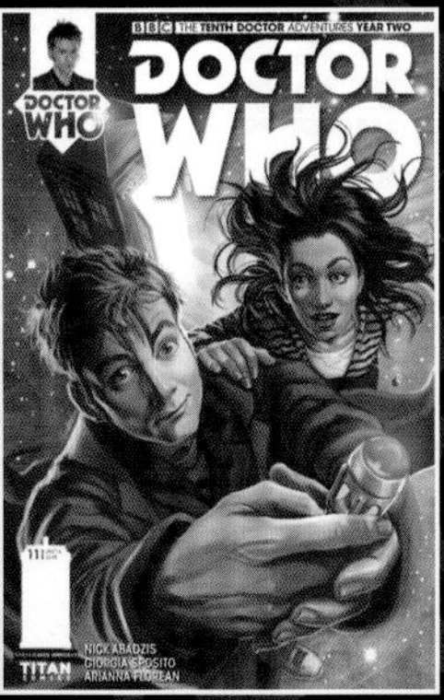
THE TENTH DOCTOR ADVENTURES YEAR TWO
DOCTOR WHO
NICK ABADZIS
GIORGIA SPOSITO
ARIANNA FLOREAN
TITAN
#2.11 A – CLAUDIA IANNICIELLO

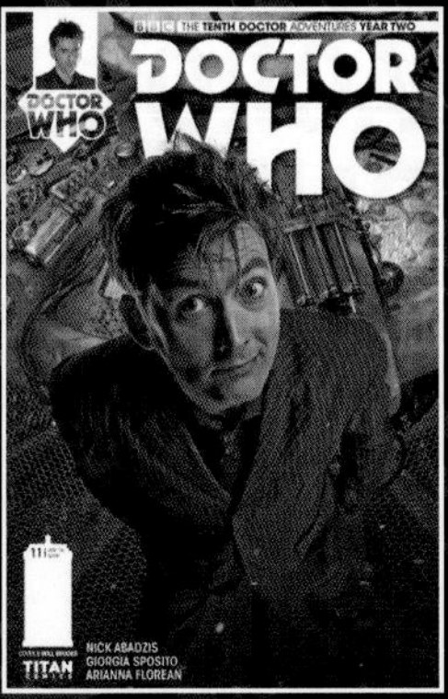
THE TENTH DOCTOR ADVENTURES YEAR TWO
DOCTOR WHO
NICK ABADZIS
GIORGIA SPOSITO
ARIANNA FLOREAN
TITAN
#2.11 B – WILL BROOKS

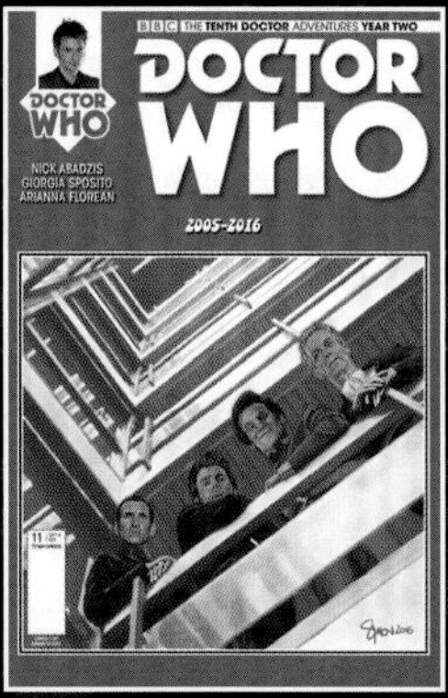
THE TENTH DOCTOR ADVENTURES YEAR TWO
DOCTOR WHO
NICK ABADZIS
GIORGIA SPOSITO
ARIANNA FLOREAN
2005–2016
#2.11 C – SIMON MYERS

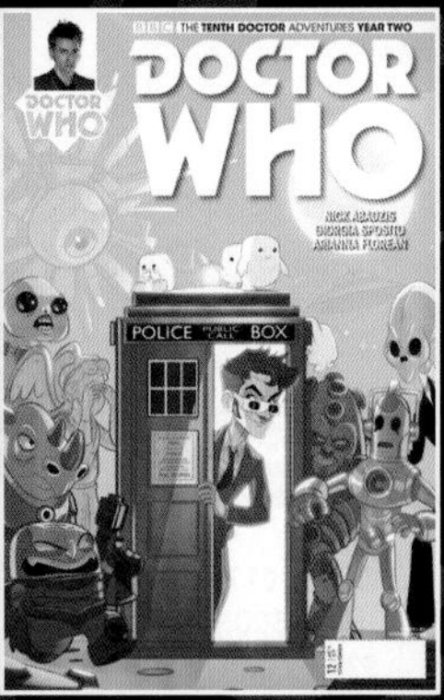
THE TENTH DOCTOR ADVENTURES YEAR TWO
DOCTOR WHO
NICK ABADZIS
GIORGIA SPOSITO
ARIANNA FLOREAN
POLICE PUBLIC CALL BOX
#2.12 C – STEPHEN BYRNE

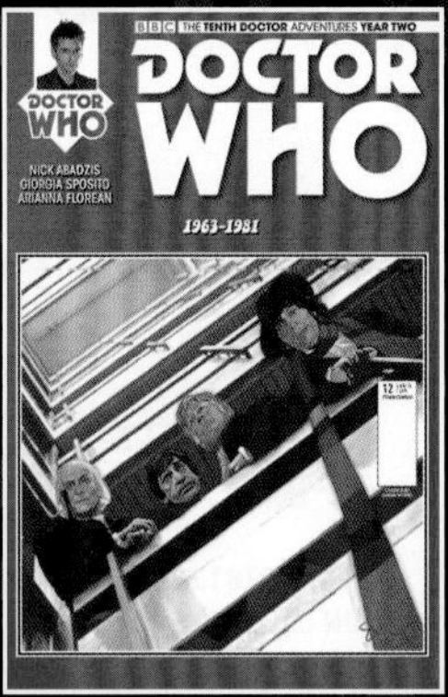
THE TENTH DOCTOR ADVENTURES YEAR TWO
DOCTOR WHO
NICK ABADZIS
GIORGIA SPOSITO
ARIANNA FLOREAN
1963–1981
#2.12 D – SIMON MYERS

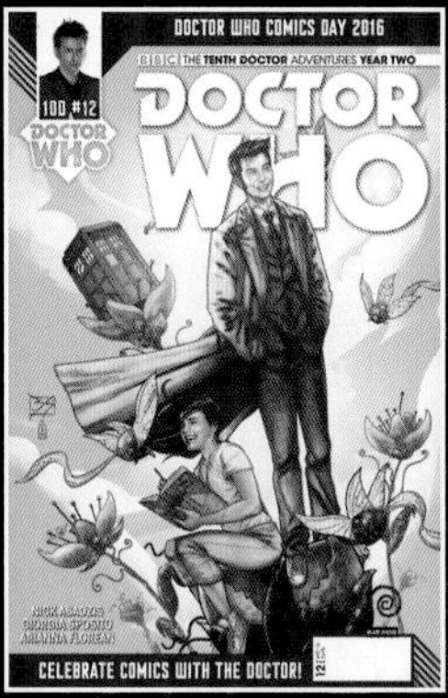
DOCTOR WHO COMICS DAY 2016
THE TENTH DOCTOR ADVENTURES YEAR TWO
DOCTOR WHO
NICK ABADZIS
GIORGIA SPOSITO
ARIANNA FLOREAN
CELEBRATE COMICS WITH THE DOCTOR!
#2.12 Doctor Who Comics Day – BLAIR SHEDD

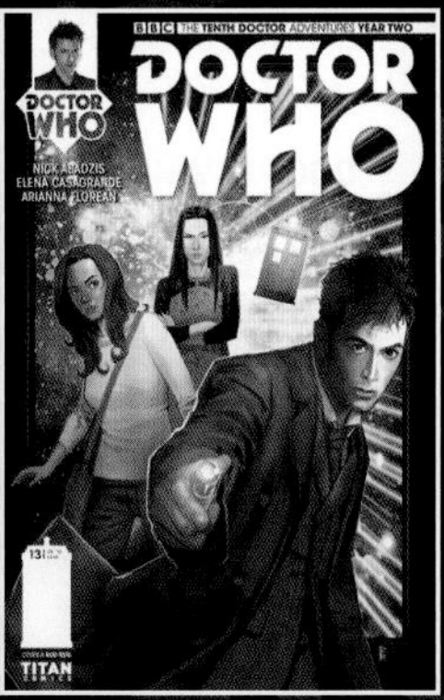
THE TENTH DOCTOR ADVENTURES YEAR TWO
DOCTOR WHO
NICK ABADZIS
ELENA CASAGRANDE
ARIANNA FLOREAN
TITAN
#2.13 A – ROD REIS

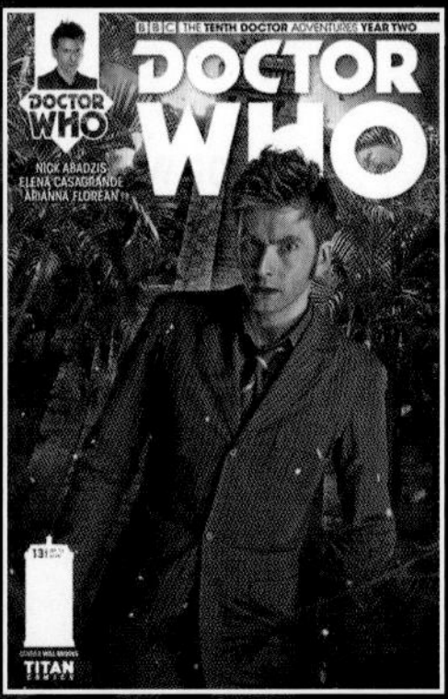
THE TENTH DOCTOR ADVENTURES YEAR TWO
DOCTOR WHO
NICK ABADZIS
ELENA CASAGRANDE
ARIANNA FLOREAN
TITAN
#2.13 B – WILL BROOKS

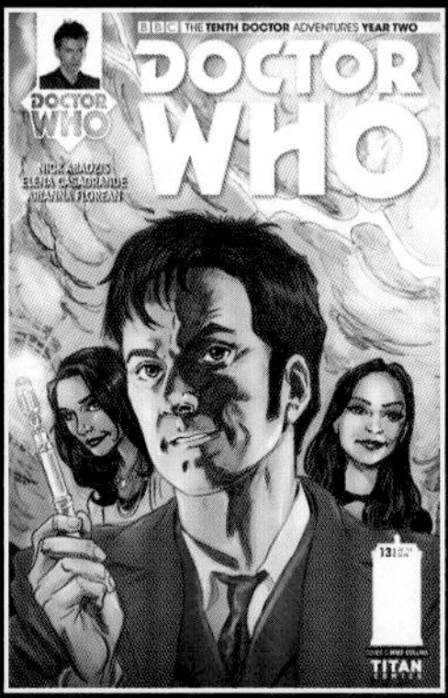
THE TENTH DOCTOR ADVENTURES YEAR TWO
DOCTOR WHO
NICK ABADZIS
ELENA CASAGRANDE
ARIANNA FLOREAN
TITAN
#2.13 C – MIKE COLLINS

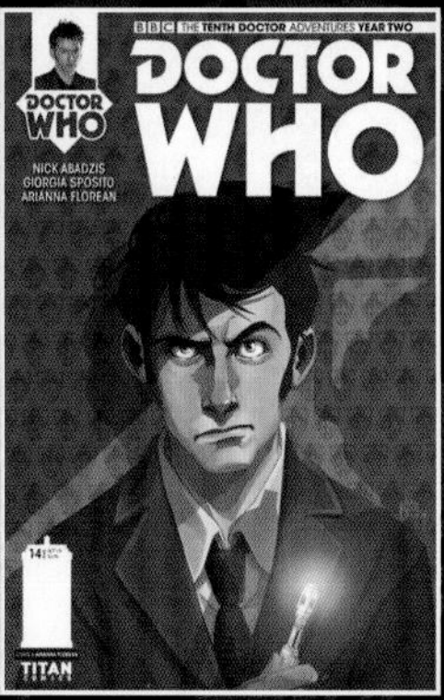
THE TENTH DOCTOR ADVENTURES YEAR TWO
DOCTOR WHO
NICK ABADZIS
GIORGIA SPOSITO
ARIANNA FLOREAN
TITAN
#2.14 A – ARIANNA FLOREAN

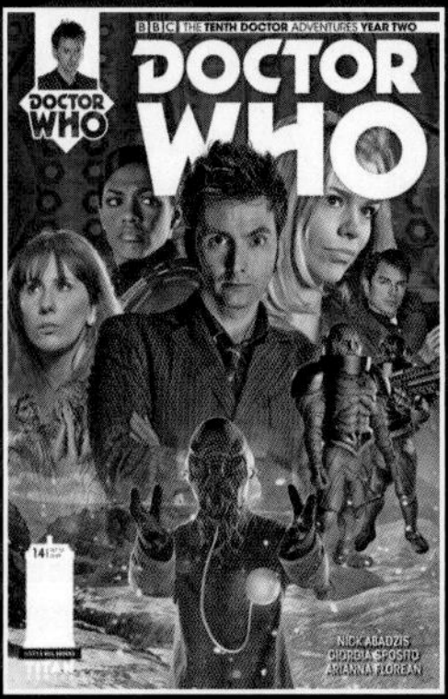
THE TENTH DOCTOR ADVENTURES YEAR TWO
DOCTOR WHO
NICK ABADZIS
GIORGIA SPOSITO
ARIANNA FLOREAN
TITAN
#2.14 B – WILL BROOKS

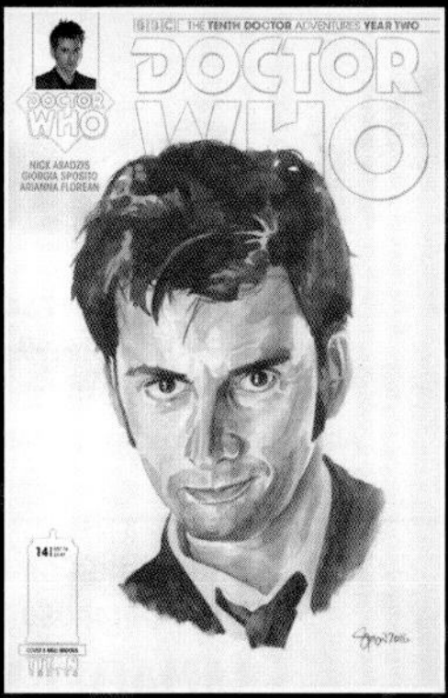
THE TENTH DOCTOR ADVENTURES YEAR TWO
DOCTOR WHO
NICK ABADZIS
GIORGIA SPOSITO
ARIANNA FLOREAN
#2.14 C – SIMON MYERS

FOLLOW YOUR FAVORITE INCARNATIONS ACROSS THESE FANTASTIC COLLECTIONS!

DOCTOR WHO: THE TWELFTH DOCTOR VOL. 1: TERRORFORMER

NEW ADVENTURES WITH THE TWELFTH DOCTOR
DOCTOR WHO
TERRORFORMER
ROBBIE MORRISON • DAVE TAYLOR

ISBN: 9781782761778
ON SALE NOW - $19.99 / $22.95 CAN / £10.99
(UK EDITION ISBN: 9781782763864)

DOCTOR WHO: THE TWELFTH DOCTOR VOL. 2: FRACTURES

NEW ADVENTURES WITH THE TWELFTH DOCTOR
DOCTOR WHO
FRACTURES
ROBBIE MORRISON • BRIAN WILLIAMSON

ISBN: 9781782763017
ON SALE NOW - $19.99 / $25.99 CAN / £10.99
(UK EDITION ISBN: 9781782766599)

DOCTOR WHO: THE TWELFTH DOCTOR VOL. 3: HYPERION

NEW ADVENTURES WITH THE TWELFTH DOCTOR
DOCTOR WHO
HYPERION
ROBBIE MORRISON • GEORGE MANN • DANIEL INDRO
MARIANO LACLAUSTRA • SLAMET MUJIONO • HI-FI

ISBN: 9781782767473
ON SALE NOW- $19.99 / $25.99 CAN / £10.99
(UK EDITION ISBN: 97817827674442)

DOCTOR WHO: THE TWELFTH DOCTOR VOL. 4: THE SCHOOL OF DEATH

THE TWELFTH DOCTOR ADVENTURES YEAR TWO
DOCTOR WHO
THE SCHOOL OF DEATH
ROBBIE MORRISON • RACHAEL STOTT • IVAN NUNES

ISBN: 9781785851087
COMING SOON - $19.99 / $25.99 CAN / £10.99
(UK EDITION ISBN: 9781785851070)

DOCTOR WHO: THE ELEVENTH DOCTOR VOL. 1: AFTER LIFE

NEW ADVENTURES WITH THE ELEVENTH DOCTOR
DOCTOR WHO
AFTER LIFE
AL EWING • ROB WILLIAMS • SIMON FRASER • BOO COOK

ISBN: 9781782761747
ON SALE NOW - $19.99 / $22.95 CAN / £10.99
(UK EDITION ISBN: 9781782763857)

DOCTOR WHO: THE ELEVENTH DOCTOR VOL. 2: SERVE YOU

NEW ADVENTURES WITH THE ELEVENTH DOCTOR
DOCTOR WHO
SERVE YOU

ISBN: 9781782761754
ON SALE NOW - $19.99 / $25.99 CAN / £10.99
(UK EDITION ISBN: 9781782766582)

DOCTOR WHO: THE ELEVENTH DOCTOR VOL. 3: CONVERSION

NEW ADVENTURES WITH THE ELEVENTH DOCTOR
DOCTOR WHO
CONVERSION
AL EWING • ROB WILLIAMS • SIMON FRASER • BOO COOK • WARREN PLEECE

ISBN: 9781782763024
ON SALE NOW - $19.99 / $25.99 CAN / £10.99
(UK EDITION ISBN: 9781782767435)

DOCTOR WHO: THE ELEVENTH DOCTOR VOL. 4: THE THEN AND THE NOW

THE ELEVENTH DOCTOR ADVENTURES YEAR TWO
DOCTOR WHO
THE THEN AND THE NOW

ISBN: 9781782767466
ON SALE NOW - $19.99 / $25.99 CAN / £10.99
(UK EDITION ISBN: 9781722767428)

TITAN COMICS

For information on how to subscribe to our great Doctor Who titles, or to purchase them digitally for your favorite device, visit:

WWW.TITAN-COMICS.COM

COMPLETE YOUR COLLECTION!

**DOCTOR WHO:
E TENTH DOCTOR
L. 1: REVOLUTIONS
OF TERROR**

**DOCTOR WHO:
THE TENTH DOCTOR
VOL. 2: THE WEEPING
ANGELS OF MONS**

**DOCTOR WHO:
THE TENTH DOCTOR
VOL. 3: THE FOUNTAINS
OF FOREVER**

**DOCTOR WHO: THE
TENTH DOCTOR
VOL. 4: THE ENDLESS
SONG**

BN: 9781782761747
LE NOW - $19.99 / $22.95
CAN / £10.99

EDITION ISBN: 9781782763840)

ISBN: 9781782761754
ON SALE NOW - $19.99 / $25.99
CAN / £10.99

(UK EDITION ISBN: 9781782766575)

ISBN: 9781782763024
ON SALE NOW - $19.99 / $25.99
CAN / £10.99

(UK EDITION ISBN: 9781782767435)

ISBN: 9781785854286
ON SALE NOW - $19.99 / $25.99
CAN / £10.99

(SC ISBN: 9781785853227)

**DOCTOR WHO: THE NINTH DOCTOR
VOL. 1: WEAPONS OF PAST DESTRUCTION**

**DOCTOR WHO EVENT 2015
FOUR DOCTORS**

ISBN: 9781782763369
ON SALE NOW - $19.99 / $25.99 CAN / £10.99

(UK EDITION ISBN: 9781782761056)

ISBN: 9781782765967
ON SALE NOW - $19.99 / $25.99 CAN / £10.99

(UK EDITION ISBN: 9781785851063)

AVAILABLE IN ALL GOOD COMIC STORES,
BOOK STORES, AND DIGITAL PROVIDERS!

BIOGRAPHIES

Nick Abadzis was born in Sweden to Greek and British parents and was brought up in England and Switzerland. He has been writing and drawing comics and graphic novels for over twenty-five years. His work has appeared in numerous books and periodicals around the world and he has been honored with various international storytelling awards, including an Eisner for his 2007 graphic novel, *Laika*. He lives in the USA with his wife and daughter.

Giorgia Sposito is an Italian artist and inker who has worked on many prolific titles such as *Independence Day, Charmed,* and *Wonderland*

Eleonora Carlini is an Italian artist on the rise, with her most recent high-profile appearance in DC's *Batgirl*.

Arianna Florean is a talented artist and cartoonist in her own right, and brings the Tenth Doctor to life with her beautiful coloring. She lives and works in Rome, Italy,

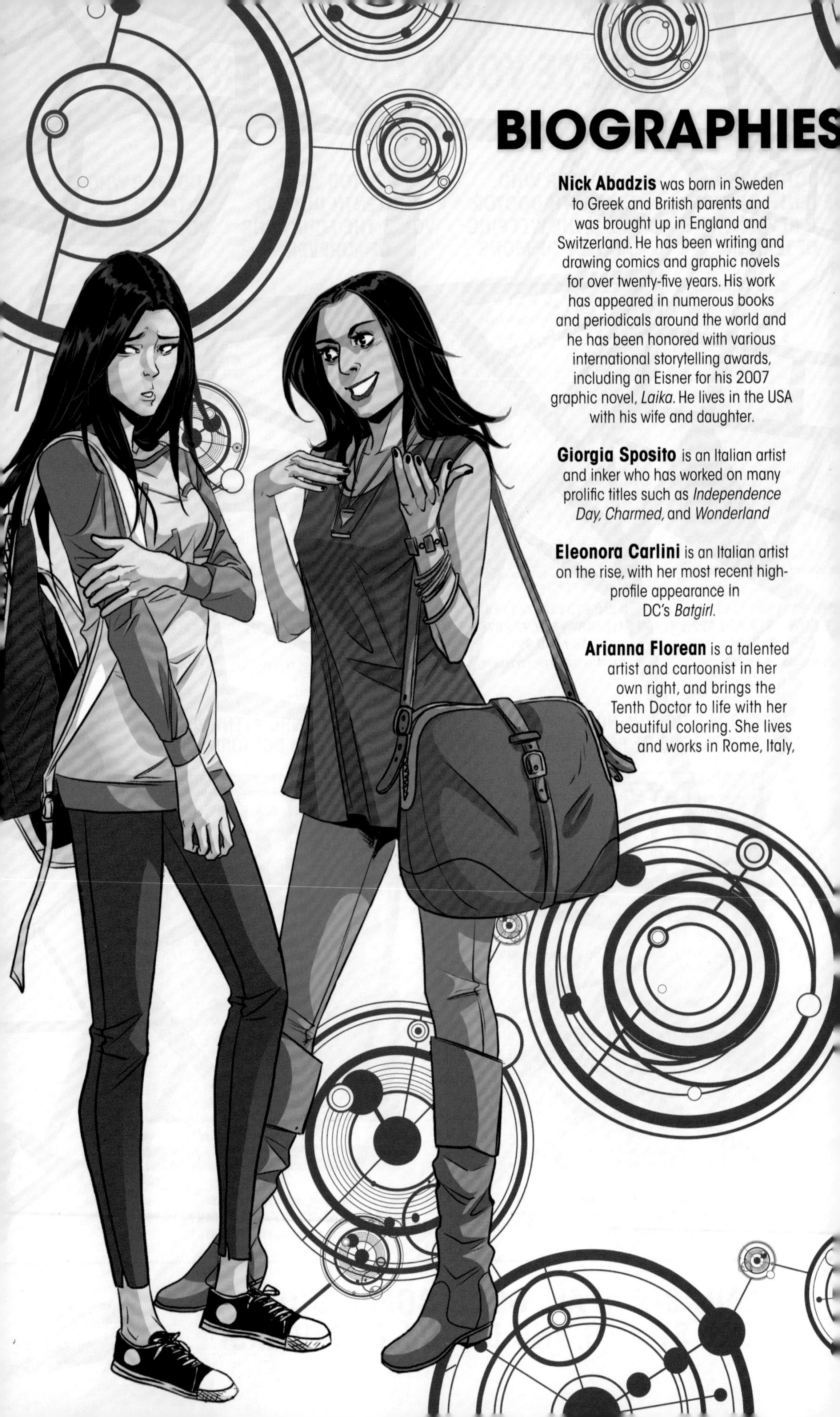